Robbie

The Biography

Also by Sean Smith

Kylie Confidential
J.K. Rowling – A Biography
Stone Me!
Sophie's Kiss
Royal Racing
The Union Game

Robbie
The Biography

'Rob is not Robbie'
ROBBIE WILLIAMS

SEAN SMITH

POCKET
BOOKS

LONDON • SYDNEY • NEW YORK • TORONTO

This edition first published by Pocket Books, 2004
An imprint of Simon & Schuster UK Ltd
A Viacom Company

1 3 5 7 9 10 8 6 4 2

Simon & Schuster UK Ltd
Africa House
64–78 Kingsway
London WC2B 6AH

www.simonsays.co.uk

Simon & Schuster Australia
Sydney

A CIP catalogue record for this book
is available from the British Library

ISBN 0-7434-6838-4

Typeset by M Rules
Printed and bound in Great Britain by
Cox & Wyman Ltd, Reading, Berks

Photo credits on last page.

Acknowledgements

One of the most pleasing aspects of researching and writing this biography was the willingness of people to share their memories and thoughts about Robbie Williams. There were some who wished to remain anonymous and I have respected that. I thank them for their help. Those I would especially like to mention are George Andrews, Bill Bache, Carol Banks, Paul Colclough, Sam Evans, Zoë Hammond, Lee Hancock, Keith Harrison, Dave Johnson, Philip Lindsay, Kelly Oakes, Jane Oddy, David and Val Ogden, Jim Peers, Tim Peers, Paul Phillips, Brian and Joy Rawlins, Giuseppe Romano, Phil Rossiter, Rick Sky, Hamid Soleimani, Eric Tams, Brian Toplass, Eileen and Graham Wilkes.

Once again Lizzie Clachan did invaluable research for me. Richard Philpott and Taryn Cass from the Zooid Agency in London did a great job finding the pictures for the book. Cliff Renfrew was an enormous help in Los Angeles. And thanks to Stephen Lenehan of the Fame Picture Agency in LA for providing a selection of pictures from Rob's new home city.

At Simon and Schuster my thanks to the publisher Jonathan Atkins for commissioning the book, my editor Rumana Haider for her enthusiasm and expertise, production controller Barry O'Connor for his energy and ideas and Darren Wall for his stunning cover design. Patrick Webster of M Rules was responsible for the eye-catching picture designs.

I am indebted to Madeleine Moore for producing a superb birth chart for Robbie. Finally, I am grateful to my wife Zoë Lawrence for her help with the manuscript and keeping my spirits up.

Contents

Introduction

Robbie Williams seems to have been around forever and yet he is still a young man. Normally, I would be reluctant to tackle a subject whose life had yet to run thirty years for fear it might end up more of a pamphlet than a decent read. A publishing mentor, when I was just starting out as a writer, advised me to make sure the chosen celebrity had 'meat on their bones'. It's all very well for a star to be featured every day in the pages of the newspapers but it doesn't actually make them interesting. They could be the most boring person in the world but have a fabulous press agent.

I never had any doubts about Robbie Williams as a subject for a book. He stands head and shoulders above the great majority of modern music stars, wallowing in their bland mediocrity. From the very beginning of Take That he had something extra, part vitality, part sense of fun and part self-awareness. He has always made the job easy for the press, wearing his mouth on his sleeve. More often than not media coverage of a famous person predominantly focuses on just one aspect of their image – it might be haircut (David Beckham), bottom (Kylie), bad behaviour (Russell Crowe), shaggability (Justin Timberlake), weight (Geri Halliwell), money (J.K. Rowling). A measure of the breadth of Robbie's appeal is that you could substitute his name for each individual in that list.

The most intriguing remark I have heard from Robbie is the one on the title page of this book: 'Rob is not Robbie'. It immediately begged the question, 'Who, in that case, is Rob?' In *Somebody Someday*, the fascinating, authorized account of his previous European tour, Mark McCrum provided us with a compelling portrait of the man now and what makes him tick. At the risk of getting my metaphors in a twist, I wanted to know what wound his clock in the first place – the how, what, who, when, why of Robert Peter Williams. I decided to go back to where it all began in Tunstall, one of the six Potteries towns that make up Stoke-on-Trent. It struck me almost at once that I wanted to write about Rob Williams, not his alter-ego Robbie. The people who knew him here and remember him with great warmth and regard, knew him as Rob.

From the moment I stepped off the train I was astonished at what a small world it was. The taxi driver taking me to my hotel told me of the time he had been waiting for a fare and Rob's mother, Jan, had turned up in her gleaming BMW car. Out walked Rob with Nicole Appleton, whom he had brought home for the weekend. At the Sneyd Arms, where I stayed in Tunstall, I was told that Rob's dad, Pete Conway, had sunk many a pint there and Rob himself had done a spot of karaoke. On my first evening in Tunstall I strolled out and found a local Indian restaurant, the Kashmir Garden. The friendly waiter asked me what I was doing up this way. When I told him I was researching a book about Robbie Williams, he announced, 'My brother was in the same class as him at school. I used to see him rollerblading down the pavement outside.' Rob and his mother, his sister Sally and family friends had regularly eaten there. I later found out that he had shown his mum his famous Maori tattoo for the first time while they were eating a curry there. On the wall is a signed picture of Graham Wilkes, a very popular figure in these parts and the father of Jonathan Wilkes, Rob's best friend. Graham is a well-known toastmaster locally and I was informed that he was larger than life and twice as funny, which proved to be the case when I had the pleasure of meeting him.

A few streets away from the Sneyd Arms is Newfield Street, where Pete Conway was brought up and where Rob spent many happy childhood hours in the company of his beloved grandmother, his 'Nan', as he always referred to Betty Williams. It's a small terraced, working man's street. I spotted a man in overalls next to a van. 'Excuse me', I said. 'I don't suppose you knew Robbie Williams's grandmother who used to live in this street?' 'Yes, I did,' came the reply. 'I bought her house from Rob's father after she died. I used to live next door.' At the local library I boldly asked, 'Anyone here know Robbie Williams?' and was answered by a shy receptionist, who admitted that her daughter had known him and he used to pop round their house when he was a lad.

And so it went on. From the very first day I felt that I was travelling on a very scenic road, of changing landscapes with plenty of places to stop and contemplate the view. These were not rent-a-quote people, making a living out of tenuous links with a superstar. In Stoke-on-Trent and beyond, I found people who really knew Rob Williams and could illuminate his life and how he came to be the person he is today. The great advantage of an unauthorized biography is that you do not have to portray someone to his or her advantage. In the case of Robbie Williams, the great majority of the people I met and talked to about him liked the man.

There is nothing more frustrating, at the end of the book, than to have unanswered questions. I therefore propose to end this introduction by answering some of the questions that I have been asked during my time writing and researching this biography.

Does he still enjoy a pint?
No he doesn't! Los Angeles is proving fantastic for Rob. He told Jonathan Wilkes's mother, Eileen, that he had never felt better. He is very proud that he is now sticking to the programme mapped out for those suffering from alcohol and drug problems. He is attending AA and NA meetings and living a healthy Californian lifestyle. It has been a bumpy ride since the bad days of the mid nineties, but he is definitely winning.

Can he sing?
Rob is such a brilliant entertainer that the fact that he is also a superb singer is easily overlooked. There was a piano in the lounge at home but Rob does not appear to have been that interested in playing a musical instrument as a child. He was not, for instance, in the school orchestra nor did any of his teenage friends sit around strumming guitars singing Simon and Garfunkel. He was much more interested in being an actor as a child and was one of the young stars of local amateur dramatics. In those days his voice was not particularly strong but he had the gift of delivering a song in a way that breathed life into it.

If you are a professional sportsman you will get better with practise and coaching. It's no different for a professional singer. Rob's vocals have improved immeasurably since the reedy days of Take That, when he made himself cringe with embarrassment by singing 'Everything Changes' hopelessly out of tune at a concert. One can only marvel at the change from that dismal effort to his *Swing When You're Winning* concert at the Albert Hall, which was a personal triumph. Of course he's not Frank Sinatra. But then, no one is.

Is he gay?

If it wasn't such a terrible cliché I would be tempted to say, 'If I had five pounds for every time somebody asked me that . . .' I don't quite understand what all the fuss is about. This question is a no-win situation for anybody in the public eye. A few years ago I wrote about Prince Edward and the whispers about his sexuality: 'There has never been one shred of acceptable evidence offered as proof that he is.' I also observed that it does not take very long for a rumour to gain momentum. The remarks apply equally to Robbie Williams.

Take That began life as a rather camp band playing in gay clubs, but Rob's friends never had any indication that he was gay. The nearest he appears to have got to a gay encounter was chatting to Jimmy Somerville in the gents. The rumours, however, originated in those Take That days and have been fuelled by innuendo over the years, particularly with regard to his friendship with Jonathan Wilkes. The difficulty is that you can prove a positive, e.g. Rob has slept with a number of women, but you can't prove a negative, e.g. Rob is not gay.

Rob has maintained his good humour over the issue preferring to be jokey and light-hearted when he is asked the question, 'Are you gay?' for the zillionth time. The important thing is that, whether he is or not, it is irrelevant to his status as an entertainer. He does not rely on his sexuality to sell 'Robbie Williams'. That image is a combination of things – cheek, wit, good music, great stage presence and those brooding eyes. He is not a Hollywood heart-throb whose reputation rests solely on his sex appeal to women and who, in the case of the late Rock Hudson for example, was living a lie.

Will he ever crack America?

We need to get some perspective over this. British artists do not have a divine right to succeed in the United States. Currently, rock music and rap music fill the American airwaves. The Rolling Stones, Paul McCartney, the Bee Gees and Elton John have iconic status across the Atlantic, thanks to the so-called British invasion of the sixties and seventies. There is no tide of British success for Rob to ride. Take That had one US top ten hit, 'Back for Good', but then split before they could achieve any long-term success. The fantastically successful song 'Angels' was the lucky break Rob needed in this country. He was, however, already one of the most famous names in British pop. In the States he was an unknown and the single did not meet with similar success there. It was too early in his career as a solo artist.

Rob has made Los Angeles his home, which is a good start. He has given good value for money on the American talk show circuit. He does not have the fan base to sell out major venues in the States, so the plan is for a series of concerts at smaller venues. Hopefully, this will gradually improve his popularity. At the moment if you mentioned Robbie Williams to the average American they would probably think you were referring to Robin Williams, the acclaimed movie star. It's bad luck for Rob that their two names are so similar.

Rob is not the first artist to claim he does not care about cracking America. Kylie Minogue, to name just one, is another who has made that statement. I cannot believe that artists with such strong inner drive do not want to achieve great success in the biggest market in the world. But lack of success does not in my view, equate to failure. After all, according to the *Guinness Book of British Hit Singles*, only four singles from this side of the Atlantic have made the US top ten in the first three years of the new millennium, which is absolutely dismal.

My feeling is that Rob just needs a bit of luck to crack America. It may not be a new, classic record. It could be something as small as a brilliant appearance in an episode of *The Osbournes* or some other popular US show. Best of all he could make a hit film. He would have been perfect for *The Full Monty*, especially as he has never been shy about getting his kit off. He could do a version of *Notting Hill* set in Stoke-on-Trent. Or he could do something like Eminem, whose semi-autobiographical debut, *8 Mile*, has proved such a hit. Rob's would have to be called *M6*.

Why is he unlucky in love?

Rob suffers from a celebrity disease – every time he speaks to a girl everyone wants to know how long it will be before they get married. He was never a great ladies' man at school and confessed that when he joined Take That he had never had a proper girlfriend. Since that time, of course, he can pretty much have any girl he wants. Celebrity relationships, however, are notoriously unstable because of the long absences that result from being on tour, making a film or honouring promotional events all over the world. It must be impossible to get a sense of perspective.

At thirty, Rob is not exactly on the shelf and any girl in his life is going to have to stand comparison with his mother. He was brought up in a very matriarchal household, with mum Jan, sister Sally and grandmother Betty, the most important people in his life from day-to-day. They are a hard act to follow. And then there is his career, which will always compete for his attention. His birth chart reveals a classic conflict between the need for freedom and independence and a desire for intimacy.

He recently remarked that he would have to go back to Stoke-on-Trent to find a girl to settle down with. Pity he didn't find one before he left.

Is he well-endowed?

Legend has it that a girl at Butlins once described Rob's manhood as resembling a baby's arm holding an orange. Moving on . . .

What will he be doing when he is fifty?

Rob has been a performer all his life. It, genuinely, is in his blood. His father has been a professional comedian and entertainer for more than thirty years. It would be astonishing if Rob jacked it all in to count his money in Beverly Hills. One of his great heroes, Tom Jones, is still more than going strong at the age of sixty-three and Rob may well go down that road. He has joked that he always does a turn when the fridge light comes on. He may combine singing and acting, or he may be in Vegas. I could see him with his own show on TV – the Tonight Show with Robbie Williams.

In her absorbing birth chart of Robbie Williams, which follows this introduction, Madeleine Moore reveals that in three years' time certain areas of his life will take on a new direction. I would be surprised and disappointed if he ever became boring.

Incidentally, Madeleine knew practically nothing about Robbie Williams before she compiled his chart for this book. She has not 'spun' the indications to fit the public perception of him in any way.

Sean Smith

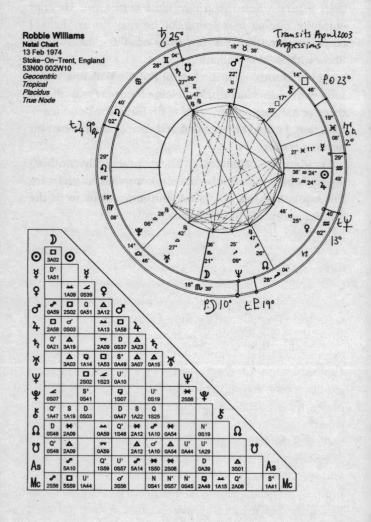

Robbie Williams
Natal Chart
13 Feb 1974
Stoke–On–Trent, England
53N00 002W10
Geocentric
Tropical
Placidus
True Node

Transits April 2003
Progressions

P.☉ 23°

t.♄ 2°

t.♅ 13°

t.♇ 19°

P.☽ 10°

t♄ 25°

t♃ 9° ℞

	☽										
☉	□ 3A02	☉									
☿	D¹ 1A51		☿								
♀		⚹ 1A09	⚺ 0S39	♀							
♂	♐ 0A59	□ 2S02	Q 0A51	△ 3A12	♂						
♃	□ 2A58	♂ 0S03		⚹ 1A13	□ 1A58	♃					
♄	Q² 0A21	△ 3A19		⚼ 2A09	D 0S37	△ 3A23	♄				
♅		△ 3A03	⊼ 1A14	□ 1A53	S³ 0A49	△ 3A07	△ 0A15	♅			
♆			□ 2S02	⚹ 1S23	U² 0A10				♆		
♇	⚹ 0S07		S³ 0S41		Q 1S07		U² 0S19		⚹ 2S56	♇	
⚷	Q² 1A47	S 1A19	D 0S03		D 0A47	S 1A22	Q 1S25				⚷
☊	D 0S48	⚹ 2A09		⚺ 0A59	Q² 1S48	⚹ 2A12	⚹ 1A10	⚹ 0A54		N¹ 0S19	☊
☋	Q² 0S48	△ 2A09		⚼ 0A59		△ 2A12	♂ 1A10	△ 0A54	U² 0A44	U² 1A29	
As		♐ 5A10		Q² 1S59	U¹ 0S57	⚹ 5A14	⚹ 1S50	⚹ 2S06		D 0A39	△ 3S01
Mc	♐ 2S56	□ 5S59	U² 1A44		♂ 3S56		N 0S41	N¹ 0S57	N¹ 0S45	⚺ 2A48	⚺ 1A15

						♇	⚷	☊	☋	As	Mc
♇						♇						
⚷							⚷					
☊								☊				
☋									☋			
As										As		
Mc											Q² 2A08	S³ 1A41

The Robbie Williams Birth Chart

This is someone whose quest is to be big – to prove his importance to himself and others, a man with a need to impress and win approval. At the heart of his birth chart the energies of a focal Sun and Jupiter combine to form a T-square configuration with the Moon and Mars. These intense, often difficult aspects provide the drive and passion that fuel his creative self-expression and ambition, confirming him in a figurehead role. He is someone with the common touch, a man who can identify with other people and speak their language, who understands the humanity of the people – but is himself a leader. He belongs with the establishment in executive class, although a little self-honouring streak of rebelliousness means he is happiest in the high ranks of the alternative establishment – for the moment anyway. Sun Aquarians vibrate to the self-willed, non-conformist energy of the planet Uranus, but should not forget their star sign is co-ruled by conservative, respectable, rule-obsessed Saturn, and each will have its day.

Robbie Williams has a chart with some classic patterns and placements, one of which is the conjunction of Jupiter, the planet known as the 'great Benefic', with his Sun, placed in Aquarius. Jupiter is ruled by Zeus and such a placement is considered to bring luck and certainly lends optimism, buoyancy and far sightedness to the person who has it. Such a person is drawn towards growth, expansion and excess. It is the mark of someone who has huge expectations of what he is due and desires attention. Indeed, he needs to be honoured. He is not a man who likes to be ignored, yet conflicting with this, there is an enormous need for freedom and privacy (*suggested by the Moon in secretive Scorpio*). These two basic drives will inevitably clash. The fun-loving, bold, adventurous side will be at odds with the need for respect – a drive towards excess undermining his sense of dignity, resulting in bouts of moody unease.

Excess can take many forms, all or some of which may be indulged, but one less obvious guise indicated in this chart, is a relentless drive to reach the highest standards. This person aspires always to do his job properly. He will set himself high standards, not always considering human limitations, either of himself or others. There is much passionate nervous energy, leading, when unchecked, to exhaustion. Sparks will fly and tantrums ensue when this perfectionism, most usually focused on self-criticism, is directed at those nearest as he seeks to improve them. Out of balance, this urge for perfection will cause great discomfort to him and to others. Disappointment with attainment will usually manifest as fire energy – anger, and sometimes depression. It is likely that the arena for such potential conflict will be in his day-to-day working life and in contractual partnerships and established relationships, which have public or legal recognition. This man may relent in such battles, partially aware of the excesses of his demands, but very often, unable to set aside his core instincts, will return to the fray.

Robbie Williams has an essential drive to know more. His life is fuelled by a desire to learn, although not in an academic sense. He will prefer experience in the raw rather than the distilled knowledge of the classroom and will seek out personal challenges. Much of his energy will be directed towards the task of working towards truth and understanding life, as he has a strong desire for purpose and a flair for leadership (*Leo ascendant*). He can lift others out of a narrow mind-set, expanding their vision and providing solutions through shifting the perspective. This panoramic take on issues can come across as a cavalier, unattractive attitude on occasions, but overall this urge to travel mentally and emotionally, to go further and fly higher will win admirers. Uranus in the area of the chart associated with education, indicates originality of thought and a thirst for knowledge – but initially a disinclination to do more than superficially skate over wide ground. The chart suggests that developing mental discipline is one of the key goals Robbie Williams may engage in after the age of twenty-nine. Highly intuitive, Robbie can tune into people's thoughts quickly, and like others of his generation, he will search for common ground within belief systems, attempting to break down religious boundaries.

In the area of relationships, this person will live out the classic conflict between the need for freedom and a desire for intimacy. His whole chart speaks of this dilemma. Many relationships will fall foul of his huge desire to pursue aspirations, visions and ideals, with complete freedom, exploring the expression of his own uniqueness. He functions best with space and independence. If he is not conscious of this then he will attract a partner who will live out this side for him, perhaps married, living a distance away or emotionally detached. This will be a likely scenario when he is acknowledging his strong need for closeness. Conversely, when he denies his desire for intimacy, claiming he needs space, his partners will be the possessive type. Zeus-inspired Robbie would be the first to acknowledge that there are no mistakes in life, only lessons, and he will find the lesson repeated over and over until he has learnt it by heart. Like many of this generation he will live singly for a lengthy period, putting off the painful learning of give-and-take that long-term intimacy exacts, so that he appears to remain at the growth stage of adolescent self-centredness – at least until his Saturn Return.

At variance with his outwardly exuberant and sexually charismatic persona, is a man with intense emotions, private about his feelings and somewhat mistrustful of opening up to another. For him emotional security often means being in control. This is the possessive side of this man who would never settle for a doormat, but needs the loyalty of a partner happy to understand his own need to explore. A tall order. Whilst Robbie may have grown beyond these painfully contradictory needs, it is highly likely that he may have grown up with echoes of these issues at home – one parent restrictive, possessive and passionate, the other more detached and independent. He is someone at ease with his own sexuality and will attract people who give him the opportunity to be brave, expressive and spontaneous. He will be honourable in his commitments. Solid and lengthy relationships will take time and be more a feature of future years.

Family life may have been difficult for this man, his parents needing to reconcile different values, views of life, and beliefs. There may have been outright conflict, which would contribute to the difficulties Robbie may experience in feeling real emotional security and solid self-esteem. It is possible he would have acted as a mouthpiece for one or both parents unable to express their real feelings. His father may have been distant either in physical or emotional terms. Saturn, which often represents the father in a chart, is linked to Uranus and Jupiter, two of the outer planets associated with separateness and detachment. The presiding feeling is of an erratic presence, an adventurous father who is a law unto himself. The image of mother (*created by the placement of the Moon in Scorpio, opposing Mars*) is one of intensity. It is likely her expectations and imposed standards were very high. It is possible that in the fierceness of Robbie's commitment to his public status and career, he is living out his mother's dreams.

Mars, the planet associated with force, energy and aggression, is situated at the top of this birth chart, joining forces with the Midheaven. This is a point connected with one's career and objectives in the world. This placement is an indication of great ambition, an instinct to fight for recognition, the audacity and ruthlessness to take the lead and win. It is a dominant feature in the charts of many self-made people. It is certainly very dominant in this chart, placed as it is in a sign (Taurus) where it is traditionally ill at ease and, at the same time, touching many other planets. One would expect people with this placement to be wilful and stubborn, with much stamina and perseverance. If crossed they would make implacable enemies. Robbie may encounter conflicts with those in authoritative positions and it can be the case that anger with an early parental/authority figure has been an instigating factor in the process of his advancement. Taken with the tight link that Mars makes to the optimistic, extroverted, adventurous Sun-Jupiter conjunction, the chart suggests a powerful drive towards career success.

This is supported by a wonderful aspect, in terms of ambition and distinction, between the Sun and the 'Great Taskmaster', Saturn. This is a contact that does much to contain the indulgence-excess thrust of Jupiter, providing boundaries to this inflationary energy. Saturn, in total contrast to Jupiter, is a planet of denial and restriction and, touching the Sun, suggests problems around the sense of identity. Those with this contact are forced to work out who they are – no bad thing with this chart because Sun-Jupiter people often feel they can be everything and when the bubble reputation bursts, nothing.

The Sun-Saturn contact in this chart, albeit a soft contact, suggests fears around identity. In youth especially, there will have been times, very likely in the classroom, when he did not feel valued. Saturn in Gemini can indicate communication problems, which can have a profound impact on study and confidence. This placement is also linked to phases of depression. The planet touches Uranus in the third house – the area which relates to early schooling. Independence in thought and an outspoken manner, mixed with insecurity and Martian wilfulness combine to present a picture of a difficult schoolboy.

It is an understatement to say that being dismissed or humbled is not something Sun-Jupiter people feel comfortable with and one reaction to such a slight would be to strive to create something to be proud of, something that bears testament to one's worth. This is the best way to use this energy and, given the drive, stamina and optimism evident in other areas of the chart, it is an aspect of eventual success. Robbie Williams may be constricted by his pursuit of excellence and his desire to avoid mediocrity. As a result, he may fail to deliver the goods.

Robbie has experienced his first Saturn Return. This is an important time when the planet Saturn has completed a twenty-nine-year cycle around the chart and returned to its place at the time of birth. It is a period when events will prompt an assessment of the progress made towards one's goals and purpose in life. These are not always the same thing.   Robbie's chart suggests an ultimate need to consolidate inner self worth, based upon a life that turns away from public display, towards disseminating knowledge and his vision of life, using his own experience and creativity. It may not be realistic to expect someone experiencing success as an entertainer to embrace this yet. But there is an important humanitarian purpose to his life. He has been tested – this is part of the function of this transit – and so far has risen, it would seem, to the challenges implicit in his chart.

This Saturn Return will be particularly important in evaluating his life to date, it will force him into greater awareness of the difficulties he has in remaining steadfast to particular allegiances. The chart suggests an established habit of keeping a foot in two camps, fearful of committing to one side in case he misses an opportunity the other side may present. He will become aware of the cost of being all things to all people, engaging with many and much but on a superficial level. It is a time when he might feel ill at ease with the struggle of dealing with so many people, details and projects in his life which seem to get him nowhere nearer a state of satisfaction. It is a call to seek greater isolation and loyalty to one enterprise, one organization and one dream.

In July 2003 Jupiter, moving across the sky (*transiting*) was opposite the position of the Sun at his birth. It heralds a time when many endeavours will be successful, although any arrogance now will land him with problems. It is the precursor of a very important year in terms of personal growth. From here, Jupiter will cross into the first house starting a new cycle, placing emphasis on the importance of this man focusing on the truth of who he is. He will find his attitudes and outlook on life expanding and the people he attracts into his life changing. He will be urged to view his life from a perspective other than that of personal self.

True to the beneficent nature of this planet, it marks a fortunate time when he will have greater security about himself and his impact on others. He will find the right resources and people drawn to him to help in the next stage of his life, with encounters consistently working to his advantage. It will unquestionably ignite focus on the spiritual dimension of his life and allow him to become involved, in a wider way, with the world.

February 2006 will herald a tougher period. Changing situations might seem to be forcing him to relinquish things he has held dear. He may find himself getting nowhere despite huge effort. This non-negotiable paring down of things, attitudes and encumbrances he no longer truly needs will ultimately be rejuvenating, forcing a change of direction in certain areas of his life.

Madeleine Moore
2003

PART ONE

TUNSTALL

1

Zoë and the Artful Dodger

The first time Zoë Hammond appeared as a solo artist was at a small, clean and bright pub in Hanley. She was using the professional name Dulcie, in honour of her sister who had died. By this time Rob was a major star. 'When I finished the song before the interval I looked up and there he was in the audience. I thought, "Oh my God! Even with everything going on in his life he's found the time to come home." At the end of the gig he got up on stage and presented me with a big bouquet of red roses and he said, "I'd like to say a few words about this girl . . ." He said some really nice things. I didn't have a clue he would come and it was just like "wow!"'

Happy accidents in the world of show business are invariably an invention of Hollywood scriptwriters or press agents. Instead, the vast majority of entertainers, singers, actors and dancers have been practising their art since they were children, enjoying their turn in the limelight and lapping up the applause of adults. They work hard for their break. The Robbie Williams story is no exception. He may have always wanted to be considered and accepted as one of the lads in his home town of Tunstall, Stoke-on-Trent, but while his mates were kicking a football around in the park he would be at the local theatre practising his lines and rehearsing his dance steps for an upcoming pantomime or musical. He seldom let on to his friends what he was doing on the grounds, he said, that they would have thought him a 'poof'.

Rob, as he was generally known, always had a strong sense of his own destiny. When he was fifteen years old he used to go with his friend Zoë to Ritzy's nightclub in Newcastle-under-Lyme to the Sunday night youngsters' disco. On one occasion he wore trainers and a very large, mean-looking bouncer refused to let him in. Rob, who was never short of front, stood up to the bruiser and said, 'I tell you, one of these days I could buy and sell this place.'

The first time Rob performed in front of a live audience he was just three years old. His father, the comedian Pete Conway, got him out of bed at the Red Lion pub, which he and his wife Jan used to run in Burslem, to perform on the bar. Jan was not impressed. 'He's not a performing monkey!' she exclaimed.

Jan, however, was always immensely proud of her little boy's capacity to entertain. Later that year they were on holiday in Torremolinos and went to a local talent night. She recalled, 'We heard that "Robert from England" was about to perform and then he stepped out from behind these curtains into the spotlight and took off John Travolta.' From a very early age Rob had an amazing aptitude for impersonation. He had listened intently to Travolta on the jukebox until he was able to imitate his voice and mannerisms. Soon Rob would get himself out of bed at the Red Lion and give impromptu performances of whatever came into his head. Pete Conway recalls that his son could do a winning Brian Clough and Margaret Thatcher.

When Rob attended the Mill Hill Primary School he took the lead in school productions, playing, among other roles, Fagin in *Oliver!* One of the teachers Phil Rossiter, recalls that he was very keen on anything remotely to do with dance, drama and the choir: 'He wasn't very athletic. He was plump and short. He wasn't everybody's favourite and some of the other children found him a bit big-headed and pushy. But he definitely stood out as taking the main parts in our plays. I was amazed, later on, when I saw he was in Take That because I remembered him as a podgy boy aged nine.'

Encouraged by his mother, Rob found an outlet for his interest in performing away from the classroom and that is how he met Zoë Hammond for the first time. They appeared together in a production of *Hans Christian Andersen* performed by the North Staffordshire Amateur Operatic and Dramatic Society (also known as North Staffs). They were just two of the chorus children sitting around listening to the fairytales but it did require a lot of singing and dancing, which the young Robbie Williams was not at all sure he fancied. When the children first had to jump in the air and clap he pulled a face at Zoë as if to say 'What's all this malarkey?' Zoë, one of the very few who preferred to call him Robbie as a boy, explains, 'I told him "You've got two choices. Do you want to be in it or not?" But he did and he knew he did and he was dead good. It's the same with everybody who wants to be on the stage. Suddenly you've got a long skirt and dance shoes on and, as a little lad growing up, I think he thought "Jeez" but he did it. By the time he had learnt what to do, he had crossed that bridge and it didn't bother him.'

Zoë was bright, vivacious and a chatterbox. She and Rob bonded from the start: 'He was one of the reasons why I loved the theatre so much. Wherever I went he followed and vice versa.' Their amazing ten-year friendship forged on the boards of the local amateur dramatics scene is like a touching love story without the frisson of sex. Zoë never fancied her leading man. People who saw them out together could scarcely believe that they had never had a real date. She explains, 'When I see him on the telly now and everyone is going "Phwoar!" I can't because I've seen him as that podgy little lad with freckles. He was bloody fat when he was a child. To me he is just Robbie and I love him.'

The two young friends won their first juvenile leads at the age of eleven in a local pantomime company's production of *Chitty Chitty Bang Bang*. The Stoke-on-Trent Charity Pantomime and Drama Company had been formed for local children who were interested in music and theatre. Carole Banks, the company secretary, put a large advertisement in the *Sentinel*, the local evening newspaper, inviting children to attend an audition at a hotel in Hanley. Jan dropped Rob off and he swaggered in to audition along with thirty other boys for the part of Jeremy. He sang the famous number from the show, 'Truly Scrumptious'. Carole recalls, 'The moment he opened his mouth, I knew he had got the part. The other kids knew it as well.'

Zoë, who secured the part of Jemima, was not so impressed with Rob's singing: 'He wasn't all that good at singing but because he was so good at everything else it didn't matter. He used to struggle with "Truly Scrumptious", which we sang together. I wouldn't say he was crap but he didn't stand there, deliver it and be spot on. I used to say, "You can tell me to shut up if you want to but that line shouldn't be like that." He'd ask why and I'd show him. He did listen. I must have been a right bossy little madam because my mum used to say to me "He's probably thinking who does she think she is!"'

Chitty Chitty Bang Bang was originally a children's story written by Ian Fleming, the creator of James Bond. It became most widely known through the 1968 film in which Dick Van Dyke played the hopeless inventor Professor Caractacus Potts who rescues a derelict car (Chitty) and gives it magical powers. The car helps Jeremy and Jemima to overthrow the government of a country which hates children. It was perfect pantomime fodder. Eric Tams, who played Potts, would rehearse with Zoë and Rob: 'They hit it off so well. Zoë would have a smile from ear to ear. You get some kiddies at that age who resent each other but there was not an iota of that. They were brilliant together. If someone else was rehearsing they would be sitting on a stair going through their lines together.' Zoë and Rob would always learn the whole script, not just their own parts, so they could act as unofficial prompters if anyone forgot a line in rehearsal. They also had no time for the 'little prima donnas', the children who would turn up to auditions or rehearsals and think they were going to sail through. The voice of Robert Williams could be heard announcing loudly, 'There's a lot more people here without talent than there are with.'

Zoë had first-hand experience of Rob's chubbiness when the script called for them to share a bed together because they were brother and sister: 'It wasn't a real bed because it was a set and it was small and not very safe. He was a stocky little bugger and when he was in the bed I could barely get in it. We were cramped together every night and we couldn't stop laughing.'

Rob managed to wind up the director, the grandly-titled Nicholas D. Florey, a Bristol-based theatrical, who contrived to mention his own name twice on the front of the production programme – 'Nicholas D. Florey, in association with Albert R. Broccoli, presents . . .' Rob had this habit of saying 'nuthink' instead of 'nothing': 'It's "*nothing* will change me", Robert,' Mr Florey would say. He would then insist that Rob go away and practise quietly until he could come back and deliver the line properly. When Rob had perfected it he would join Eric and announce, 'I'm going to do *nothing* wrong, Eric.' He would then go out and do his line: 'And *nuthink* will change me . . .' Eric would invariably get a fit of the giggles at his young co-star's antics. Another of Rob's tricks was to hide Eric's shoes two minutes before he was due on stage, causing a mad dressing-room panic. He was just a prankster. 'We used to call him Rob when he was good, and Robert when he wasn't,' laughs Eric.

To try to drum up interest in the production, the pantomime company would attempt various tricks to get a piece in the *Sentinel* or on television. Zoë appeared on the local news telling the presenter that she was looking for a 'brother' to play Jeremy: 'He's got to be able to learn a script in a week and learn songs and not be shy.' She was basically describing Rob, which was just as well because he already had the part! And then there was the car, the original one used in the film. Eric had to pretend the car had a puncture and that they could not get it into the theatre. It worked and he was pictured with the car in the paper. Every night Rob and Eric, who was like a father figure to the children in the cast, would clean and polish the car, making sure it was in tip-top condition. They would sing or go through their lines as they did it because there was such a lot to learn. It was hard work but Rob would often turn to Eric and say, 'I absolutely love the theatre.'

Eventually the first night arrived, attended by the Lord Mayor, Jack Dimmock. It was a triumph for Rob and Zoë, although not for the car. The sound effects failed when it was supposed to start up for the first time, which left Eric on stage feeling a bit stupid. Quick as a flash Rob piped up, 'Get a decent car!' Eric was full of admiration for both Rob and Zoë: 'There wasn't one performance where they forgot any line. There was no hiccup at all. When they sang "Truly Scrumptious" it made the hairs on the back of your neck stand on end.' Afterwards they both came and said, 'Hasn't it gone quick, Eric?' The Mayor went back-stage after the show to congratulate all three. 'Well, Eric', he declared, 'all I can say is that the theatre is in safe hands with these children.' Zoë and Rob stood there, all smiles, absolutely overjoyed.

The Mayor was not the only one who was impressed. David Ogden, who played the Toymaker, maintains, 'Everybody felt that they were better than the kids in the film.' Eric Tams thinks their success was because the mischievousness they needed for the roles came naturally to them. He, however, gave everyone the biggest laugh of the night when his roller skates ran out of control and he nearly careered into the orchestra pit. Rob proved himself to be a trouper by not letting a stomach upset ruin his performance despite having to make frequent dashes to the toilet. One of the girls in the chorus still has her programme for the night signed by 'Robbie the Toilet Man'.

One of the disappointments of the night is that none of the cast has ever seen the video of the performance, much to Carole Banks's annoyance. She had arranged for a professional to video the show but Jan Williams insisted that her current boyfriend could do it. Carole has asked Jan on numerous occasions to see it but with no luck. Perhaps it never came out properly.

Flushed with his success, Rob was now keen to do more musicals. He turned up at the Theatre Royal in Hanley, to join Zoë in an audition for *Annie* for North Staffs. She had to tell him that there were no boys in *Annie*. 'I can always wear a wig,' he countered, showing off his American accent. In the end, he helped Zoë pass the audition which was problematic for her. All the children had to pass a height test by walking under a bar. However, Zoë was too tall. She went home and changed into a pair of jodhpurs to disguise the fact that she was bending her legs to get under it. Even though he was not in it, Rob would still turn up at the theatre. 'He just loved it,' observes Zoë. 'He used to tell us ghost stories and he'd have everybody right there in the palm of his hand. It was like *Jackanory* but ten times better – even the adults would sit round and listen to him. He was brilliant.'

Rob kept his acting interests well away from his new school, St Margaret Ward Roman Catholic High School, just round the corner from his house in Greenbank Road,

Tunstall. There was no school play and his school friends had absolutely no idea of his hidden talents. This was the start of the splitting of the Robert Williams personality. On the one hand, there was the sensitive lad Zoë Hammond knew. He was still fun and a laugh but he was troubled by his parents' break-up and he was fuelled by ambition. And then there was Rob the class clown, always joking, up for anything, a boy who would while away his schooldays in aimless tomfoolery.

Rob the actor appeared in *Fiddler on the Roof* and *The King and I*, in which he was just one of the children at the court. 'He always made an impact,' observes Zoë. 'He could have a two-bit part but you'd know he was there.' He wanted to play the title role in *Bugsy Malone* but, for once, failed to get the part. He had better luck with *Pickwick* for the North Staffordshire Amateur Operatic and Dramatic Society, the biggest group in the region. For the audition at the Queen's Theatre in Burslem, Rob had to sing a song from the show, recite a piece of script and do some dancing in front of the society's committee of some twenty people. All that and at the end of it Rob was given the role of Fat Boy, a two-line part. North Staffs was big news for a seriously aspiring actor, even one with just a two-line part. It was also very businesslike. Rehearsals started almost immediately and Rob had to attend two or three times a week, quite a commitment for a boy of twelve. Ironically, Rob was a little slimmer by this age and needed to be padded out to make a realistic fat boy. *Pickwick* played to full houses for ten nights at the splendid old Queen's Theatre.

The following year when he was fourteen Rob went to audition for what has so far proved to be the pinnacle of his acting life. He wanted to be the Artful Dodger in the North Staffs production of Lionel Bart's Oscar-winning musical *Oliver!* The role of the leader of Fagin's gang of pickpockets is one of the great children's roles in musicals and one for which everyone agreed Robbie Williams was born to play. The competition to play the part was literally around the block but Rob's version of 'Consider Yourself' won him the day. Zoë Hammond was there and turned to her mum and dad and said, 'That one's in the hat.' She was convinced he would be Dodger because 'nobody else was anywhere near his league. It was like lighting a firework. There was never a part like Dodger for Rob. It was just like his God-given gift.'

The rehearsals under the stern eye of the director Ray Jeffery were serious business and an ordeal. This was no 'Anyone for tennis?' type of amateur production. Jeffery treated both adult and child equally harshly. Brian Rawlins, who played Fagin and worked very closely with Robert as he called him, maintains, 'Robert found it very difficult being bawled out by the director. Ray was a perfectionist in his work and he could be very hard on people and very scathing. If you didn't get the inflection just how he wanted it, he could be bloody rude in front of the whole company. Robert found that a bit hard to take. On a couple of occasions at least I found him outside really quite upset after he had been bawled out in public.' And if it was not the director giving the children a tough time then it would be the chorus mistress: 'She was a huge lady and she would scream at them if they didn't get their words right. The song "Be Back Soon" was quite complicated for me and the boys. The trouble was that while they were concentrating on their feet, they were forgetting to sing. It was tough.'

Zoë Hammond, who played the teenage prostitute Bet, says that both she and Rob hated the director: 'I used to think "that bastard". I used to want to tell him what I thought but I never dared to. Rob just took it – most of the time. I can't remember what Ray said once but Rob goes and puts his trainers on and says, "That's it" to me and I said "Alright then, see ya." And he started walking off and I said, "When am I going to see you again then?" I was upset but I wasn't really showing it because I thought, "You don't go running after a bloke do you?" He walked all the way down to the door and turned to me and said, "I've had enough. He's not talking to me like that." I told him, "Calm down a bit, go and have a cup of tea and think about it." I knew he was the sort of person, if he was really upset, who would have just gone. He would have done it. If he had walked out, the show would have been crap without him. By the time he did Dodger he was a star as far as I could see. He was just brilliant and everybody loved him. I loved him.'

Whatever the merits of Ray Jeffery's methods, he succeeded in extracting a fabulous performance from Rob as Dodger. He had the jaunty walk, the swaggering style, the cockney boy mannerisms and he was wizard at pickpocketing – a skill for which he received special coaching and which enabled him to nick the wallets of fellow cast members. Zoë recalls, 'It was thrilling the way he did his lines. It's never left me to this day.' The big first night arrived on 19 October 1988. Rob did suffer from nerves. Most people, who did not know him that well, were impressed by his apparent confidence but, much more than that, he had 'bottle', the courage to go on. Only someone as close as Zoë Hammond knows that behind the bravado Robbie Williams can be just as scared at the prospect of performing as anyone else. 'There were times when he had nerves,' she explains. 'Then he would say "Fucking hell. I can't fucking remember. Can you remember?" I'd tell him to calm down and take a chill pill and then he'd find it. I told him he knew every last line but if he went on like that he would be shit: "Are you going to be good or are you going to be crap?" And then he'd go, "I'm going to be good." And I'd gee him up with, "You are going to be the best!"'

Rob has often needed a special person to spur him on. In those early days it was Zoë. She was also the person to whom Rob could get things off his chest. She would always sit and listen to what he had to say, confident that he would feel better if he had a talk about what was troubling him – often his mother and her boyfriends – until he was ready to pick up his bag, pack up his gear and declare, 'Right, what are we going to do next?' That easy going but close relationship continued away from the rehearsal rooms when the two friends would meet up in nearby Newcastle-under-Lyme, where Zoë's family lived and where Rob's mother ran a small coffee shop. Invariably it was Zoë who would suggest doing something together: 'It was weird because he would never come up to someone and assume anything. In a funny way he was insecure. If I mentioned doing something on a Saturday then he would ring me on that day and say, "Right, what time are we going?" He was a brilliant lad but he needed a bit of a shove.' Often the two of them would go swimming at the local Jubilee Baths before going on to Jan's café. Their hair would still be wet and Jan would say to Zoë, 'Your mum will go mad with me.' On one occasion Jan gave them some truly scrumptious gateau and asked them what they wanted to drink. Rob piped up, 'We don't want any of that cheap coke.' His mother, who always wanted him to speak nicely, said, 'I beg your pardon Robert?' Zoë recalls that when Jan addressed him that way his eyes would roll upwards to the heavens.

The first night proved to be one of the most emotional nights of Rob's life. He had no idea that his dad, Pete, had taken a break from his summer season to surprise his son on his big night. Zoë, whose role was only a minor one, helped Rob get ready in his dressing room. 'I got all his gear out and he put his blue tail coat on. I dressed his hair up and said "How's that?" and he piped up in his cockney accent, "That will do just nicely".' Rob waited off stage for his cue. Zoë was there with him and whispered, 'Go get 'em' so that he would get an adrenalin buzz and Rob swept out on stage.

Back in the 'den' Zoë could hear him on the backstage tannoy: 'I knew the moment he started singing "Consider Yourself" that he was upset. You know when somebody's upset and they can't sing properly.' The other children in the production did not notice but Zoë, who knew Rob so much better, sensed all was not well. 'What's up with him?' she asked. When Rob came off stage for his first break and went back to the den Zoë put her arms around him and asked him what had happened. The answer made her cry: 'He said, "I just put my arm around Richard [Oliver] and said my spiel and looked down into the pit like and bugger me but I've looked up and there is my fucking old man in the front row. How I remembered that song and how I remembered any of the words I don't know. I've got to get a grip before I get back on."'

And Rob cried. He may have been fourteen but, as Zoë observes, 'He put his dad on a pedestal. He was very emotional. I thought it was lovely that he shared it with me because he was a lad and not many lads would open up. They would want to be big and bolshie with it but he didn't. He was all tearful and I just gave him a little squeeze and said, "Right, come on. He's there. He's come to see you. So give him something to be proud of." And he went back out and was brilliant. It made me cry because I loved him so much at this time.'

A group of Rob's mates from school went to see him perform. One friend Giuseppe Romano comments, 'This was the first time we had any real indication of him doing anything like this. I was really impressed.' Perhaps Rob himself had realized just how good he was and wanted to show his friends his achievement. Rob was so sure of his destiny at a youngster. He would play truant from school with his mates but while many of them faced uncertain futures he would say to Zoë, 'Who's going to make it big first then, me or you?' Zoë would always answer, 'Me.' The two friends would have that conversation time and time again over the years. Sometimes it would be, 'Who'd you reckon will have a number one?' Growing up many thought Zoë had a better chance of stardom especially when she reached the final three for a leading role in the Hollywood film version of *Annie*. But sometimes an extra ingredient of luck or choosing the right direction on the career signpost is needed to turn promise and potential into fulfilment. As 17-year-olds Rob was in Take That and Zoë was working the Midlands pub and cabaret circuit as part of a singing duo. She appeared once at the Mill Hill Tavern, now called the Ancient Briton, directly across the road from Rob's house in Greenbank Road: 'It was a dead ordinary night and he just walked in with his dad. I told him, "I really want you to go home!" He said, "Don't be silly, I've come to see you, mate." All I could say was, "This isn't really how I wanted you to see me. I wanted you to see me do something a bit good." He just laughed.'

'He'd walk in singing and he'd go out singing. He just loved it.'

2

Hi-De-Hi

When Pete Conway was the resident MC at the Holme Lacy House Hotel near Hereford he kept a card, which had been sent with a bunch of flowers, stuck into the corner of his dressing-table mirror. Written in black felt tip pen, it read 'Dad, I love you, Rob.'

Rob idolized his father Pete Conway. After all, his dad had been on the telly and was something of a local celebrity. He could sing Sinatra songs, tell jokes and hold an audience in the palm of his hand whether they had paid to see him or not. Years before she became friendly with Rob's mother Jan, Eileen Wilkes was standing in a long, damp queue to get into a dance when a young man started entertaining everyone: 'He had us all laughing and had such a sense of fun. When the doors opened no one wanted to go in. We wanted to stay listening to him. It was Pete.' When Pete Conway walks into a room he owns it. He has a charisma you would not expect to find in an ordinary working man's boozer in Stoke-on-Trent. Eric Tams used to play darts with Pete in a pub in Hanley: 'We got on famously. Within five minutes of walking into any room, Pete was your friend. It's just the same with Rob. He was the most lovable child – I think it must be inbred.'

One of the popular myths about the life of Robbie Williams is that he was born in a pub, the Red Lion at Burslem. Rob himself added to the myth when he announced in a television documentary, 'This is where I was born. I was born in a pub on Oliver Reed's birthday.' Only he wasn't. His parents did briefly run it but their son was already two years old when they took over the licence. Rob was actually born in the maternity wing of the North Staffordshire Hospital in Newcastle Road on 13 February 1974. His parents had been married for nearly four years – a second marriage for both – and Jan had a daughter, Sally, who was ten years older than the new-born Robert Peter. Pete had first started going out with flame-haired Jan when Sally was just eighteen months old.

The first family home was a dark, gothic-looking house in Victoria Park Road, on the west side of Tunstall Park. From the bedroom window at the front the view took in a lake packed with swans and Canada geese and a bandstand where brass bands would strike up at weekends. The three-bedroom Edwardian semi has an atmosphere that the current owner, Sam Evans, attributes to 'ghostly happenings', although she is not sure if there were any poltergeists to disturb the infant Robbie Williams. In the early seventies, in this part of town, you were more likely to encounter doctors and solicitors and young couples on their way up in life. Pete Conway, winner of the television talent contest *New Faces* and his wife Jan fell into that category.

Pete Williams, his real name, was born and bred in Tunstall, the most northerly of the six towns incorporated into the new borough of Stoke-on-Trent in 1910. The village of Tunstall was described in 1795 as 'the pleasantest village in the pottery'. In 1829, Tunstall had a 'very respectable literary society, unassuming in character but assiduous in research'. That conjures a picture a world away from the sprawling, post-industrial area of today. Small-scale coal mining and iron works left their mark on the area but it was as one of the pottery centres that Tunstall gained much of its character. Working-class streets made up of terraced houses were built as homes for the pottery workers. Pete was brought up in just such a house in Newfield Street, just north of the old market place where the Sneyd Arms, an old coaching inn, still dominates the square. These days the inn is run by Maureen Flowers, the former world women's darts champion, and Pete still enjoys propping up the bar from time to time. It is no coincidence that despite a working life of itinerant entertainment Pete can still be found five minutes from where he was brought up. He regards his years in Newfield Street as 'very happy times'. There is a strong sense of community spirit in Tunstall and in Stoke-on-Trent as a whole and Rob, like his father, has, for the most part, retained strong links and affection for his home town. Tunstall is very much a 'small town' in that families have lived there for generations and you are always likely to bump into someone you were at school with while buying your morning paper. That newspaper is unlikely to be *The Times* – the local newsagent's in the High Street does not even stock it because there is no demand.

His grandparents' house in Newfield Street became a second home to Rob while he was growing up and he would join other children to play in the street while they waited for their tea to be put on the table. Pete's father, Phil, was a bricklayer and his mother, Betty, a very popular woman adored by her grandson, worked in a pottery factory. Young Pete was all set for a career in the police force and after he left school at sixteen he joined the cadets. He stayed in the uniform for seven years but found that life as a bobby on the beat in late sixties Stoke-on-Trent did not fire his imagination in the same way as the applause of an appreciative audience. He had won a commendation for tailing a gang of post-office robbers while he was off duty but those plaudits were not enough. He became a well-known face in Potteries pubs and clubs, and was soon successful enough to pack in the police to pursue his dream of a career as a professional entertainer. At the time, Stoke-on-Trent was a thriving centre on the club circuit. It did not 'happen' for Pete immediately. Instead he found work at a local firm which supplied electrical components. He chose the stage name Conway by looking at a list of all his fellow employees and putting Peter next to them to see which was the catchiest. In those early days he used to pretend to be a Liverpool lad because 'every comic came from Liverpool. I used to talk down my nose and say how great it was to be here from Anfield, even though I hadn't been to Anfield.'

The promise of a long-term career became a reality when he won *New Faces*, a seventies alternative to *Opportunity Knocks*, where wannabes would sing their songs or tell their jokes before being either congratulated by a panel of 'experts' or, more entertainingly, 'hatcheted' by Tony Hatch, songwriter and the Simon Cowell of his day. Pete came third in the all-winners grand final, just behind another up-and-coming comedian, Les Dennis (from

Liverpool). Eric Tams observes, 'He did the rounds, got the feel of the thing, the love for it and then went to *New Faces* when he thought he was good enough. Pete had a great natural ability to be funny. You would say something and he would always come back with something comical. He would never belittle you though or make a joke at your expense. He would just be amusing.' Rob has inherited that ability – especially in interviews where he will always have something witty to say. Sometimes he is funny and sometimes not, but he is never dull.

When Rob was two and just twelve months after winning *New Faces*, Pete made a decision to put the family first and became the licensee of the Red Lion in Burslem, an unprepossessing pub just down the road from the Port Vale football ground, which was handy as he was an avid supporter. He explained, 'I phoned around all the agents and managers and said I couldn't do any more bookings because I had become a licensee. I didn't stop doing cabaret but only performed in Stoke because the pub was now the first concern.' It did not take Pete long to realize that this was a big mistake: 'I became unhappy. It just wasn't me. I missed the goings on and the atmosphere of the entertainment business even though I was still doing a bit.' Jan's dream of a settled family life was about to be shattered. Ironically, she had urged him to become a pub landlord because she was concerned that all the travelling involved in being a comic would mean a great deal of time when Pete was not at home. She could not have predicted that when their son was three Pete would walk out on his wife and family and Rob would spend his childhood as part of a broken home. Only Pete can say for sure if he truly achieved his dream. If all he wanted was to be a professional entertainer, as he himself has affirmed, then he has lived up to those aspirations. But the reality is that he became a 'nearly man' of British entertainment, a Hi-De-Hi character with a grim mullet, doing the rounds of Butlins and Pontins or hosting the nightly entertainment in a variety of large resort hotels where a few gags and a spot of crooning would keep the punters happy. He was once the warm-up man for Norman Vaughan (a Liverpool comedian) on the television classic, *The Golden Shot*. But the big time remained tantalizingly out of his reach.

One can only speculate on the lasting effect his parents' split has had on the life of Robbie Williams. Rob's flippant dismissal that his dad was some bloke who came round every so often, took him to Woolworth's and bought him a toy car can assuredly be taken with a large pinch of salt. Pete did not see his son for several months after the break-up but says that when he first saw Rob again he was watching *Batman*. 'Hiya Dad,' he said without taking his eyes off the telly. At the time Pete was sleeping on a pal's floor and is adamant that no one else was involved in his split from Jan. He was, however, always a ladies' man and soon took up with a young barmaid from Hanley and they became a popular couple in the local pubs.

Inevitably, the young Rob would see the glamorous side of his father's life and brag a bit about it to his friends back in Tunstall, especially if he had been in the spotlight as well. He wanted to be part of that life and, of course, he wanted his dad to be proud of him. When Pete was in a summer show – he did four seasons, for instance, at Perran Sands, a Cornish holiday camp – Rob would visit in the school holidays, sometimes for as long as six weeks, and always watch the acts and make a mental note of what the audience liked. Pete's friend Pat Brogan, a boxing promoter, recalls, 'He would watch his dad work and you can't buy people that sort of experience. Pete was a great pro and I'm sure a lot of it has rubbed off on Rob.' From the age of twelve Rob would tell his father that he was going to leave school at sixteen and become an entertainer. Like most parents in that situation Pete told him to go to college first and then try his luck but the young Rob was having none of that.

Pete's work took him to the seaside resorts of Britain and Rob, who loved the lifestyle, would be there in Scarborough, Great Yarmouth or Carmarthen Bay. There were times when it was not quite as glamorous as Pete might have hoped. On one occasion in Cornwall, when Rob was visiting, Pete went into his caravan to discover the future multi-millionaire standing underneath a hole in the ceiling catching the rain in a bucket. During one of those traditional seaside rainy days in Scarborough Pete taught Rob how to play backgammon, a game which remains one of his hotel favourites. One of Pete's best memories is when one of the camp entertainers, Bill Wayne, in a leotard without his trousers on – as was often the case to get some laughs on stage – spotted Rob watching from the wings and beckoned to him to follow him on and copy what he was doing. The act was that he would pretend to be doing keep fit. Rob went on stage, bold as brass, and did exactly what Bill did, copying him precisely and expertly. 'The place was in uproar,' says Pete, proudly.

Rob's nan remained a figure of great importance in Rob's life throughout his childhood and beyond. Even when he joined Take That, he would still be going round to his nan's for his dinner. Paul 'Coco' Colclough, who used to live one street down from Betty Williams, recalls, 'We would go round his nan's to borrow two quid to go to the Power House Gym. That was what it was like; even when he was in Take That. They saw this person on stage but back here he would be round her house and she would always be asking if you wanted some biscuits. "You're all right," he would say. "I'm going to the gym in a bit." She was always for fattening you up. She was a very nice person.'

Pete's mum Betty was clearly a remarkable person. Eileen Wilkes, the mother of Jonathan Wilkes, recalls that she would always have his tea ready for him after school when Jan was working: 'She was a lovely lady. The two boys loved old people. They loved talking to them and hearing all their stories.' When Jonathan first had a piece about him in the local paper, Rob's nan rang up Eileen and said, 'Oh, I am so proud of him. Send him my love.' Ever supportive, Betty even travelled up to Manchester to see her grandson perform with Take That, although the loud screams of the young female fans made her temporarily deaf. Later, when her grandson was a superstar, Rob was absolutely distraught when she died in 1998. He wrote the touching 'Nan's Song' as a tribute to her. It is on the phenomenally successful *Escapology* album. It is the first song on any of his albums that bears the name Robbie Williams as a single writing credit. In it he describes how his nan used to teach him the kings and queens while she stroked his hair. And how, since her death, she is watching over him, by his side every day. Pete was thrilled to be in Los Angeles when his son recorded the song: 'I've been proud of everything he's done but I am really proud of this one. The song for his nan, my mum, is a real tear-jerker.'

While Jan struggled at home to get her son to help with the gardening or do the dishes – 'My worst thing is washing the dishes and wiping them' – and keep his room tidy his father Pete was able to be the hero in absentia. Rob would enthusiastically tell his friends when he was off to stay with his dad at whichever holiday camp he was appearing in at the time. He first got drunk watching his father perform at a camp in Scarborough when he persuaded the barman to slip him bottles of Newcastle Brown, despite not enjoying the taste. A mutual love of beer enabled father and son to become the best of pals during Rob's teenage years. His washing-up, however, did not improve when he was staying with his father at the camps. Pete recalls, 'I would do the cooking and he would do the washing-up and then he would go out and I would do the washing-up again.'

Pete also introduced Rob to boxing. He had been an enthusiastic amateur boxer in his younger days and still enjoyed going to the fights locally. He roped his son in to sell programmes for his promoter friends so that Rob could make some extra pocket money. He, in turn, used to take mates like Lee Hancock and Giuseppe Romano along to help, either at the King's Hall in Stoke or the Victoria Hall, Hanley. The boys would also do the music and the lights when the boxers made their 'grand' entrances towards the ring. Afterwards they would adjourn to the Wagon and Horses, which was run by a friend of Pete's. Rob would get up and do a turn with his dad. The second time Rob got drunk he unintentionally smashed his picture of Muhammad Ali. He was able to replace it a few years later with an Andy Warhol print of the world's most famous sportsman.

Friends continue to point out the similarities between Rob and his dad but they tend to be superficial ones based on the fact that many of Pete's mannerisms as a professional entertainer have rubbed off on his son. They both have great charm and a twinkle in the eye. A friend once described Pete as wearing a smile even when he wasn't smiling. Eileen Wilkes observes, 'Pete is Pete. He'll never grow up.' Kelly Oakes, who met Rob's dad when she used to appear in amateur dramatics with Rob, recalls she thought Pete a bit self-centred: 'I think he liked being in the limelight.'

The poet, Philip Larkin, famously wrote, 'They fuck you up, your mum and dad, they may not mean to but they do.' Rob's parents have had an immeasurable effect on his life, one that he has, perhaps, been able to examine too much through his recent years of therapy. There is his father Pete, a Jack-the-lad character and a great companion whose presence and style clearly influenced the creation of Robbie Williams the public performer. Rob's bi-polar personality is never better illustrated than by his chaotic appraisal of his relationship with his father. On the one hand there is the affectionate tone of his hit 'Strong' in which he says that when he gets drunk he dances like his dad and that he is starting to dress like him. And then there is the lyric to 'My Culture' in which he rages that he is the boy whose father reduced him to tears and who has been lonely for twenty-seven years.

To suggest that there is bitter resentment forever bubbling underneath the surface in Rob's relationship with his father is to simplify his unique personality. It is the height of pathos, however, that it is Pete, who walked out when Rob was so young, who is now the one grabbing the crumbs of contact with his son. A 2002 television documentary entitled *Robbie Williams Is My Son* followed Pete as he found himself out of a job when his long-standing gig as an entertainer in a stately home turned luxury holiday camp in Nottingham came to an end. He was shown packing up his belongings, in preparation for his move back to Stoke-on-Trent, musing on the fact that he had not spoken to his son for over a year. Rob's new lifestyle aimed at overcoming his well-chronicled problems with drink, drugs and personal demons did not include his father, who appeared to be part of the problem rather than part of the solution. Eventually, after eighteen months, Pete received an invitation to visit his son in Los Angeles where, at the time, he was recording *Escapology*. They played table tennis in the garage and rediscovered the comic banter that always existed between father and son. Intriguingly, after originally being frank and honest with the camera crew, he has clearly been told by 'Robbie's people' to watch what he says in the future – and not to talk about Rob. Although privately he might think this is a bit 'precious', he is happy to go along with it if it means regular contact with his son.

Pete, now fifty-eight, has not made a career out of being the father of our most famous pop star. He has been in the entertainment business himself for more than thirty years. The first and last time he has bragged about it was when chatting to some young Take That girl fans in a bar where he was appearing. The DJ was playing the Take That song 'I Found Heaven' on which Robbie sang the lead vocal.

'I'm Robbie Williams's dad,' he announced proudly. The girls looked at him sceptically before one of them replied, 'Are you? Well, I'm the Queen Mother,' and with that they marched off.

'Pete and Robert are like peas in a pod.'

3

Mum

When Rob was earning some decent money with Take That, he decided to surprise his mum on her birthday. She was working in her florist's, Bloomers, in May Bank, Stoke-on-Trent, and was not expecting him. He surreptitiously set off all the alarms so she came running out of the shop to see what was going on. There, parked outside, was a gleaming white BMW with a great big bow on the bonnet.

While Pete Conway always maintained a home base in Stoke-on-Trent and strived to see as much of his son as he could, it was left to Rob's mother, Jan, to play the thankless role of single parent. She had to rely a great deal on the kind hearts of Pete's parents to help out while she endeavoured to make a success, first of a boutique followed by a coffee shop and then a florist's. She always appreciated the value of money and was quite shrewd about business. When she decided to sell the coffee shop, she waited until she had secured a licence to sell alcohol so that she could increase its attraction to potential buyers. Eileen Wilkes, who has been a friend for twenty years, says that Jan still has some of the furniture she had when she was first married, despite the grand homes she has since enjoyed thanks to her son's relatively recent wealth.

As well as having to raise two children by herself, Jan faced the dilemma of trying to have a life as well. Inevitably, this led to some family conflicts and heartbreak for her son, although Rob has always remained 100 per cent loyal to his mother. They moved in to a smart post-war semi in Greenbank Road, Tunstall, opposite the Ancient Briton pub, a dream location for a teenage boy. Behind the pub, a sprawling council estate ran down towards Burslem and Hanley but on the Williams's side of the street the houses were privately owned. Their house was kept tidy but friends remarked that it was a bit higgledy-piggledy with things here, there and everywhere – very much a family home where everyone would sit watching a television that was kept in a dark wood cabinet in the lounge. The three-piece suite was green and in the front room there was an upright piano for Christmas sing-songs and the creation of one-finger classics. It was very homely. Rob even kept a couple of parakeets. One morning he went into school and told his mates that one of the birds had died the previous evening. They never told him that when they had been round his house the day before they had been persecuting the poor thing by poking it with a pencil.

The house in Greenbank Road was ideally placed for both the Mill Hill Primary School and the St Margaret Ward Roman Catholic High School. It was also a short stroll to the High Lane Oat Cake Shop, one of young Rob's favourite places. Oat cakes in this part of the world are nothing to do with biscuits for cheese. Instead, they are belt-busting savoury pancakes filled with cheese and bacon and other ingredients that have no place in the faddy diets of celebrities. Rob loved them.

Jan has always tried to involve herself in her son's life, mindful that he did not have an ever-present father to join him. So Jan took up golf when Rob became interested, playing with him at Burslem Golf Club. She was a left-hander and, according to Tim Peers, who used to play golf with Rob, she 'wasn't bad at all'. She joined the amateur dramatics society to keep her son company and she became a drugs counsellor when he showed a little too much interest in narcotics. She was not a great actress – she was consigned to the chorus – and preferred the more relaxed good humour of the Olde Time Music Hall. She also involved Rob in one of her own passions, horse racing, particularly when she went out for a couple of years with a man who was an owner and knew the England and Manchester United captain Bryan Robson, definitely something to grab the attention of a young lad. Rob was much more interested in football than racing although, when he was old enough, he routinely spent the afternoon in a bookie's in Burslem with his mates.

Tim Peers remembers Rob's mother as being very 'down to earth'. He adds, 'She was very realistic about things but very supportive at the same time.' Kelly Oakes was struck at 'how chilled' Jan always seemed: 'Nothing fazed her.'

'His mum was lovely, a very generous person,' remarks Lee Hancock, Rob's best friend at school. 'There were no rules in the house but she was definitely not one of the lads. She was very much a mum. She would have been an attractive woman in her day.' She was certainly attractive enough to have a number of boyfriends over the years, not all of whom met with the approval of her son. And not everyone shared Lee Hancock's high opinion of her.

Pantomime organizer Carole Banks observes, 'I think Jan thought she was the bee's knees when Robert was young.' She remembers he 'kicked off' as a 12-year-old when it was suggested the family go to stay with one boyfriend from Nottingham: 'He didn't want to go and I heard him say "I'm fed up with your boyfriends."' She also recalls dropping Rob off at his grandmother's house after rehearsals and his nan saying to her, 'Oh, you picked him up again!' David and Val Ogden, who were also involved in *Chitty Chitty Bang Bang*, often saw Rob waiting at the bus stop on his own and they would give him a lift back home because his mum was unable to make it.

'His mum did leave him to come on his own,' recalls David. 'She did pick him up sometimes but often she would be late and one of the things I best remember was when I had a conversation with him one time about getting home: "Robert, is your mum picking you up tonight?" "Yeah." "Well, where is she?" "Oh, she's out with her new fella."'

Zoë Hammond recalls his mother turning up to the Queen's Theatre in Burslem: 'She was wearing a fur coat and she's standing there with more lip gloss on than Boots the chemist have and there's this bloke with her looking as smarmy as you like and there was Rob – he just had that look of "here we go again".' Zoë was present at a heartbreaking scene at the after-show party when Rob, then fourteen, achieved his greatest amateur triumph as the Artful Dodger in *Oliver!*: 'His mum turned up with a brown paper bag and she said "Here you are Rob", and tossed it to him. And he just looked and I knew by his face he was upset. He walked down the stairs from where we had the party and sat on the steps outside where we used to rehearse. I followed him down and said "What's up?" He was really upset and he said, "It's really difficult for me because I love my mum to bits but I don't always agree with her choice. You know what's in the bag? My pyjamas – I'll have to sort something out for tonight." My heart went out to him. I think his mum was trying to find a bit of happiness, looking for Mr Right, but he didn't always agree with who she picked if you know what I mean. He protected her like you'd never know and it took a lot that night for him just to tell me that he was upset. You know how some lads are but he was never like that. He was just down in the mouth about it but never nasty.

'I always felt dead sorry for him because he loved his mum but he felt in the way, sometimes, of what she was doing at the time and yet, despite all of the feelings and all of the confusion he was going through on a personal level, he never went funny with his mum. I found that really weird because I used to say to him, "If it was my mum I couldn't be doing with it. I don't know how you can just stand by her like you do." He just got on with his life even though inside it hurt. That was the way it always was. No matter what feelings she gave him as a kid, he never retaliated.'

When Zoë told her own mum, who was at the party, about the incident with the pyjamas she asked her why she had not asked Rob to go home with them. 'I didn't like to because he was that het up about it,' she replied. 'I just said to him, "What are you going to do?" and he said, "Oh, I'll be all right." Reading between the lines, I was sure he would go round to his nan's. He was very close to her.' Rob would often talk about his grandmother to members of the cast in his amateur dramatics. Brian Rawlins, who played Fagin to his Dodger, was struck by the bond that existed between the two: 'He used to talk an awful lot about his nan.'

The observations and recollections by those who knew Rob reveal a degree of emotional turmoil in his adolescence. Intriguingly it is the female of the species who noticed the sensitive side to his nature, certainly where his mother and father were concerned. He would never have dreamt of opening up to the 'lads', which would almost certainly have been considered a mark of weakness. Instead, Rob had to bottle up these feelings while maintaining the veneer of bravura for his mates at school. Under these circumstances 'having a laugh' became a method of protection, a form of defence that he continues to use in public.

Jan never planned for her son to become a superstar – that would be impossible. But she did try and instil basic values in him. She was from a strong Irish Catholic, working-class family. Her great-grandparents had escaped from the poverty of Kilkenny in the south-east of Ireland to try to find a better life in Staffordshire. Her father, Jack Farrell, a well-known local character in Tunstall, was in the building trade. He had married her mother, Janetta, in the Church of the Sacred Heart, just a mile from the home in which Rob grew up. It would be stretching credibility to suggest that Rob had a Catholic upbringing in a strong sense but his secondary school, St Margaret Ward, was a Roman Catholic school where it was compulsory to take classes and a GCSE in RE (religious education). There was a chapel in the school and Rob had to join other pupils to celebrate feast and saints days. One of his best schoolmates, Giuseppe Romano, says, 'The Catholic faith did play a significant part in the education.' The most obvious religious link for Rob came when there was a weekend away to a Catholic retreat called Soli House in Stratford-upon-Avon. The then deputy-head, John Thompson, was impressed with Rob's contribution to a day spent discussing moral issues including poverty: 'He always led the discussions and helped act out the playlets to illustrate the concerns. He thought very quickly and could ad lib well.' Mr Thompson's considered recollections of Soli House are a little different from those of Rob's mate Lee Hancock. 'It was a weekend away boozing – a day or two on the pop,' he observes. Another friend, Phil Lindsay, confirms, 'We used to sup beer until we fell asleep. You were free to do what you wanted.'

The schoolmates, however, were overawed by a glimpse of Rob's talent, which, up until then, had been hidden from them. On the last day, each of the 15-year-olds had to do a little turn, a mini talent competition with no prizes. Rob sang a song quite beautifully. It was 'Every Time We Say Goodbye', the haunting classic by Ella Fitzgerald and a slightly less inspiring hit in late 1987 for Simply Red.

Robert Williams was one of the politest boys you could find in Stoke-on-Trent. Everyone remarked on it. While there was a side to Rob which enthusiastically embraced the contemporary teenage culture of drinking, drug-taking and scallywag behaviour, the other, hidden face of Robert Williams was one who always treated people – especially his elders – with the utmost respect and courteousness. That element never formed part of the image that became Robbie Williams, a bad boy off the rails, a cheeky schizoid pop star. Nothing encapsulates this secret side of the superstar more than his membership of the Burslem Golf Club. Belonging to a golf club and observing the rules and traditions of the game is not going to bring street cred or working-class hero status.

The nine-hole course was only a five-minute walk from the house in Greenbank Road so Rob could easily pop up after school or in the holidays. Sometimes he would play with his father, sometimes his mother but more often than not he would muck in with Tim Peers and his fellow juniors. Rob was a useful player but, more importantly, he was elected junior captain when he was fifteen, in 1989, the year before he joined Take That. Jim Peers, Tim's father and the man who was responsible for organizing the junior team, explains, 'Robert was responsible for the conduct and etiquette of the other juniors particularly when they played other clubs in competitions. He was always very polite and had to wear a jacket and tie just as the senior members do after a competition. He also gave a speech at the junior captain's day.' Tim confirms, 'Rob took it seriously. His persona on the golf course was nothing like the Robbie Williams we read about but it was still a good crack when we played.'

Although there was not a huge amount of money to splash around when Rob was growing up, Jan always did her best to provide him with the trimmings he wanted. He had a set of good golf clubs, a BMX mountain bike, and a Sega games console in his room, which was the box room at the front of the house. He could open the curtains and see the pub sign opposite. Giuseppe Romano observes that Jan probably spoilt him like any single mother would her son but adds, 'If she did spoil him, it didn't show in his school uniform. He was a right scruffy bastard.' Rob was far from hot on the domestic front but Giuseppe does recall the time when Rob was starving and decided to impress everyone by cooking an omelette after school: 'We went round there one afternoon and he made this huge omelette and had it in the pan. I got this chewing gum which I was chewing at the time and chucked it in there when he wasn't looking. When it was cooked he put it on the plate and started eating it. We were all killing ourselves so I had to tell him it was a spearmint-flavoured omelette. He went right off it and chucked it outside in the backyard. He wasn't very happy.'

Jan always wanted her son to achieve something which is why she made him respect the value of manners, speaking proper English and doing his schoolwork (something she soon gave up on). Eventually she realized that she was going to have to accept his show-business ambitions and that it would be better to work with them rather than face the same struggles she had during her marriage to Pete. When Rob was coming up to ten they were watching television together when the dire eighties group Kajagoogoo came on. Jan suggested playfully that Rob must want to be a pop star like them but Rob surprised her by saying that his ambition was to be an actor and he had no interest in being a pop star. In the end it would be Jan's impetus that turned Rob towards a musical rather than an acting career.

Both Rob's parents have obviously had a profound effect on his life, perhaps more so because of their own troubled split. But it is his mother Jan, there day in and day out, who has always been the biggest influence. Lee Hancock confirms, 'He didn't chat about his dad – it was always his mum. He loved his mum.'

Rob's elder sister, Sally, has always been a rock of dependability for him. Quietly, she has got on with her own life while supporting him as much as she can. She was always very popular with Rob's mates, who regarded her as his attractive elder sister – forever unattainable. 'Sally was nice,' says Lee Hancock, simply. Rob has always regarded her as his sister and never introduced or referred to her as his half-sister. For her part she was happy to indulge him and his mates. She never went in for amateur dramatics but would sometimes go to watch him perform. Zoë Hammond met her in Jan's coffee shop in Newcastle-under-Lyme, where Sally had a part-time job: 'She was a pretty girl. He would always refer to her as "My Sally" or "My mum and Sal". He never said she was his half-sister. It was always "Sally, my sister". She was all right.' Sometimes Sally would join Jan and Rob for a kebab in the Tersatolis restaurant, round the corner from the Theatre Royal in Hanley. The proprietor, Hamid Soleimani, recalls that sometimes Jan would have a man in tow and that they were always very polite and friendly. He would sit down and have a chat with them about how things were going. He has never forgotten the night when Rob asked if he could get up and do a Frank Sinatra song for the clients. Hamid is a great fan of Rob's mother, whom he calls 'a wonderful lady, modest and down to earth'. Ironically, he still sees Pete for a social drink and was as pleased as punch when Pete told him that Rob had asked after the kebab restaurant when he visited him in Los Angeles.

By the time Rob had joined Take That, Sally had moved out of the family home. She still lives in Newcastle-under-Lyme with her partner Paul Symonds, a local golf professional who is useful for family golf lessons. She used to help run the Take That fan club, which had 70,000 members – but that became unworkable after Robbie left the group. With all the bad feeling flying around it was inevitable that someone would suffer in the fallout. She was suspended on full pay after the split and then fired the day after the band itself called it a day. These days she is a full-time mother. Her favourite indulgence is riding her horse, a mare called Shannon, which Rob gave her for Christmas a couple of years ago.

After the birth of her son, Rob was so chuffed at becoming an uncle for the first time that he devoted one of his Brit awards in 2001 to baby Freddie. He said, 'Your mum can play this video tape back to you of when your uncle was famous.' It was at this time that Sally had a serious conversation with her brother about what was truly important in life. They had both agreed that it was family and friends: 'It is especially important for someone in the music business like Robbie. It doesn't matter how successful you are or how famous, what really counts is your relationships with those that are closest to you.'

Jan Williams has thrived on Robbie's success. Whereas Pete is still, broadly speaking, the same man now as he was thirty years ago, money and prestige within the family appear to have given Jan stature. Sometimes the media have gently poked fun at Rob's reliance on his mum as if to suggest that a grown man should not be as close to his mother as Robbie Williams is to his. Rob is absolutely steadfast in his appreciation of his mother's role in his life. One of the few instances where Robbie Williams has ever been serious in an interview was when a journalist suggested that his mother must have nagged him when he was a kid. 'No she didn't,' was the sobering response. 'She just worries about me.' And she has had plenty to worry about!

In the early days her son's fame was more of a nuisance, disrupting her life. She would complain bitterly about the girl fans, sometimes as many as 300, who would deprive her of her privacy at the family home in Greenbank Road. They would come from all over the world to sit on the wall outside, carve messages of love including their phone numbers or, sometimes, the bolder ones would knock on the door demanding to know the whereabouts of their beloved idol. Jan was forced to put up a handwritten notice on her front door asking them to keep away. But there would always seem to be thirty or forty outside, even on a slow day.

Sometimes it would all get out of hand. Once, Rob was in the Ancient Briton pub across the road enjoying a few beers in the company of friends. He decided to adjourn to the comfort of his home with a young woman friend, who was most definitely 'up for it'. The tipsy pair pushed their way through the throng of fans and into the house, firmly bolting the door behind them. Just as they had dispensed with their clothes and were getting down to things there was a loud knock at the door. Rob, thinking it was another lovestruck fan, shouted out, 'Why don't you just fuck off!' A voice from beyond the door bellowed, 'Robert. It's your mother. Let me in!'

Eventually, Jan put the house up for sale at the end of 1994 for £57,950 and Rob bought her a house on the posh side of Newcastle-under-Lyme where she had always fancied living. It was not just to try to escape the headlamps of celebrity. Jan had begun to realize that her son had a serious drink problem and she did not want photographers to have an easy opportunity of catching him drunk whenever they happened to be passing.

She gave up the flower shop and devoted her life to her son in two main ways. Firstly, she enrolled at the Stoke-on-Trent College in Shelton to do a social studies course, which would enable her to act as a drugs counsellor. Secondly, she became chairwoman and main mover and shaker of the Give It Sum charity which was set up to channel some of the Robbie Williams millions back into his home town. Over the years she has become an accomplished and authoritative speaker on both issues – Rob and drugs and Rob and good works – not for her the glib one-liners which so characterize the conversations of her son and his father. The Give it Sum charity is administered by Comic Relief, and their experts, with a proven track record, make up the majority of the London-based committee. This is a very serious concern and not, in any way, the idle plaything of a celebrity mother with too much time and money on her hands. One of the biggest projects so far has been a six-figure donation to Rob's old school, St Margaret Ward. The idea is to promote the school as a centre for performing arts for children in the area. It is a far cry from the days when Rob was there and, according to his mate Giuseppe Romano, the only musical instrument they were taught was the recorder.

Jan, quite the politician, told the *Sentinel,* 'Robert has a very strong affection for his school and for Mr Bannon, his headmaster. He has a vast admiration for him and for his other teachers.' Rob certainly had a 'vast admiration' for the PE teacher, Mrs Gittings, whose athletic derrière was the object of much young masculine fantasy.

Give it Sum has so far given well over a million pounds
to all manner of community projects from toddlers to
pensioners throughout the north Staffordshire region.
Many areas of Stoke-on-Trent remain quite depressed –
some houses, not too far from where Rob used to live, still
have tin roofs. There is no doubt that the charitable
initiatives in Robbie's name have greatly increased his
personal standing within the community. All he needs to
do now is invest in Port Vale Football Club and the man
would be a Midlands Messiah.

In real terms Give It Sum is more a reflection of his
mother than himself. He lives practically full time in Los
Angeles and relies on Jan to keep him informed. She told
the *Sentinel*, 'The charity isn't something I am doing as
Robbie Williams's mum. This is me. It's very much in my
heart and I'm doing it because I want to do it. It's a vehicle
for me to be able to channel my own thoughts and
feelings and desires into something. Robert isn't here and
I can oversee things and feed them back to him and the
committee.'

Her influence was also vital in his acceptance of a role
as patron of the Donna Louise Trust, which raises funds
for a children's hospice. Donna Louise Hackney had died
of cystic fibrosis when she was sixteen. One of the trust's
committee members, Keith Harrison, was a policeman
who, by chance, lived close to Jan Williams and he asked
her if Rob would be interested in helping: 'I thought it
would be a terrific idea for him to consider us.' Both Jan
and Rob were sufficiently impressed to visit the Treetops
hospice at Trenthams Lake, Stoke-on-Trent, which cares
for up to eight dying children. Keith was delighted that
Rob showed a genuine interest and was quite obviously

moved by what he saw. One eyewitness reported that he was 'almost overwhelmed' by the courage of the sick children. The trust is well on the way to reaching its appeal target of £5 million. Although a platoon of corporate suits keep Rob cocooned from day-to-day life, the Donna Louise Trust is one thing in which he does maintain a personal interest. Coincidentally, Donna Louise's mother, Christine Hackney, used to know Betty Williams and met Rob when he used to visit his nan in Newfield Street.

You get the impression these days that Jan Williams would walk it if she stood for Parliament. Some things connected with her son's fame do still irk her. When the headmaster, Conrad Bannon, introduced her to the school, when she was presenting a cheque on behalf of Give It Sum, he asked, 'Do you know who this is?' 'Yes,' shouted a chorus of young voices. 'It's Robbie Williams's mum.' She has just had to get used to it, although intriguingly it is Pete Conway, a minor celebrity all his career, who professes to not minding a bit that he is now universally regarded as Robbie Williams's dad. Jan Williams has the precious gift of tolerance. While her son's life resembled a pinball on speed, she seemed to find a new serenity. The last time Hamid Soleimani spoke to her she was sitting by herself in a restaurant in Newcastle-under-Lyme quietly reading a book.

Robbie's success has been a life changer for Jan. She has been able at last to indulge her passion for travel with trips to India and Cuba – and she plans to visit China. She has been liberated whereas the boundaries of Robbie's life have grown smaller. He has continued to buy her expensive gifts because he can afford to. In 1999 he paid Jeffrey Archer £20,000 for an Andy Warhol portrait of

Grace Kelly and gave it to his mother. 'Robbie might be a pop star with a reputation for wild ways, but I found him very charming and well-mannered,' said the soon-to-be-jailed novelist. He upgraded the family home to a remote and stunning million-pound residence in the village of Betley near Newcastle-under-Lyme. It boasted five bedrooms, five reception rooms, three bathrooms and twenty-four acres of landscaped gardens. It even had its own lake with an island in the middle, ideal for boating and picnics. And, of course, there was a games room for Rob. The property afforded Rob the privacy and opportunity to indulge his 'little boy' fantasies such as driving his brand new Ferrari at breakneck speed round the driveway – the only place he was allowed to drive because he did not have a licence.

Jan may not have enjoyed the pressure of Take That or her son's descent into drink and drugs purgatory but her grip on her son's life shows no sign of weakening. For a while their relationship was strained when Rob first moved to London – her little boy leaving home – but Rob said after he realized his addiction problems that they were getting back their mother–son relationship. By way of apology, he wrote a song for her called 'One of God's Better People'. The change in Jan's own life was not an overnight one. School friends of Rob who used to see her in Tesco in Newcastle-under-Lyme recall that she would always speak and say hello. But the sheer magnitude of Robbie's fame has meant that she is more likely to be seen shopping in Notting Hill or Beverly Hills than in downtown Newcastle-under-Lyme, and never in Tunstall. Rob rented a huge mansion for her when she visited him in Los Angeles. He also spent more than £1 million on a

five-storey Georgian house for her round the corner from
his London home. In her exclusive birth chart on Robbie,
Madeleine Moore reports, 'It is possible that in the
fierceness of the son's commitment to his public status
and career, he is living out the dreams of the mother.'

**'Your mum's your mum and you've only got one
mum.'**

4

Willwogs

Rob's drug of choice at high school was Lynx spray
deodorant. He and his mates would put a towel or a tissue
over the top, shake the can and bring the gases out gradually.
They called it 'toiling over the nozzle'.

Rob's teenage life revolved around what can best be
described as a 'lad's culture'. He was desperate to be part
of it, to be considered one of the boys, a paid-up member
of the gang of schoolmates who had a 'life's a laugh and
we don't care' attitude. It was a philosophy in direct
contrast to his female-dominated domestic life at
Greenbank Road or his 'acting' life where he would reveal
his sensitivity and hurt to his first real love Zoë Hammond.

At home, his mum called him Robert. At school, he
rejoiced in the nickname of Willwogs – occasionally
Willywogs – a most un-PC moniker, which not surprisingly
failed to find its way on to his Take That curriculum vitae.
'He is the junior captain of the golf club and he answers
to the nickname of Willywogs' are not the sort of titbits
that are going to encourage young girls to stick your
poster on their bedroom wall. Everyone had to have a

nickname at school. It resembled the cast list of *Auf Wiedersehen Pet*. Rob's best mate Lee Hancock was Tate, and then there were Giuseppe Romano (Gius), Peter O'Reilly (PO 2) and Philip Lindsay (Lino). Sometimes Rob would get away with being called plain Will or, on other occasions, Swellhead because he literally had a big head, although some thought it fitted him perfectly because he was so full of himself.

Rob unintentionally stood out when he first arrived at St Margaret Ward because he started school a few days' late, always a mistake because it becomes that much harder to be accepted once initial cliques have been formed. The start of term had clashed with his appearance in *Chitty Chitty Bang Bang* at the Theatre Royal in Hanley. Philip Lindsay recalls seeing him for the first time in the school foyer sporting a ridiculous haircut: 'He must have had his hair dyed for the play because it was in streaks.' Rob did not tell the other boys then that he had been in a musical, preferring to suggest that he had been on holiday. The boys responded by nicking his BMX bike, which had Rob weeping and wailing that his grandma had bought him the bike but she was dead: 'We felt that sorry for him that we brought it back,' recalls Giuseppe. 'Then he legged it home.'

Lee Hancock confirms, 'He was full of that much crap!' Lee and Rob were not the best of friends at first because they fell out over a girl, the first real object of desire for pubescent young Rob. Her name was Joanna Melvin, a very pretty girl with mousy brown hair: 'We both fancied her. She was in my class. We were in the top band and Rob was in the dunces' class. I asked her out and she said no. Then Rob asked her out and she went with him for a bit and then she changed from Rob and went with me. She chose me over Rob. I ended up courting her for three or four years when we were about eleven to fourteen. I remember that she was the first girl in school to have one of those frizzy perms when they first came in years ago. Rob and I used to have fights over her – we hated each other! I would say looking back that our fights were even.' The rejection by Joanna obviously rankled with young Rob. Years later, when he was hugely famous, he told Phil Lindsay, 'I bet Joanna Melvin would go with me now!'

The saga of Joanna obviously did not help Rob's efforts to break into the ring of friends in the lower years of senior school. Tate, Gius and Peter O'Reilly were inseparable, although there used to be a 'massive gang' of boys they all belonged to. He and Peter were soon at loggerheads over another girl, Sharon Fernley. Once again it was Rob's precious bike that suffered. Giuseppe Romano recalls, 'We had decided to get revenge on him and let down the tyres. He kicked up this big stink about them being special tyres with special valves, which meant you couldn't just pump them up with any old bicycle pump. We all got into trouble with the headmaster who made us run round the football pitch.'

Rob discovered that the only way he was going to be allowed into the lads' circle was by making them laugh. As a result he swiftly gained a reputation for being a bit of a clown. He used to walk home with Phil Lindsay and his sister, Leah, who lived near Greenbank Road. Phil recalls, 'He was always messing about, being the class clown. At the time the Rambo films were really big and he used to put his tie round his head as if he were Sylvester Stallone. And we would always walk past this row of hedges and most nights he would dive over them pretending to be Rambo.' Rob also managed to fall out with Phil over a girl, Leanne Cox, whom they both fancied: 'We didn't actually fight over her but we had some serious arguments.'

Girls, in these early teenage years, were not a priority. 'We used to take the piss out of them,' remembers Giuseppe. 'There was a big posse of us who would hang out and we would have a laugh at the girls' expense. We would speak to the girls and that was about it. There were a couple of fit girls – Joanna was all right. It was a lad's culture. I can't remember him having any birds at school. We just had a good time, really, and girls didn't come into that.'

Perhaps for that reason Rob was quite secretive about losing his virginity. He never told Giuseppe or Lee for fear they might take the mickey out of him. But he did confess to Phil Lindsay as they chatted at his house the day after the deed was done: 'He said it was in his bedroom at home. I don't know if any drink was involved because they were never going out or anything like that.' Rob's only recollection of it is that it was not his best performance, although he was delighted.

Eventually Rob became accepted as one of the boys. 'He was still the show-off, even though he was now one of the gang,' observes Lee. Their own close bond was forged when they discovered they both shared the same off-the-wall humour and, in particular, a love of the satirical northern band, the Macc Lads, a now defunct rock group from Macclesfield. Lee remembers, 'We used to sing all their songs which had lots of swearing in and were degrading to women. We used to love them.'

And then there was Vic Reeves, who became Rob's schoolboy hero. Later the pair would become firm friends when Robbie appeared on Vic's *Shooting Stars* programme on television. At this time in the late eighties the 'in' show was *Vic Reeves's Big Night Out*. Willwogs and Tate, like many a school friend before them, would laugh themselves silly recounting the previous night's show to each other, literally line by line. Lee observes, 'We were always reciting Vic. We just discovered we had the same sense of humour. We talked about Vic Reeves, Macc Lads, beer and football. We never talked about school work. We never worried about exams. It didn't matter and we didn't care.'

One of the reasons Rob was not too bothered about school work was because, academically, he was not the brightest apple in the barrel. He was in the lower stream and he never particularly shone. Lee recalls, 'He was that thick in French that the person next to him told him the answer and Rob stood up and said "Je suis un jardin" – I am a garden.' He did poorly in exams, never taking them seriously. What the school did for Rob more than anything else was to give him a sense of belonging. Throughout his life there is a thread running through of someone with an enormous need for approval and acceptance. Clearly his ability to communicate through lyrics and humour was not something which could flourish in a school environment. Indeed one teacher famously derided Rob, declaring that he would never amount to anything – a prediction that Rob took great pleasure in throwing back at him on his *Life Thru a Lens* album with a devastating poem which began 'Hello Sir, remember me?' Rob was never a candidate for sixth form college, something his mother and father had to accept. His friend Kelly Oakes, who was two years above him in school, observes, 'I don't think he ever had a plan in mind. He was just going to be an entertainer and that was it.'

Rob and Lee became Tunstall's answer to the Chuckle Brothers. At this time Jan Williams was running a florist's and the pair would go in and make a nuisance of themselves. On one occasion they sent jokes to all the other Interfloras on the fax machine, clogging up the whole system with jokes from Bloomers, May Bank, Stoke-on-Trent. 'He got bollocked for that,' laughs Lee. They went babysitting for one of Jan's friends: 'We were smoking as you do and we decided to ring 1471 to see who'd phoned. Then we used to ring the people up and tell them jokes. We phoned up this chartered accountant and told him jokes on his answer machine for a quarter of an hour until his tape ran out.'

The two 'Likely Lads' would also ring up advertisements they saw in the paper: 'We once saw this car for sale in the *Sentinel*. It was for a Lada Estate. We rang it up and pretended we were funeral directors, as you do. "Hello," says Rob. "We're very interested in this car you've got for sale. The thing is we need it in a bit of a hurry 'cos we're undertakers and the hearse has broken down. What I need to know from you is will it hold a dead body in the back?" Rob was so brilliant at voices; we used to have great fun on the phones.'

Their *pièce de résistance* was repeatedly ringing up some poor bloke. Rob would run through his repertoire including Frank Spencer and a loud black man, which Lee recalls was his particular favourite. 'Some bloke would answer and Rob would ask, in a voice, "Is Pete there?" The bloke would say, "No, never heard of him." Rob would put the phone down and then ring back, using a different voice, "Is Pete there?" "No!" This would go on for four or five times, one after the other. Then, finally, I would ring up: "It's Pete here. Have there been any messages for me?" We used to do stupid things.'

Now that he was a fully paid-up 'lad' Rob was able to participate in two of the favourite pursuits: football and curries. He joined games in Tunstall Park, just a kick-around after school, but in summer it would be three or four evenings a week. One of the boys who played, Paul Phillips, never knew Rob's real name until he was in Take That. He was just known as Willwogs. Whenever it was one of the lads' birthdays half a dozen of them would pile over to an Indian restaurant in Shelton called Al Sheiks. Lee remembers, 'There would be quite a few of us. We would go across the road to the Norfolk Inn and get all the beer because the restaurant didn't have a licence. We paid fifty pence deposit on the glasses and took them to the curry house. We always ended up drunk and throwing all the food about, as you do. I don't know why they used to keep letting us back in – we used to cause that much of a nuisance.'

Towards the end of the school time Rob took up smoking with the rest of the lads. He would trot down to behind the school water tower where the hardened smokers would fill their lungs with their cigarette of choice. Rob's preferred schoolboy inhalation was Silk Cut Ultra Lights. Zoë Hammond recalls that he was smoking when he played Dodger in *Oliver!*: 'You could smell it on him. He was about thirteen when he started hanging out with his cronies and smoking. He would have smoked whatever he could have got his hands on, being a dead ordinary lad.' There was always the hint that Rob was a lot less cool than he would have liked to have been. He discovered rap music. His record collection read like a coffee shop menu – Ice T, Ice Cube and Vanilla Ice. He loved Vanilla Ice, a one-hit wonder whose number one 'Ice Ice Baby' is unlikely to find a place in any play list which includes Eminem.

School was a bit like a holiday camp. Rob has always said how much he enjoyed it and it's true that he seldom got into any trouble even though the headmaster, Conrad Bannon, had a fearsome reputation among his ne'er-do-well flock for being very strict. Giuseppe observes, 'He was pretty decent really although we all had the cane. We just used to take the piss out of a lot of the teachers.' One favourite trick for Rob and Lee was walking behind the French teacher Mr Openshaw, who had a hearing aid. The boys would start whistling so the poor man would start tapping his hearing aid thinking it was on the blink. Lee laughs, 'Rob loved all the messing around.'

Certainly Rob was doing his share of 'bobbing off' as playing truant was called. If there was a lesson they didn't fancy they would scoot down towards the gates at the bottom of the school grounds where there were temporary classrooms and loads of trees in which they could keep out of the way, have a smoke and chat about things. Very occasionally they would talk about their aspirations. Giuseppe wanted to be an airline pilot, Lee an air traffic controller or stockbroker and Rob a redcoat at Butlins. The students were not allowed out of the grounds at lunchtime; instead they would eat chips and kick a ball about in the yard. Lee and Rob used to have a competition where they would put all their chips on a fork and see how many they could get in their mouth at the same time.

The 'lads' were a bunch of masculine plonkers at school. Lee and Rob used to have sweating competitions. The idea was to see who could get their shirt to smell worst by wearing it day after day. It got to the stage where they would sit next to radiators all day to get more of a sweat on and deliver those lovely wet patches under the arms. Then Giuseppe and Rob had a bet which involved shaving off their pubic hair. 'I remember it was very itchy. The bet was that we would each shave off half our pubes. It was something we arranged in the changing rooms after PE. We both did it but the funny thing is I can't for the life of me remember what the bet was for!' Occasionally the girls would get their revenge on the lads, like the time they told the lads there was going to be a great party in a local community hall. The boys arrived, clutching alcohol and shouting out, 'Hey, we've got the beer!' only to discover that they were gatecrashing an evening karate class. The girls also ran a 'fit list' in the fifth year to determine who the 'fittest' boy in school was. Rob didn't win, nor did Lee, Giuseppe or Phil.

By the time Rob was fifteen, booze was a major part of his teenage life. A lot of his contemporaries would have parties and he and his friends would go round and get drunk. It was easy to get booze. The tallest of the gang, Richard Kirkham, would be designated to go into the local off-licence and buy it. If there was no party, they might sneak into the school gym and play on all the equipment. PE was a lot more appealing after a few cans of beer. On a Friday or Saturday night the big thing was the disco. Jan used to drive Rob and a couple of his mates to the Zanzibar (now the Ritzy) in Newcastle-under-Lyme and another called Norma Jean's in Hanley. Sometimes there might be a fight, sometimes not. Phil Lindsay remembers a fight on a bus with some Stoke lads on the way back from Hanley. It is still fresh in his memory because he was the only one who got hit. Giuseppe Romano remembers another time when they were chased through the streets by the boys from the rival James Brindley High School, known locally as Chell School, who had 'the biggest lad in the city' on their side: 'At the time we were probably more scared of our dads than the chasers – in case we got into any trouble.' Later, when he was in Take That, Rob remarked that this was one of the advantages of having parents who had split: 'If I get told off by my mother I can go and tell my dad. And if I get told off by my dad I can go and say "Mum, me dad's been telling me off".' Rob was always lucky to avoid fights because young men and boys getting involved in a spot of bother was pretty much the norm in Stoke-on-Trent. As the Elton John classic goes, 'Saturday Night's Alright for Fighting'.

The drugs culture at school was not huge. Besides sniffing gas the kids used to do some 'blow' and sniff amyl nitrate (poppers) in class. Phil Lindsay remembers, 'I don't know if the teachers knew but they never said anything. They must have noticed us with the bright red face on. We were lucky to get through it I suppose.' On the very last day at school in July 1990 about ten boys and girls, including Rob, snuck away at lunchtime. They crept down to the back of the school, where the grassy banks swept down and hid them from view, and sat down on the grass. There they all shared an end-of-school joint. Phil observes, 'We didn't actually get stoned. It was school kids' stuff but it was a nice way to go out of school.'

When school finished Lee was waiting to start college and Rob was waiting for a break. They both got jobs selling double glazing. The first one was with a firm called Abacus Windows, just round the corner from Rob's house. It paid £50 a week and was money for jam. Lee recalls, 'The gaffer used to drop us off in the morning in one place and say "knock this area lads" and we just sat on the wall smoking all day until he picked us back up. We didn't do any work. They paid you extra if you made a sale. I made one but I can't remember Rob making any. We did a few of the window companies – Staybrite was one – because it was dead easy money.' Another company was Outlook Windows where Paul 'Coco' Colclough also worked, filling in between jobs. Coco was a couple of years older. It was always a laugh with the boss of the sales reps thinking up ways to forge a bond between the staff – team building. On one occasion he suggested they should go to Lawton Hall and try a seance: 'We had all had a drink so Rob said "Alright, let's go." It was an old school and when we went inside we heard this rattling sound coming from upstairs. Next thing we hear there's stamping and we all start panicking. The candlelight was flickering and we were all focusing on this opening. Then we saw this silhouette and a person appeared in seventeenth or eighteenth century costume. It was just like something out of a scary ghost movie. So we were all off then. Rob was one of the first to go out the window. It turned out it was a salesman called

Barwick wearing a stocking on his face but it had us all going.'

When they were not working Lee and Rob would raid Jan's drinks cabinet. They would get an empty two-litre plastic Fanta bottle and fill it up with everything they could find – gin, vodka, whisky, mixers – literally anything. They would then put the top back on and shake it all together and go up Tunstall Park for an hour or two, getting 'rat-arsed'. 'We were big drinkers when we left school,' says Lee. No wonder Jan was getting desperate to find something for her son to do.

Rob has often said that he felt he missed out on his teenage years because he joined Take That when he was just sixteen. That can only be partly true because all the evidence shows that he had a very full and happy time with his contemporaries. He may have had to play the fool initially to get accepted but that was always part of his nature. He had been a prankster from a very young age. Where Rob may have been different from his peers is that he always had something extra in his life. Being a 'lad' was only part of his day-to-day existence. There was the Artful Dodger, the youngster who was so certain he could make it. There were his friendships with Zoë Hammond and Jonathan Wilkes which were completely separate from the world of sweating competitions and shaving off his pubic hair. He had a secret drive that would raise him above the norm.

One of the heart-warming things about discovering the real world of Willwogs is that the friends he left behind still have enormous regard and affection for him. When they heard him sing 'Mack the Knife' or 'Every Time We Say Goodbye' they thought it was 'absolutely fantastic'.

They were knocked out by his performance in *Oliver!* They did accept him, both at school and in the local community, which is one of the reasons why Rob's roots have always been so important to him. The tricks they got up to still raise a smile and a laugh today without any hint of 'I Went to School with a Celebrity'.

Nothing better illustrates that bond than when Rob was famous and in Take That and he joined Lee, Giuseppe and the lads for their Monday night jaunt to the bars in Hanley. Lee recalls the night, 'Monday night was student night. It was 50p a pint in loads of places and most of them you could get into for free. Rob came out with us this one night. There were loads of people in this one bar giving him aggro because of who he was. So we put him in a taxi, which carted him off home. And then we had a fight for him outside the kebab house in Hanley. We won!'

'We were just retarded basically.'

5

The Beautiful Game

Rob loved leading the chanting at Vale Park. 'Can you hear
the goalposts sing?' he would shout to the rest of the crowd.
'No!' they yelled back.

Whisper it softly on the terraces of Port Vale FC but Rob
is secretly a big Manchester United fan. He may be the
most famous supporter of the Valiant, as Port Vale are
nicknamed, but it was the inspirational Bryan Robson,
skipper of United, whose picture he had on the wall of his
bedroom. His friend Paul 'Coco' Colclough explains, 'If
you are a lad living in Stoke-on-Trent you have two teams,
Stoke itself and Port Vale. You support one or the other –
that's a local team. But everybody's fickle and you've also
got the big, famous teams that you also support. Rob's –
and mine – was Manchester United.'

Rob had actually met Bryan Robson through one of his
mum's boyfriends. They both had an interest in a horse
called Taylormade Boy and, to his great delight, Rob was
introduced to his idol at Haydock Park racecourse and
had his picture taken with him. The teenage Rob looks
like a member of the Young Conservatives wearing a

buttoned-up shirt and a jumper with lurid horizontal stripes that only your mother could make you wear. It makes a vivid contrast with another photo opportunity just a couple of years' later when Take That met Robbo as part of a charity event and were pictured with him posing with the premiership trophy which Manchester United had just won. The now cool Rob is wearing a leather jacket and sideburns.

Rob never bothered with pictures of scantily dressed girls or rock gods like Jim Morrison or Jimi Hendrix on his bedroom walls. He was a lad and only interested in his football heroes. There was another one of him taken with Neil McNab of Manchester City after he and Lee Hancock had gone up to Maine Road, Manchester. That partially explains why he was so star-struck when he met David Beckham. Rob went bright red and started doing his nervous walk where he moves his right arm and right leg at the same time followed by his left arm and left leg. He is also a great admirer of the way Beckham handles the pressures brought by that adulatory fame – keeping cool when people abuse you because of their jealousy at your star status and the material benefits that brings. Rob has always hated the hard time he got from Stoke City fans when he used to go out in his home town. They would threaten him with all sorts of bodily harm. Giuseppe Romano observes, 'When he was in Take That he was out for the evening with a friend of ours and got chased through Hanley by a group of Stoke City fans. I think that was the last straw as far as going out was concerned.'

When his parents ran the Red Lion pub in Burslem, Rob lived less than half a mile from the Port Vale ground, Vale Park. He was too young to appreciate that good fortune, however, although his father Pete did introduce him to the joys of supporting a club in the lower divisions. Pete's family had long been loyal Vale fans. When he was young Rob always had a dream of playing on the left wing for his local team and scoring the winning goal in a big match, often the local derby with Stoke. Just a couple of years ago he listed that wistful ambition as being one of two dreams he had always had – the other was winning a Brit award. One suspects he would have preferred to realize the football dream. He used to sit in his room at home playing the Sega football game hour after hour.

One of the best ways of being accepted into a lads' community is to join in the almost obligatory after-school games of football. As a sportsman, Rob has always favoured the flamboyant approach. Tim Peers, his golfing chum, recalls that Rob would always go for the extravagant shot in a game of golf. He was much better at pool at which he excelled. Tim observes, 'He was pretty good but he had the strangest grip in the world. He would bridge over the knuckles instead of over his thumb.' But it was as a footballer that Rob wanted to impress and he would privately practise little tricks in his back garden ready to try them out in Tunstall Park. Coco Colclough assesses his ability: 'He's all right but he thinks he's a lot better than he is. He would always be trying something, little flicks and stuff like catching the ball on the back of his neck or juggling it with his feet.' Lee Hancock remembers that, surprisingly, Rob did not play for the school football team. Both Lee and Giuseppe Romano were in the school team for their age but they recall that Rob was not picked. He would kick a ball around with them in the playground at lunchtimes. The games after school were never organized but the lads used to roll up and there would always be enough for a kick around. These became quite serious if they were split between the boys from St Margaret Ward and the nearby Chell School. There was no love lost between them. 'Willwogs' would always take up his customary position on the left wing. Phil Lindsay recalls, 'He was a bit of a show-off at football but he wasn't bad at all.'

Rob didn't go to every game at Vale Park. He was often too busy. He had his commitment to amateur musicals and, as a 13-year-old, he became the Saturday boy at Signal Radio, the Stoke-on-Trent commercial station. George Andrews, one of the best-known names in local football broadcasting, recalls that Rob's job was to get the coffee: 'He was just an ordinary kid. He was always polite and courteous and very enthusiastic. He liked his sport.' Rob would start at ten on a Saturday morning and finish at six, so there was no chance of catching a home game. George remembers that Rob was just as keen on the broadcasting side of things as the Saturday afternoon sport. He says, 'Rob was always interested in the mechanics. He would always be sitting there, watching how it was done. He had a broad Potteries accent and I suspect he could still slip into that even now. Sometimes he would go into the studio and DJ by himself and you could tell he really enjoyed that. But we didn't see a musical side to him – he didn't go round the office singing!'

Rob stayed at Signal for a couple of years but had more time for watching football when he left. Lee Hancock was a Stoke fan but he would join Rob to watch the Vale because they were guaranteed to have a laugh. They used to go in the railway stand and keep everyone amused on

damp and grey December days by making up songs, or
more precisely chants, from the advertising hoardings.
Lee's favourite, which they would do every time they went,
involved the board for the Langport Fish Bar. The whole
crowd would join in: 'Langport Fish Bar'; clap, clap, clap.
'Langport Fish Bar'; clap, clap, clap. It must have been a
little disorientating for the opposing teams. Another was
'High Lane Oat Cakes'; clap, clap, clap: 'It was crazy and
great fun.'

He played traitor one afternoon when he was in Take
That and went to support the Vale's bitter rivals Stoke City.
He would not have dared roll up to a Stoke home game
but this match was away at Preston North End. Lee drove
up with his friends and picked Rob up at Manchester: 'He
wore my mate's Stoke City socks and shirt. After the match
we went back to his hotel where he was stopping, a nice
posh place with a bloke on the piano, and played snooker.
All of us, including Rob, were still wearing our Stoke
shirts. He never gave my mate his top back. He's still got
that.'

Rob has always liked to wear a football shirt when he is
not on show. His collection ranges from the national strip
of Brazil, to a Glasgow Rangers shirt, to a local lads and
dads team in Silverstone Crescent which Rob sponsored by
providing them with kit. And, of course, the Port Vale
strip. He also has a Barcelona shirt which he bought in a
Los Angeles branch of Niketown. Football was the
inspiration for the front cover of his third solo album *Sing
When You're Winning*. It was shot at Stamford Bridge,
Chelsea's football ground where Rob played a number of
charity games alongside other celebrities who thought
they could play a bit. Rob has always said that pop stars

want to be footballers and vice versa. The blue strip he wore on the album cover, as well as a signed jock strap, made £2300 for his charity Give It Sum when they were auctioned in London. He has also played for the Stick and Whistle pub team in the East End. They play Sunday mornings in the Hackney/Leyton league.

Rob seems to be a more ardent supporter of Port Vale since he has moved away from Tunstall. If he wore a Vale shirt while on tour with Take That, it would almost guarantee an extra £1000 in weekly takings at the club shop. He brought Port Vale FC, founded 1876, to the attention of the masses. For a while he even had a seat in the stand with his name on it. Jonathan Wilkes is a big fan as well and the two of them were always glued to *Final Score* when they were sharing a house in Notting Hill. In the early days of Take That Rob would stroll down the hill from Greenbank Road to call in to see his friends who worked in the Port Vale shop and marketing offices. Brian Toplass recalls, 'He used to wander in for a cup of tea and a chat and then I would give him a lift back home.'

Rob has played in three testimonial games for his favourite Vale players. Each time the crowd has been bigger than for a normal home game. The legion of girl fans that turned up would not normally be flogging down to Vale Park on a Saturday afternoon. His debut for the Vale was a testimonial match for Dean Glover in 1995 against Aston Villa. The rain was lashing down and halfway through the first half some joker in the crowd shouted out, 'Come on Robbie, entertain us!' Just after the interval he had his wish when Vale were awarded a penalty. Rob, wearing the number nine shirt, stepped up and scored with a sweet left-footed shot that gave the goalie no chance. Minutes later he got involved in an argument with the referee who showed him the red card for 'foul and abusive language'. Rob bowed theatrically to the crowd and marched off. It was all pre-arranged because a Mercedes was waiting to whisk him back to London. Coco Colclough recalls, 'It was ever so funny. There was probably more of a police presence for that match than there was for the Vale–Stoke derby.' After Rob left the pitch, Coco went back to the dressing rooms to say hello and was told Rob would be out in a few minutes: 'By this time there were two or three girls there. They were from Crewe. And they said, "Do you know Rob?" Within ten minutes there were 500 girls there. And me. Rob comes out and says, "Excuse me, excuse me, I've got someone here I want to speak to." And they just cleared a path for him. He comes up and says, "Alright Coke," puts his arms around me and says he has to shoot off to London. He says, "Give me your new address and phone number." I said, "Rob, do you seriously think I am going to give you my address and phone with all these girls here? I'd be having hundreds of phone calls every day for a month asking 'Is he coming up?'" He just paused for a second and looked at me and said, "I understand."'

After the game Vale manager, John Rudge, tongue firmly in cheek, said, 'He's not the quickest in the world. His agent is talking about a £5 million signing-on fee but I'd really need another look.'

Fame has allowed Rob to indulge his love of football. He has had plenty of practise over the years and is, by all accounts, a more useful player now than he was as a Tunstall teenager. A familiar sight while he was on tour was him relaxing backstage by practising his tricks with a

football, surrounded by his 'yes people', the hangers-on
ready to light his every cigarette or, in this case, throw the
ball back to his feet if he lost control of it. In May 1999,
not long after his solo breakthrough with 'Angels', he flew
in from Chicago – he was on a promotional tour of the
United States – just to play in a game for Vale skipper, Neil
Aspin, who had been with the club for ten years and was
one of Rob's favourite players. The opposition was
Leicester City. Rob scored one and made one for a more
famous footballing Robbie, the Wimbledon forward
Robbie Earle, who is now making a new career as a
television pundit. Paul Gascoigne had been due to play
but failed to turn up. Rob was jet-lagged but wanted to
make it for Neil because he was 'a hero and a top bloke'.
He even managed to find time to drop his shorts for the
benefit of the crowd. After the match, Rob kept phoning
Neil up to find out if he had got the video of the match yet
because he wanted to see his goal again. Neil recalled, 'He
kept saying "Did you see my goal Neil? It was a good goal."
I just felt that Rob had done really well for me.' The last
time he played at Vale Park was in May 2001, when
another great club stalwart Martin Foyle was the
beneficiary. Jonathan Wilkes played, too, and they
persuaded their great friends Ant and Dec to join them.

Football is a great provider of a sense of belonging. To
be a loyal fan of a football club is to belong to a huge
family with thousands of people in it, all sharing a
common bond. A true fan will soldier on even if their
beloved team is losing ten matches in a row through a
slump which affects even the best clubs occasionally. At
the beginning of 2003 Port Vale had gone into
administration with debts of more than £2 million. People

kept on expecting Robbie Williams to step in and become the celebrity face of the club rather like Elton John did at Watford. Articles in the *Sentinel* discussed whether Rob would be getting involved. They did not take into account the fact that Rob has not been seen in the stand at Vale Park for several years after an alleged falling out at one of the testimonial games. The rumour on the terraces is that Rob was not happy after an incident at a post-match drinks when, it is alleged, someone suggested he had had one too many and should give it a rest. That did not go down well. And once Rob feels crossed, nothing will make him change his mind.

As a result of this high-level frostiness it is most unlikely that Rob will ever adopt a high-profile rescue of Port Vale. Elton John has already warned him of the pitfalls of becoming a celebrity backer. His days as chairman at Watford were a nightmare because whenever word leaked out that his club were interested in a player, the price doubled. Coco Colclough observes, 'Round here people say Rob should help Vale because of all his money. These ordinary people read the papers and think he's just got £80 million so, if he was a true Vale fan, he would come in and save the club. I can understand why he doesn't want to throw money at the club. It would be nice if he considered putting some in to make sure the club wasn't abused in the future and there were people running it who he could trust.' Rob has already put more than a million back into his home town for charitable causes. And Port Vale FC is not a charity. He is unlikely to ignore its plight altogether in the future although he may well never publicly reveal that involvement. Conspiracy theorists have already noted that the club has recently

£80 million man on stage at the NRJ Music awards ceremony in Cannes, January 2003

Left: Zoë Hammond as Jemima in the local pantomime company's production of *Chitty Chitty Bang Bang*

Right: Robbie as Jeremy in the same production, the first time the two friends worked together in lead roles

The highlight of his amateur dramatics career, as a 14 year-old Artful Dodger in the North Staffs production of *Oliver!*

Class of 1990. Rob is hard to miss in the back row, fourth from right. Lee Hancock, Rob's best friend, is second left in the fourth row with Phil Lindsay next to him on the right. Giuseppe Romano is in the row in front of them on the left and Peter O'Reilly is next to Rob on the right. Joanna Melvin is in the second row second from the right.

Robbie leans out of his bedroom window, to announce to the world he is going to be a star, after signing with Take That, August 1990

The boy band look – an early publicity still for Take That

Take That show off their pecs appeal

Take That at the 1993 Brits where they won their first award for Best British Single

. . . on stage with Lulu at the 1993 Smash Hits Poll Winners Party

At a Nordoff Robbins awards lunch in 1995, the 'real' Robbie Williams is starting to emerge

When Robbie met Liam . . . the 1995 Glastonbury Festival was a landmark event in his life

An almost unrecognisable Robbie at a press conference **(right)** and playing football **(below)** in 1996. The effects of his hedonistic lifestyle are becoming obvious

With his mum at a charity awards lunch in 1998, as far as Robbie is concerned she's the most important person in his life

With his dad in November 2002 at the *Top of the Pops* studios

Nigel Martin-Smith, manager of Take That, and Robbie on their way to battle it out in their high profile 1997 court case

received a pledge from an unidentified Manchester benefactor. At the end of April, control of the club was assumed by a supporter's consortium group, Valiant 2001, and with a new board in place, the future for the Vale is a little brighter. A member of the group said, 'There's one thing Robbie Williams could do for the Vale, with him obviously being a supporter. If he was to wear a Vale shirt on stage or do a concert for us once a year then he could be the saviour of the club.'

Rob's support of Port Vale while growing up in Tunstall was an extension of the feeling of family that his home town provided. He thrived on the sense of community and has been loath to give it up. Sadly, but inevitably, as fame took a firm grip on his life, the bond with his home town was weakened.

'David Beckham's the dog's nuts.'

PART TWO

TAKE THAT

6

Fame Academy

When he first got into Take That, Rob's mate Lee Hancock
gave him a letter and asked, 'Will you sign us this Rob?' So
he trustingly signed it. When he turned it over the other side
read, 'I, Robbie Williams, being of sound mind and heart
declare half my earnings to Lee Hancock.' 'He owes me forty
million quid,' laughs Lee.

Opportunities when they arise need to be taken with both
hands. Rob had determination and guts and an absolute
certainty that he was going to be somebody in the
entertainment business. But that sense of ambition counts
for nothing if all you are doing is smoking your days away,
sitting on a wall, while you are supposed to be selling
double glazing to some hapless punter. Fortunately for
Rob, his mother Jan shared his belief in his abilities and
she understood that her 16-year-old son was unlikely to
make much of a life for himself if he stayed in Tunstall.
Not surprisingly it was Jan who spotted the story in the
Sentinel in which a Manchester-based talent agency was
seeking a candidate for a newly formed boy band. She
pressed Rob, who, at the time, was more likely to be

reading the back of a fag packet than the local newspaper, to send in the details of his experience on the stage and try to get an audition.

The agency in question was run by a thirty-something go-getter called Nigel Martin-Smith. In the late eighties he had seen the American teen sensations New Kids on the Block at a television studio and cared little for what he saw. He told the rock journalist Rick Sky, 'I couldn't help but feel how obnoxious they were. They seemed to be very big-headed, strutting around the studio as if they owned it.' Even though he was unimpressed by the group in person, Nigel was very taken with its enormous success. It was a rare bedroom wall that was not filled with a poster of the band from Boston – Jordan, John, Danny, Donnie and Joey. In 1990 alone – the year Take That was formed – they grossed a reported $861 million making them the highest earning boy band of all time. That year they had eight top ten hits in the UK charts. No wonder Martin-Smith felt there was room for a home-grown band to take some of the action. Fortunately for him, by the time Take That were trying to make a name for themselves playing small clubs around the country, New Kids were old news.

Crucially for the future career of Robbie Williams, New Kids on the Block had five members. If they had just had four then it might all have been different because Rob was almost an afterthought in the band. Martin-Smith had already recruited four before he auditioned the lad from Tunstall. His notion was that the boys should all be down to earth, ordinary lads, perhaps unemployed, but likable and not big-headed. (He obviously had no idea that one of Rob's nicknames at school was Swellhead.) He also wanted a fifth member because he knew the amount of hard work and graft that the lads would have to put in to make the project a success and he feared someone would drop out, unable to take the pressure. So Rob was hired as an insurance policy. With the benefit of hindsight, Nigel should have had a closer look at Rob's small print. The irony was that the other four, Gary Barlow, Jason Orange, Howard Donald and Mark Owen, were absolutely dead ordinary and Rob was anything but.

The decisive meeting in the story of Take That had nothing to do with Rob. It was between Nigel and Gary Barlow, a young northern musician. Gary, who is three years older than Rob, was brought up on a council estate in Frodsham, a small town in Cheshire about twenty-five miles from Manchester. When he was ten years old, his father Colin offered him a choice of Christmas presents – a BMX bike or a keyboard. Gary chose the keyboard, partly because he had been impressed by watching Soft Cell performing their 1981 number one 'Tainted Love' on *Top of the Pops*. The singer Marc Almond understandably took most of the attention but Gary's eye was drawn to David Ball on keyboard: 'I thought it sounded amazing. Thank God I chose the keyboard.' One suspects that if Jan Williams had given Rob the same choice he would have chosen the BMX bike every time.

Within a couple of weeks Gary was able to hear a tune on the television and play it on his new keyboard. His father decided to buy him a better model and sacrificed his holiday pay to buy a £600 version, quite an investment in an 11-year-old. Gary literally spent every waking moment playing "this bloody organ". In recent years knocking Gary Barlow has been a national pastime but he was undeniably a precocious talent. Unlike Rob, whose ambitions were vague within the broad parameter of entertainment, Gary was always completely focused on being a singer-songwriter. By the time he had left school his hero was George Michael and he was determined to write songs of the quality of 'Careless Whisper' and 'A Different Corner'. He was already a seasoned performer of a style that would not have seemed out of place in *Peter Kay's Phoenix Nights*. At the age of twelve he could be found every Saturday night at the Connah's Quay Labour Club in North Wales delivering a medley of cheesy standards. He came third in a local talent contest for his rendition of 'A Whiter Shade of Pale'. Club chairman, Norman Hill, recalls that Gary was a polite boy while others remember him telling them that he was going to be a star – the new Elton John. Remind you of anyone? The young Gary was, rather like Rob at the same age, distinctly chubby. The ironic thing is that for all the animosity of future times Gary and Rob were actually quite alike in that they shared the same inner certainty of success and were prepared to work at it even at a very young age.

By the age of fourteen Gary had moved on from the Labour Club to the Halton British Legion near Runcorn. He did four gigs each weekend, finishing at 2 a.m., but for his efforts he was earning £140 a night, a very fair wage for someone just discovering the joys of acne. This was exactly the sort of venue one might have expected to have found Rob's father Pete Conway plying his trade. Gary recalls that Ken Dodd, Jim Davidson and Bobby Davro were three of the 'household names' whose acts he would accompany. Just like Rob, Gary benefited from having a mother who realized early on where her son's ambitions and talents lay and was prepared to support him. Marjorie

Barlow was a science technician at Gary's school which meant that if he was ever in trouble he would be threatened with 'being sent to see his mum'.

When he was fifteen Gary entered a BBC Pebble Mill competition called 'A Song for Christmas'. He came up with a ballad entitled 'Let's Pray for Christmas', which his mother Marjorie thought too slow and dull but that Cliff Richard would have loved. To his amazement the song was short-listed and he was summoned to a recording studio to sing the song with an orchestra and backing singers. Although he failed to make it past the semi-finals Gary made some useful contacts including Rod Argent who had been on the music scene since the sixties and had written a seventies' classic called 'Hold Your Head Up'. Gary used to send songs to Rod for advice and he became very influential in the development of the songwriting style which would eventually become the Take That sound. Amazingly Gary had written two of Take That's hits, 'Why Can't I Wake Up With You' and the memorable 'A Million Love Songs', before he had reached his sixteenth birthday.

Unlike in Tunstall where money was scarce for the teenage Rob and his mates, Gary had wads of cash. In addition to what he made performing, he would make pirate tapes of himself singing popular songs and sell them. But his efforts to make the record companies sit up and take notice were getting nowhere. They thought him too young. And, anyway, Rick Astley was from up north and the thinking in London seemed to be that there was only room for one singer in the charts with a northern accent. Ironically Astley had originally been the drummer in a band that Gary had once worked with.

The difficulty for the ambitious Gary Barlow was that he was not cutting edge in any way. He admits that he was the squarest teenager in the world: he was podgy, boss-eyed and could not dance. He also had one of the least cool names in the history of the charts, overtaken only recently by David Sneddon. Gary Barlow actually sounds like the name of a northern comic – Gary 'Chubby' Barlow appearing nightly at the Legion Club, Runcorn. When he travelled down to London to try to drum up interest in his songs he wore a suit and carried a briefcase. At one publishing company an executive listened to his cassette, stood up, removed the tape and threw it out of the window. Someone did recognize the potential in Gary Barlow, however. Nigel Martin-Smith, like just about everybody else in the music business, had received a demo tape from Gary Barlow but he shrewdly realized that here was someone who could write the music for his northern New Kids, thus generating a much greater income from music publishing royalties.

When they met, he played Gary a tape of New Kids on the Block – Barlow had never heard of them – and told him that was the sort of sound he was looking for. He also said he wanted to build the group with Gary very much the singer: 'I told him I was crap at dancing and could only do a few hand movements. But I was very keen to be a star.' Nigel persuaded him that it was too soon for him to be a solo artist. Gary may have been reluctant at first to have the band built around him but he was desperate to follow in the footsteps of George Michael who had used Wham! as a stepping-stone to becoming a solo superstar. That was the path that Gary dreamt of following. It would be him and four Andrew Ridgeleys. The problem was finding the right four.

Gary and Mark Owen had met and become friendly before they fell under the influence of Martin-Smith. They had chatted at Manchester's Strawberry Studios where Gary was given some studio time as part of his BBC prize and where Mark used to hang out with a friend of his sister's, making tea. He and Gary found they got on well together and Mark would trail along to Gary's gigs, carrying equipment and making tea. Eventually they formed a half-hearted band called the Cutest Rush to perform a mixture of Gary's own songs and some of his corny standards.

Surprisingly, Mark did most of the singing then. The rather sickly name for their group was quite apt in that Mark was always small and cute, a quality that was very important in the development of Take That. Girls just wanted to pick him up and cuddle him.

Mark, who was brought up in a small council house in Oldham, near Manchester, was only two years older than Rob and would be the member of Take That who became closest to him. Like his mate from Tunstall, Mark went to a Roman Catholic school and was mad about football. He had hoped to make it as a professional footballer but trials with Huddersfield Town, Rochdale and even Manchester United failed to provide the career breakthrough he had hoped for. A groin injury put paid to any long-term plans and he settled for a job in a local boutique and then with Barclay's Bank, which is where he was working when he met Gary.

One of the reasons Mark and Rob would hit it off so well was their similar backgrounds. While Gary was hard at work on his organ they would be acting or playing football. And while Rob was practising Frank Sinatra, Mark was mad keen on Elvis, even dressing up as the King which must have been quite funny to witness because Mark has always been a wee lad. Although he was naturally cute – a description he himself always loathed – Mark was prepared, even in these pre-Beckham days, to work at it. One of his schoolteachers, Fred Laughton, observed, 'He was very good at soccer but he was a little bit of a poser. He used to prepare his looks and comb his hair before and after he went on the football pitch.' At the Zuttis Boutique in Oldham, where he worked, Mark was well known for being fashion conscious and spending most of his wages on clothes.

When Nigel Martin-Smith met Jason Orange and Howard Donald they were already a double act. They were athletic, muscular and six-pack heaven. They were also two of the best break-dancers in Manchester, a kind of dancing which now seems decidedly prehistoric although for a couple of years it was a form of high-energy gyro-technics that every young man in clubland aspired to master. Rob was no exception. He loved it. He would go down to Ritzy's nightclub in Newcastle-under-Lyme at weekends with a bunch of mates to polish up his technique. Zoë Hammond, who used to see him down there, recalls, 'Everybody used to clear the floor because they were bloody good I tell you. Rob was amazing and I always used to stand on the edge of the dance floor. He used to say to me, "What do you think of that move, I've just learnt that." I'd say, "It's great".'

While Rob was then an enthusiastic amateur break-dancer, Jason and Howard were professionals. Jason was the son of a Manchester bus driver and one of six brothers. He had little interest in school but was always mad keen on dancing. While working on a YTS scheme as a painter-decorator he started busking in the city centre as a dancer. Howard was also from a large Manchester family. He had bunked off school regularly to practise his dancing. When he left school he too had a YTS painting job as a vehicle painter. The duo met in the Manchester nightclub, the Apollo, they were dancing with rival break-dance crews but both considered themselves the best of the bunch. Howard's father was a latin dance teacher and so he had grown up with dancing, even appearing on *Come Dancing* on television. When Jason and Howard teamed up to form Street Machine they entered competitions, even achieving a third place in a world championship. This background would be invaluable when they set about working out the dance steps for the flamboyant Take That routines.

Jason and Howard went to see Nigel Martin-Smith to try to interest him in professional representation. Spying an opportunity he put them with Gary and Mark. He would then have a chorus line to back up Gary: Two dancers to obscure the fact that Gary was hopeless in that department; a babe magnet in Mark and, in Gary himself, a highly promising singer-songwriter. His northern New Kids was almost complete. The missing ingredient was 'on the knock' in Stoke-on-Trent.

Jan drove Rob to Manchester herself for his audition with the band. The other four were there and Gary introduced himself with a 'Hi I'm Gary Barlow and I'm the singer', which did little to impress Rob. But everyone seemed friendly enough. Nigel asked Rob to prepare the Jason Donovan song 'Nothing Can Divide Us', a piece of chart fodder from Stock, Aitken and Waterman. It had been the Australian soap star's first UK hit in 1988 and was not quite in the class of 'Mack the Knife'. Rob, however, had the priceless advantage of being an old hand at auditions and he managed a very passable interpretation. At least, it would have been very difficult to be worse than the original. Nigel said he chose the song because it was a hard one to sing and he wanted to see how Rob would stretch himself. Meanwhile Jan went in to see Nigel to find out exactly what it was all about and what he intended to do. Jan's astute sense of business has been invaluable to Rob as his career and his wealth have grown. And right from the start she was not going to let him sign up to something dodgy. Nigel admitted, 'She fired twenty questions at me and gave me the hardest time.' Eventually Jan was reassured by the size of Nigel's own personal investment in the band – £80,000.

All Rob could do was go back home to Tunstall, kick his heels and wait to see if he was given the thumbs up by Nigel and the rest of the band. He had been drinking the 'Fanta bottle cocktails' and playing drunken bowls on the bowling green with Lee Hancock the afternoon the phone call came. They staggered back in the early evening and his mother excitedly told him, 'Nigel says you're in!' Lee recalls, 'His sister Sally ran down to Bargain Booze to get some beers.'

Originally, Nigel called the new five-piece group Kick It, hardly a memorable choice. Rob would be very much the baby of the band. At not much more than sixteen he was four years younger than Jason, three years younger than Gary, two years younger than Mark and fully six years younger than Howard. There is a world of difference between being sixteen and twenty-two. Gary, who was born middle-aged, described Rob as 'quite a likeable young lad'. Rob would appeal to the very young fans as the group's cheeky monkey, a good all-rounder with no special talents; at least that was the mistaken first perception. Rick Sky met the band when they were launched on the national press. He was impressed by Gary's talent; Mark was 'very lovable', Howard and Jason were 'body beautifuls' and Robbie, as he was now known professionally, 'was 100 times more charismatic than the rest of them'. Was there room for more than one star in Take That?

Breaking through was not a doddle – far from it. Rob was thrilled at the news that he had got the job. There is a very famous picture of him leaning out of the window of his bedroom at Greenbank Road shouting to the world that he was going to be a star. Not everyone was so convinced. On the day before he was due to leave for Manchester he was with his mother in the Trent Vale branch of Tesco when they bumped into Brian Rawlins, who had played Fagin to his Dodger: 'He told me what was happening and that he was off to join this group. I can remember saying, "Do you think it's wise?" I wouldn't have let him go and I remember saying that. At the time I was running a youth theatre group and I saw so many kids go off and think they were going to be a star. I told him that. I worked in education and I would have preferred him to stay on at school. I remember asking Jan, "How well do you know these people you will be handing him over to?" and she said she hoped it would be all right because she had made quite an investment in it all. She had bought him new clothes and that sort of thing. And she would have to pay for his accommodation in Manchester.'

One common thread running through Rob's life is the need for approval, the desire to be accepted and to belong. He was the last to join the group just as he was last boy to start senior school. He needed to be accepted at St Margaret Ward by the 'lads' and it was a similar story at Take That. His Tunstall mate Coco Colclough observes, 'I think they must have been a bit cliquey in Take That. Rob always felt like he was an outsider.' Ironically, by the time he was fully accepted he had outgrown the environment. He would outgrow Take That just as he had outgrown Tunstall. One of the first requirements of his new life was to be called Robbie, something he has never enjoyed and which, very early on in his career, meant that the entertainer Robbie Williams became separated from Rob Williams, the lad from Stoke-on-Trent. Coco observes, 'His manager named him Robbie and I must tell you he hated it himself. It surprises me a bit that he has kept it. I imagine it's because it has made him so successful. And I suppose changing it now would be impossible. If he walked past you in the street and you called him Robbie he wouldn't take any notice. But if you went "All right Rob?", he would turn around straightaway because he would know it was one of his mates.'

Robbie Williams is such a boy band name. It conjures up a youngster with a floppy fringe and a toothy grin. There was more to come. Suddenly Robert Peter had acquired an extra name – Maximilian – a total invention but one which still pops up under researched newspaper articles as one of the names he was born with. Rob went along with everything, partly because he has admitted he was a little scared of Nigel and partly because, despite his weekly efforts at Ritzy's nightclub, he was well behind in the dancing department, more on a par with Gary than with Howard or Jason. He recalled, 'I was terrible. I kept getting everything wrong.'

The name Take That came about, as these things inevitably do, by accident. They saw a sexy picture of Madonna with the caption Take That and liked it instantly. Mark Owen explained, 'We thought it was snappy and had a punch to it. We wanted to make sure our name was original.' First of all they called themselves Take That and Party but dropped the extra two words when they heard of a minor American group called The Party. Instead *Take That and Party* became the title of their first album.

The dance training seemed to last an eternity. Rob was under strict instructions to get fit and stay fit. The fags and boozing mentality of Tunstall Park was, at least temporarily, out the window. Even when he was at home for a spell he was under strict orders from Nigel to go the gym. Coco, who used to accompany him to the Power House Gym on the Newfield Industrial Estate, laughs, 'It was always like a muscle man's gym. Rob was not really a big lad, although he had a good physique. We used to go down there and there were all these blokes with veins popping out of their heads, really giving it some with all these big, chunky weights. Rob and I had to search around just to find something we could pick up!'

Rob was also hung up about his weight, which would shoot up the moment he had a bag of chips, a couple of oat cakes or some cans of lager. Zoë Hammond recalls seeing him one weekend after he had evidently been having a difficult time in Manchester. He turned to her and said plaintively, 'I'm not a fat bugger am I?' One time when the going was particularly tough he told her, 'It's not hard but there are times when you could just say sling your hook and walk out.' Zoë advised him, 'Just promise me that you'll just count to ten and stand back before you do or say anything you don't need to.' Good advice, but Rob hasn't always followed it.

Eventually, after six months of constant rehearsal, Nigel believed the boys were ready to do their first gig. In the best traditions of pop legend just a couple of dozen people turned up to Flicks in Huddersfield to watch the fledgling band blunder their way through their first public outing. The first incarnation of Take That was very camp. Nigel dressed them up in tight leather so they all looked like the biker guy in Village People. Nigel began booking the boys into gay clubs up and down the country, a move that would have important repercussions for the future of both the band as a whole and Robbie Williams as a solo artist. From this humble, small-time beginning the group was able to build up a very substantial gay fan base, one which Robbie Williams has been able to carry with him to this day.

The gay impression given by Take That was further emphasized by the group's early television appearances. Nigel was friendly with a former *Smash Hits* journalist called Ro Newton, the producer of a short-lived music show called *Cool Cube* that aired on the BSB channel. He persuaded Ro to see the boys and he was very impressed by both their dance routines and their singing voices. Gary wrote a couple of new songs for their first appearance but, most importantly, Nigel was determined that they make the most of their opportunity to get noticed. They proved popular enough to be asked back a few times. For one show they wore red velvet bomber jackets and skin-tight black cycling shorts that left little to the imagination and that Ro admitted to being 'a little dubious about'.

Nigel was unable to secure the boys a record deal so decided they would bring out the first single, a very catchy disco track called 'Do What U Like', on his own independent label, Dance UK. It reached an unspectacular number eighty-two in the chart. Far more significant was the first video, which was co-produced by Ro Newton and Angie Smith, who had worked on the cult television programme, *The Hitman and Her*, hosted by Pete Waterman and Michaela Strachan. The notorious video, a camp classic, became known as the 'jelly video'. The boys did a breathtaking dance routine dressed in their leather gear. It was originally intended to end with a close-up of one of the boys' bare bottoms surrounded by some wobbling red jelly. The problem was which bum to choose. The boys, competitive as ever, started to argue about who had the most photogenic derrière. In the end, Angie decided to audition each behind. 'It was amazing,' she recalled. 'I have never seen five people strip off so quickly in my life. Robbie was very keen!' In the end we saw the cheeky side of them all in the video.

They shot the video in Manchester and afterwards Nigel treated everyone to a meal at Bredbury Hall in Stockport. Gary, being the talented one, got up and serenaded the guests with some of his cheesy favourites, including songs by Barry Manilow and Lionel Ritchie. Afterwards Angie remarked that even the waiters thought he was great. 'I realized what a talented singer and musician he was,' she gushed. While Gary was Mr Talent, Rob adopted his classroom persona as band clown.

The video, which had an adult and children's version, was seen for the first time on *The Hitman and Her* in July 1991, just ten months after the five-piece band had officially been formed. Rob's sister Sally admitted to Rick Sky that she and Jan were rather shocked by what they saw. Although the final chart position for 'Do What U Like' was very disappointing, to get things into perspective, Rob was only seventeen and he had a record, he was appearing on TV and more people than he could ever have imagined had seen his bare bottom. Radio 1, typically, was not interested in the track or in having the boys on the Radio 1 Road Show. Fortunately, their other television work and the constant stream of gigs were gradually producing a groundswell of interest, which prompted Nick Raymond, the head of A&R at RCA records, to take a trip out to a small gig in Slough to see them. He liked what he saw. The winning ingredient, for him, was their natural enthusiasm. RCA offered them a deal but despite this massive stroke of good fortune the success of the band had yet to be guaranteed.

A record deal with RCA was signed and sealed in September 1991, one year after the official birth of the group. It had been a tough year for Rob and the others. Rob had relied on his mother Jan to pay his train fare and digs. They did not travel to their shows in any style, piling in to Gary's car or, when he sold it to buy a new keyboard, using a battered old van. Back at home, Rob was always complaining that he was broke to Coco Colclough and his mates: 'He used to tell us that he'd been paid £25 for a gig. And he was only getting something if they had done a bit of a gig. It was paper round money. Three hundred miles up the road, three hundred miles back, dance your heart out and whatever, all for twenty-five quid. Half the time we'd go out and we'd have to give him the taxi fare home. I used to say "Rob, you're mad!"' Rob did have the luxury of one home-town gig, an outside event in Stoke where it poured with rain, which made the floor of the wooden stage extremely treacherous. It became hysterical when the lads came sprinting on to much applause and promptly all slipped on to their bums.

Although the RCA deal meant the van was replaced by a limousine Rob still had very little money. And the momentum generated by striving to 'make it' quickly repaired any cracks in the united front. Their first press officer Carolyn Norman recalled how they all picked on Rob one night for messing up a dance step even though he was obviously trying his very best. Even at an early stage, it seemed that if there was going to be any needle it would be aimed at Rob.

Gradually in 1991 young girls began to notice Take That, thanks to a concerted media blitz in teen magazines like *Jackie* and *Just Seventeen*. There was a conscious effort to promote the band as fan-friendly, always happy to give interviews – with Rob usually making everyone laugh – or participate in competitions. One teenage girl, who had won a competition to spend the day with Take That, was forbidden from going by her father when the lads turned up at her house driving a rickety old yellow van. It took all Carolyn's powers of persuasion to cajole him that it would be all right because they were only going to Alton Towers. It also did no harm for the band's reputation when girl fans smashed a plate-glass window at a nightclub in a bid to see the new teen idols – at least that's the story that kept interest running high.

Take That were now firmly marketed towards an audience of under-eighteen girls. The first thing to be ditched on signing their deal with RCA was the Village People leather look. Instead, they wore string vests on their whistle-stop promotional tour for their second single. This was another Gary song, an overproduced disco track called 'Promises'. It debuted on the chart at number thirty-eight, better than 'Do What U Like' but nothing to get too excited about, although everyone thought it was a good start. Next week it went out of the top forty. The third single 'Once You've Tasted Love' was a flop, failing even to make the top forty, managing instead the poor position of number forty-five. They just were not going forward. If that dismal failure had been in 2003 it would be odds on that it would have spelt curtains for Take That. The patience of record companies today is notoriously short – just ask Rob's great friend, Jonathan Wilkes. But, in 1991, a top ten hit was a much greater achievement. They had also recorded their first album – a sizeable investment for RCA – but there was little point in releasing it when the band was 'cold'.

Nigel hit upon a brilliant strategy. He hooked up with the Family Planning Association and sent the boys on the *Big Schools* Tour preaching a safe sex message and plugging the band relentlessly, sometimes with four mini concerts in a day. It proved to be a ground-breaking success with the boys getting the message across to 50,000 kids before the release of their next single, a cover version of an old Tavares song from the seventies, 'It Only Takes A Minute'. Once again it was more *Saturday Night Fever* than New Wave. It entered the charts at number sixteen but this time it continued to improve its position finishing up at a highly creditable number seven. They celebrated at a restaurant called La Reserve in Fulham with, a portent of things to come, a mass of girl fans outside with their noses pressed up against the window. They had arrived and things were only going to get better.

Rob met Princess Margaret when she was guest of honour at the Children's Royal Variety Performance. It was good publicity for Take That when she told them how much she had enjoyed their dance routines. They also appeared for the first time on *Top of the Pops*, singing live in June 1992, very much the start of the Take That era for the famous television pop show. TOTP producer, Jeff Simpson described Take That as a 'godsend': 'At last there was a buzz about music again. They regularly delivered what the show desperately needed – excitement.' Rob could not believe it when the group first appeared on the show: 'Everybody looked so bored. I couldn't understand why they weren't excited to be working on *Top of the Pops*. I was!'

The excitement that Rob felt as a fully fledged pop star was being slightly tarnished by what was happening to him back home. His home was still in Greenbank Road but his efforts to carry on as a normal Tunstall lad were beginning to be thwarted. Rob belonged to Stoke-on-Trent. He was accepted and felt happy there. It was his home turf and the sense of community spirit and easy friendship were enormously important. As that began to disintegrate for him so a vital piece of the bedrock in his personality and well-being was eroded. From being a member of the cast of his home town he started to become a guest star.

At the start it was just relatively insignificant things. He went to put some sounds on the jukebox in the Talisman pub and someone shouted out, 'Don't put on any of that Take That rubbish!' One weekend he bumped into Zoë Hammond's dad, Tony, outside a club in Newcastle-under-Lyme: 'Do you know what Mr Hammond? I've got a problem here. This dickhead won't let me in. They've said no trainers and no jeans. He knows very well who I am but he was on my back saying "Not tonight sunshine" before I had even opened my bloody mouth.' Tony went up to the doorman to try to plead Rob's case: 'Just let the lad in. Just because he's doing all right. He's come a long way.' But the bouncer, a classic example of a bonehead, was not budging. Tony suggested the two of them should find another bar for a drink but Rob said, 'No, you're alright. Its knackered my night now.' And with that Robbie Williams took off his coat, swung it over his shoulder and swaggered, whistling, down the street with an 'I don't give a sod' spring in his step. But Tony Hammond thought differently, that behind the bravado Rob was really thinking, 'I've popped in to see my mum and I can't even go for a ruddy pint.'

'I'm still the boy next door – until I move.'

7

Dizzy Heights

One afternoon, on his way home from school, Rob spotted Joan Peers in her garden. He shouted across: 'Mrs Peers, I am going to an audition tomorrow for a group.' Joan laughingly replied, 'When you become famous, come back and give us an autograph.' About two years later, with Take That at the top of the charts, there was a knock at the door and it was Rob. He had an autograph in his hand and said to Joan, 'I hope I'm famous enough for you now.'

'Hello Brian,' said the familiar voice cheerfully. Brian Rawlins was queuing for coffee and sandwiches in the buffet car on the train home from London. He turned round to be confronted by a youth wearing 'a silly woolly hat' whom he could not place. 'It's Robbie,' said the voice helpfully. And Brian realized it was Robert Williams whom he had last seen in Tesco, Trent Vale, on the day before he left to find fame and fortune with a boy band. That was only a couple of years before but he had not recognized him and apologized: 'I said I was sorry especially as I had just read he had won some award for something or other. I remember being surprised he called himself Robbie. We went back to the carriage together and talked the rest of the way back to Stoke, much to the amazement of the man sitting on my inside who clearly recognized him and was listening in intently.

'One thing I remember us talking about was money. I was asking how it was all going and he said one thing that wasn't true was that he was making lots of money. At that point he clearly wasn't. He was already quite famous but I had the impression he was struggling. He was still travelling second class on the train up to Stoke. Famous people don't travel second class on a train in case ordinary folk annoy you.'

At the time what Brian Rawlins did not realize was that Rob craved to be ordinary himself. He would travel home, as he was that afternoon, to relax and try to maintain a grip on normality. He would play pool with his old golfing buddy Tim Peers in the Ancient Briton. Tim recalls the time he popped in with Mark Owen for a game on their way to play a gay club in London. 'They had a helicopter standing by but they wanted a game of pool first. Mark Owen was a very small fellow but a good lad.' Rob would take his father Pete up to Burslem Golf Course for a round before they enjoyed a couple of pints together. He went to karaoke nights at the Talisman and sang 'Mack the Knife'. He would rollerblade round the familiar streets of Tunstall. He would go out to local clubs and bars with his mates. That would astonish Zoë Hammond: 'He'd just turn up and I'd say, "I don't think I'd dare" and he just said, "Well, most of these people know me" because it was Stoke-on-Trent, but I used to think there's still dickheads about who would glass you. I said "You're braver than me."' He liked to go out dancing. One time, when his mates went to pick him up to go to Shelly's in Newcastle-under-Lyme they were astonished by the sight that greeted them. Coco Colclough recalls, 'He was wearing a little black vest top, black cycling shorts, and black Reebok boots with his socks rolled down. He looked like the dancer off *The Hitman and Her*. He was going out to dance!'

The sudden burst of overnight fame in 1992 – after all the hard graft – culminated in the band practically sweeping the board at the *Smash Hits* Poll Winners Party, even though they had yet to achieve a number one hit record. They won seven awards – the modestly named Best Band in the World, Best British Band, Best Album, Best Single and Best Video. Mark Owen, as would become the norm, won Best Haircut and Most Fanciable Male. Mark, with his easy grin, was predictably by far the most popular member of the band with the teen fans. His walkover win in the 2002 *Celebrity Big Brother* was a testament to his phenomenal popularity just a few years before – the media, it seems, forgets far more quickly than a generation of adoring fans.

The first album *Take That and Party* peaked at number two, while the video of the album was number one in the video charts for fourteen weeks. They embarked on a nationwide tour of HMV shops but several thousand girl fans created madness and mayhem at the first couple of appearances. In Manchester, where 5000 turned up to see their idols, the boys had to be smuggled out of the shop disguised as policemen to avoid being torn to bits by the adoring masses. HMV cancelled the rest of the tour for safety reasons, which did the band's growing reputation no harm at all. More importantly they had managed to convince the record company to release 'A Million Love Songs' (much to Gary Barlow's pleasure). It was a big ballad that Rick Sky compares to George Michael's 'Careless Whisper'. The song, which boasted a soulful saxophone opening, was several divisions above the class of their dance fodder and opened the eyes of critics and the record-buying public, who had too easily dismissed Take That as one-dimensional disco.

In some ways 'A Million Love Songs' is a smaller mirror image of 'Angels', the hit which would later transform the solo career of Robbie Williams. Neither reached number one but have subsequently become arguably their best-loved songs. There is nothing like a classic ballad to transform public perception and expand appeal. Gary Barlow acknowledged that the song changed the career of Take That: 'A lot of people thought it would be the kiss of death and there were a lot of rows but in the end we got our way and it was released.' It soon became common knowledge in the media that Gary had composed the song in just five minutes when he was only fifteen which greatly improved his and the band's credibility. Today, much of the Take That canon appears quite dated, very much set in the early nineties. But 'A Million Love Songs' is a timeless classic.

This was the perfect time for Take That to abandon the small gay venues and school classrooms and go on a proper tour for the first time, starting in Newcastle-upon-Tyne City Hall. The *Daily Mirror* review was ecstatic, declaring that the boys 'could give Michael Jackson a run for his money when it comes to dancing'. Rob's voice had gone AWOL just before the tour was about to start which meant a speedy trip to the doctor. The approach of Take

That to a concert, one that Rob still embraces as a solo artist, was to regard it like an important football match. Nigel would get the boys in a huddle as if he was a manager about to send them out on to the pitch at Old Trafford: 'Work for each other and no prisoners!' Sometimes that enthusiasm went too far. For example, Rob accidentally got his finger caught in Howard's nipple ring, which was complete agony for the body beautiful and resulted in him spending the rest of the concert trying to kick Rob very hard during the dance routines. The tour was a fantastic success.

Rob's own personal star was very much in the ascendant. He had sung lead for the first time on 'I Found Heaven' earlier in the summer, then at Christmas he took centre stage again for 'Could It Be Magic', which gave the boys their first top three hit. Rob, complete with sideburns, also hogged the attention on the accompanying video. As a result of this enormous exposure, the attention of the fans in Tunstall was soon out of control. Nigel had, in fact, warned everyone right at the start that when they broke through their lives would change, privacy would be out of the window and they would have to make sure their whole life was ex-directory, not just their phone number. Changing his own phone number every couple of months was just the start for Rob. What do you do when the telephone operator is a fan or some fan's father is a policeman? It becomes impossible to keep it a secret. Even his nan had to change hers. Friends used to seeing Rob happily whiling away time rollerblading would now witness him speeding down the pavements pursued by a small army of frantic girls. He received sackfuls of mail simply addressed to Robbie

Williams, Stoke-on-Trent. Girls from all over Europe and beyond would turn up outside his home. They would trawl the telephone book to phone people up at random and ask them if they knew where Robbie was. Or, failing that, they would just try the dialling code for Stoke-on-Trent and then add a random number in the infinitesimal likelihood of getting Rob's number.

On one occasion Rob was in a pub in Tunstall called the Cheshire Cheese when the bar phone rang. The barman answered before shouting over to Rob's table: 'There's a phone call from Italy and they're asking for you, Rob.' Everyone was amazed that the Italian girl had achieved a million-to-one shot in ringing a random bar just as the object of her affection was enjoying a pint with his mates. 'I don't want to take that', he said firmly. Taxi drivers in Stoke-on-Trent were celebrating an unlikely lottery win as customers asked to be taken to Robbie Williams's house. Sometimes tourist fans would ask to be driven onwards to Oldham to try to catch a glimpse of Mark Owen. The wall outside the house in Greenbank Road still bears the 'scars' today of girls' names, messages of love and their phone numbers scratched into the brickwork for all the world to see, much to the delight, no doubt, of their mothers.

Rob had problems adjusting to the reality that he was becoming public property. His own feelings were exacerbated by those of his mother Jan, who was feeling like a prisoner in her own home. The way Rob dealt with it then remains the way he deals with it now. If he is being Robbie Williams then he embraces stardom and the inconveniences it might bring. If he is plain old Rob Williams from Tunstall he hates it, especially if they start asking him for an autograph while he is having a pee. One male fan put his arm around an astonished Rob when he was in mid flow. One supermarket manager even closed his store so that 'Robbie Williams' and his mother could do their shopping in peace without getting harried by fans. In this case, Robbie found it funny, even posing for a picture for the manager to hang on his office wall. 'It was hysterical because it was a Monday morning and there wasn't a soul in there anyway,' said Rob.

When Robbie Williams is working he will go out of his way to speak to the fans but if it is a 'day off' they have little chance of a friendly greeting. He has been that way from the very beginnings of Take That with the girl fans outside his house. He would ignore them hour after hour and go about his life inside his home in Greenbank Road. When he eventually emerged he would refuse to have his picture taken or sign any autographs. Instead he would tell them gruffly he was not 'at work' and they should go away.

That aloofness does conceal, however, the occasions when Rob does have a soft heart. One evening he was drinking in the Ancient Briton with his mate Tim Peers. They decided to carry on drinking with some girls they knew at Tim's house round the corner. Tim recalls, 'Rob went home at about one o'clock and everybody else went soon after. About half an hour later I was getting ready for bed when there was a knock at the door. It was Rob. I said, "What's up mate?" and he said, "Do you know any bed and breakfasts Tim?" I told him I thought there was one at the bottom end of town but wasn't sure. I asked him why and he said, "There's these girls asleep in the driveway and I want to fix them up." He made sure he found them a place before he called it a night. And he paid for it. People don't get the right idea about what he's like.' Rob had to keep that particular good deed very quiet or else every teenage fan of Take That would have been sleeping in the driveway of his home in the hope that he would rescue them. He preferred to keep the fans at arm's length.

It would be different for friends and family. He would happily sign a plethora of paper napkins for Jim Peers to auction for charity at the Burslem Golf Club. For the first time, Rob was receiving some decent money, enough to buy his mother a present or two, settle his nan's bills and do some mad shopping for himself. He was also able to fix up his mates with precious tickets or do a good turn for a friend. Lee Hancock recalls that he had free tickets left on the door for the gig at the Manchester Apollo. At first they could find no trace of them until he said, 'Try looking under Tate', and sure enough, Rob had left them under his mate's nickname. Rob would make a point of supporting Zoë Hammond when he knew she was performing. He made a special effort to make it home for birthdays and parties, including a memorable appearance at the fortieth birthday party of Eileen Wilkes, mother of Jonathan, where he sang 'Mack the Knife', even though he was under strict instructions to rest his voice when not performing with Take That.

Nigel had ambitions for them far beyond these parochial shores. Soon after the success of the UK tour, they embarked on a series of concerts and promotions all over the world. Rob enjoyed Japan and Hong Kong but pride of place went to Amsterdam because 'You can get the best curry in the world there.' He entertained the Dutch crowd at the Bulldog Bar to, unsurprisingly, 'Mack the Knife' and received a standing ovation. The group tried to make headway in the United States by visiting New York when their first album was released over there. It was hard because the school-age group they were hoping to attract in the USA were mainly interested in rap music. At the time they were opening their show with 'I Found Heaven' (lead vocal: Robbie Williams) which went down like a lead balloon. The band was destined to have just one US hit single, 'Back for Good' in 1995.

A UK number one hit record eluded them. Their seventh single, 'Why Can't I Wake Up With You?', reached a tantalizing number two in February 1993. That same month the boys were nominated for their first Brit awards. They were up for Best Newcomer and for Best Single. So far so good, but Nigel was furious when the band were not invited to appear live on stage at the awards ceremony itself. With understandable pique they boycotted the night altogether and went to the United States for some promotional work. In the event they lost out in the Best Newcomer category to Tasmin Archer, a one hit wonder if ever there was one. She had, however, achieved a precious number one with 'Sleeping Satellite' the previous September.

The thing about the Brits, a good showpiece event, is that it seems to be a carve-up among the big record labels, the corporate suits as Rob has referred to them. It may or may not have been coincidence that Take That's record label, RCA, picked up the prestigious Best Female Artist with Annie Lennox, leaving Tasmin's label EMI with the rather less noteworthy Best Newcomer category. At least the boys won Best Single with 'Could It Be Magic' – an award voted for by members of the record-buying public, in this case the listeners of BBC Radio 1.

The much sought-after number one finally came with another Gary Barlow song, the uplifting, up-tempo 'Pray'. It went straight to the top of the charts on 11 July 1993 as the band began their second sell-out UK tour at the Manchester G-Mex Centre. The song, upbeat and uplifting, had been written by Gary during a break in rehearsals for the previous year's tour. He used to relax and compose on a keyboard belonging to Mark Owen. He knew it well because he sold it to Mark for £1000 so that he, too, could learn how to play. The only problem with that was that Gary continued to use it as if nothing had changed. 'Pray' stayed at number one for four weeks, a very fair achievement which cemented Take That's position as the premier UK boy band.

Rob had been to so many places all over the world he could have written his own (very) Rough Guide to the world. He and Mark would stick together on tour, playing football on Acapulco Beach one day, checking out the remains of the Berlin Wall the next. Getting to the top is such a fantastic adrenalin buzz that nothing else seems to matter. It is only when you get there and draw breath that the enormity of your position dawns on you. Kylie Minogue once said, 'I climbed the ladder of success. Now I'm right at the top but when I look down from the dizzy heights there is no one there except me.'

But Rob was only nineteen and it was a bit early to become spoilt by success. His local paper the *Sentinel* declared after Take That's G-Mex concert that 'Robbie is undoubtedly becoming the star member. He possesses a cheeky, almost irritating, self-confidence and star quality.' Just the sort of observation which would not be music to the ears of Gary Barlow. The concerts were more overtly sexual than before with the boys finishing their encore of 'It Only Takes a Minute' by bending over in their underpants on which the letters of Take That were spelt out. Each of them had two letters of the band's name on their pants – Rob had TH – except Gary, in the middle who just had a star on his. At least they were not written in felt tips on their bare bottoms. Banners in the audience proclaimed 'Robbie – I want your babies' and 'Robbie I want to be your babe'. Rob's popularity had grown since he had come into his element on stage where his theatrical training was of enormous benefit, even when he made a cock-up. At the Wembley concert he launched into his lead vocal of 'Everything Changes', the title track of the second album, and proceeded to sing it completely flat, much to his discomfort. He admitted that it was made even more embarrassing because he knew Elton John was in the audience. At the after-show party he asked Elton if he had heard his horror. Unfortunately, he had.

Rob also gave the best interviews. It was absolutely no contest with the rest of the band. A journalist asked Mark, Jason and Rob about the video they had shot for 'Why Can't I Wake Up With You' Mark: 'It's a bit dreamy and you can get taken in by the dream.' Jason: 'It's so sensual and sexy looking.' Robbie: 'An essential part of the video was finding the dead stoat in the middle of the lake, don't you think?' Another question asked if a film or book had ever changed their lives. Gary: '*Star Wars*.' Mark: '*The Outsiders*, which is about friendship and staying loyal.' Robbie: 'My life as a male prostitute by Robbie Williams.' Rob was a winning combination of the quick wit of his dad Pete Conway and the zany, off-the-wall banter of Vic Reeves.

At the end of 1993 Take That claimed eight *Smash Hits* awards. The following February they won two Brits, for Best Single and for Best Music Video. This time they did perform, in a spectacular tribute to the Beatles. At the time Take That's success and status were being compared to the Beatles, surprising as it may seem now. Sell-out tours, number one singles, screaming, fainting fans were the established ingredients of superstardom. It was a golden age. Take That had four singles in a row go straight in at number 1, 'Pray', 'Relight My Fire', 'Babe' and 'Everything Changes'. At the time, pre-Westlife, this was a record. The only slight hiccup had occurred at Christmas when 'Babe' was knocked off the prestigious seasonal number one spot by Mr Blobby. (There's fame and then there's TV.) All that was needed for the band to achieve iconic status was internal division and strife.

'You've got more chance of seeing the real Loch Ness monster than the real Take That.'

8

The Melon Man

Rob was feeling apprehensive as he travelled alone to the Glastonbury Festival in June 1995. He had a case of champagne in the boot and was meeting a friend who knew Oasis but he wondered how the Gallagher brothers would take to a member of a boy band and their only serious chart rival. He walked in to where they were having a drink. Liam turned round, took one look at Rob and declared, 'Take fucking what?'

How did it happen? It was all over so quickly. From riding the crest of the wave Rob was sunk. The previous twelve months could not have been any better for Rob or for Take That. Or so it seemed. The reality, of course, was nothing like the bland victory parade portrayed in the saturation media coverage that the group now enjoyed. The highs are very easy to list. Between July 1993 and July 1995 the band had enjoyed six number ones, all of which had gone straight to the coveted top spot. They would have needed a removal van to ship their awards. They had appeared before Prince Charles at the Royal Variety Performance and in front of Princess

Diana at the Concert of Hope at Wembley Arena. They were all millionaires.

Like many front-page overnight sensational stories, the seeds of the Take That split were sown many months before the actual day of division. The first and most obvious factor was money. Gary Barlow, and to a lesser extent Nigel Martin-Smith, made all the money and the other four lads were given a jobbing wage of £600 a month. That was only the pocket money though and a much larger sum was being looked after by the money men – with Rob's mother Jan looking intently over their shoulders. Rob's only songwriting credit on a Take That hit was as one of the co-composers on the 1994 number one 'Sure'. Although Jason, Howard, Mark and Robbie all had a share in the Take That franchise, it would be no exaggeration to say that Gary made four or five times as much. He was the principal songwriter in a group that by the time it was all over had sold 9 million albums and 10 million singles. Rob had made a great deal of money by Tunstall standards but Gary, thanks to the Take That catalogue, was one of the richest performers in popular music. In retrospect, it seems incredible that Robbie Williams only sang lead vocal on three Take That hits – 'I Found Heaven', 'Could It Be Magic' and 'Everything Changes'.

And then there was envy. Rob resented the fact that Gary received all the plaudits and he was still perceived as nothing more than the group clown. It was Gary who picked up four Ivor Novello Awards for songwriting. It was Robbie who would feature under headlines about the crazy things he said: he would be the winner of any 'Daftest Person in Take That Award'. He admitted, 'I was the one who'd sit back and take the piss out of the others or the situation. I wasn't expected to say anything serious.' He would have much preferred to win an award for being the most talented, the richest or the most famous. On the reverse side of that, Rob was becoming more of a threat within the band. He had always had the biggest personality and the others had the charisma of tadpoles next to him. Rick Sky observes, 'Gary Barlow was perceived as the talented one. But Robbie had talent as well, and he had charisma. He also had an arrogance about him.'

The third reason was constraint. Nigel Martin-Smith had ruled the band with iron discipline. Rob said that at times he felt as if he was back at school. The problem for Rob was that he always had a touch of the naughty schoolboy in him, bobbing off lessons, smoking and getting drunk and not bothering with exams. Rob was very young when he joined Take That and though he was far from a virgin in the sex, drugs and rock 'n' roll stakes, he wanted a lot more of all three. Rick Sky says, 'Robbie Williams is a natural rebel, just like Liam Gallagher and Keith Richards, in that he likes to buck the rules. Things were being made very hard for him within Take That.'

Here is a typical Take That day when Rob was eighteen or nineteen while the band was on tour – according to the PR machine. Half past seven: get up, breakfast and chat about last night's gig. Pack up. Half past nine: on the coach for what might be a couple of hundred miles to the next hotel. Discuss business, play cards. Three o'clock: check in and have lunch. Half past four: sound check at the venue. Half past five: local interviews and photographs to plug concert and any record out at the time. Half past seven: meet and greet fans backstage. Eight o'clock: make-up and costumes; Half past eight: Take That on stage. Ten forty-five: back at the hotel, a late supper and a few beers. Midnight: lights out.

Who are they trying to kid? Rob was young, free and single. From the beginning he felt like a prisoner, stuck in a chain gang, cut off from the outside world. He learnt a harsh lesson at a promotional appearance in Derby when he gave his phone number to a pretty young actress who caught his eye and was told off like a naughty schoolboy all the way home. It is little wonder that he felt oppressed by the joyless professionalism on which Take That prided itself. He was assigned his own security guard on tour specifically to keep an eye on him because he was such a handful. He spent most of his spare time trying to give his minder the slip, even resorting to hiding under a table in a bar until the minder gave up and left.

If you chose to look, the signs were clear that Robbie was being marginalized within the group. He did not sing a single solo on their third album, *Nobody Else,* which sold 250,000 copies in its first week of release in May 1995. Rob gamely parried questions by saying that he was concentrating more on the writing side of things. According to Gary Barlow, Robbie had been given twelve songs to learn but did not do any of them. The reality was that Rob's untrained voice had cracked up under the abuse of late nights, boozing and cigarettes. 'I abused my voice and I paid the price,' he would later admit.

Rob's persona as the maverick of the group almost crept up on them by accident. He started being a rebel in small ways. The band was staying at a hotel in Dunadry, near

The Melon Man 129

Belfast, and, as usual, a large gaggle of teenage girls gathered outside, shouting their names for them to come out and make an appearance. Rob appeared at an upstairs window – or, at least, his bare bottom did. Once again the least mysterious bottom in the world made an appearance as Rob mooned to his fans. The press coverage suggested that everyone was deeply shocked, although this was a bit hysterical. The gesture almost certainly made it a day to remember for the fans. Another time, he plunged, drunk, into the fountain in the lobby of an Italian hotel and cut his head open, resulting in the scar he now bears just above his forehead.

The most overexposed bum in the history of popular entertainment was out again in May 1995, two months before the final split. Rob turned up to the MTV show *Most Wanted*, complete with new bleached blond hair-do, and proceeded to take over. The presenter Ray Cokes asked the band if they would ever pose naked. Rob immediately said he would do it for a tenner. A female member of the audience promptly brandished a ten-pound note to call Rob's bluff. Mark Owen loyally tried to stop things getting out of hand by saying Robbie would only do it for ten old pound notes but Rob, now with the bit between his teeth, was having none of it. 'No, I'd do it for new pounds,' he said. 'As long as it's ten pounds I don't care.' And, with that, he dropped his trousers and pants, showing his backside to several million viewers. It was deliberately provocative, although it was little more than an extension of the behaviour of the 'lads' back in Stoke-on-Trent.

One of the saddest aspects of the whole Take That saga is that Rob genuinely thought everyone was friends. He told Piers Morgan in 1993, 'They're like my best friends. There's not one I couldn't tell my problems to. I suppose that's good because a lot of bands have friction between themselves, and I couldn't cope with that sort of tension.' It's a slightly pathetic misconception from a naive teenager. Rob needed to have friends, he wanted mates and he wanted them to tolerate his bad lad behaviour, pat him on the head, say he was a laugh and carry on. The reality of Rob's progressive isolation was that Jason and Howard, the oldest pair, had little to say to Rob. Gary, forever sensible, tended to socialize with that more mature pair. That left Mark, who was Rob's ally initially. Mark however, had his own problems and grew increasingly introspective, embracing Buddhism. He thus had less time for sharing Rob's youthful antics, which had been so amusing in the early days of the band. Gary observed, 'Mark grew up and became a very truthful, good living person. He got into Buddhism and became very interesting. I think he left Robbie behind and Robbie resented that.' Tellingly, after the Take That split, Rob and Mark spoke just three times in six months.

Although a combination of factors led to Rob's departure from Take That, the actual blue touchpaper was lit not by his now-famous shambling, shocking, drunken appearance at the 1995 Glastonbury Festival but by his secret, skulking, clandestine trip to the event a year earlier. The rock, pop and new age jamboree is the premier summer event for Rob's generation, a three-day extravaganza of drinking, drug-taking, fabulous music and police arrests. It represented the absolute antithesis of everything Take That stood for. To be seen at Glastonbury would be the ultimate transgression for a member of the

band. Rob was left in no doubt that under no
circumstances should he go. So he went anyway. But
nobody knew. He spent the entire event hiding in a tent,
getting drunk with Irish singer Feargal Sharkey. He had a
sniff of what the air was like outside his prison cell in Take
That and he wanted a jailbreak.

From that moment on, dissatisfaction and restlessness
set in and Rob began hinting to the others that he wanted
more from life than Take That. He was fed up with having
to stay in a room all day, only being allowed out if a
security guard was holding his hand, even when he went
to the toilet or backstage. He had other ambitions,
perhaps in acting or in television. He was always getting
offers, although he had no firm masterplan.

By the time Glastonbury came around again, he
appeared to be past caring what anybody thought and
there were strong hints of the decadence and debauchery
to come. On a visit home he was drinking in the Ancient
Briton with a female companion when Coco Colclough
walked in. Coco recalls, 'He had obviously been
drinking for a while because he was quite slaughtered. I
don't think he had a clue who this girl was because his
eyes were like half open. I did the usual and went to buy
him a drink. He just sort of whispered "whisky". I was
looking at this girl and she has just got her hand down his
trousers, fondling him in the middle of the pub. I was like
talking to him and he was going, "Alright Coke, how are
you going? And I said, "Rob you look like you're
hammered." He said, "I'm alright mate." In the end I just
said to this girl, "Excuse me love, do you mind if we just
have a chat for a bit." But she was just as out of it as he was
and carried on doing what she was doing down his

trousers. I thought, "Leave him alone for five minutes and
come back to him.'"

More publicly, he was regularly pictured coming out of
nightclubs the worse for wear but nothing quite as radical
as his now legendary appearance at the 1995 festival. It was
just the incongruity of it all. Glastonbury was cool, a
melting pot of the cutting edge of youthful culture
whether it was pill-popping clubbers, naked hippies or
mums and dads getting stoned. The last thing you might
expect was a member of Take That off his face. But there
was Rob in sublime drunkenness, peroxide-blond hair, a
front tooth blackened out with tape, making a total prat of
himself by jumping on to the stage where Oasis were
performing a set and, beer bottle in hand, becoming their
dancer for the night, rather like the peerless Bez from the
Happy Mondays. Liam Gallagher had pulled him on stage,
although Rob was unlikely ever to recall how it
happened. The *Face* magazine memorably described the
event as the day Robbie Williams 'leapt from being
popcorn to pop idol'.

Gary and the boys were less impressed. The bond
between the five northern New Kids had been one of
shared ambition. In the beginning it had been a laugh
sharing a room in a bed and breakfast. Now they could
barely stand being in the same room as one another.
Jason, in particular, had a barely concealed antipathy to all
things Robbie Williams. He was threatening the whole
secure, reassuring cocoon that had bred Take That's
success. Rob was simply becoming too dangerous for the
band. Rob's divisive presence within Take That was
nothing new in pop music. The same thing had, for
instance, happened in the 1960s when Brian Jones of the

Rolling Stones was famously jettisoned after drugs and psychological problems escalated to such an extent that he threatened the fabric of the band. Rob thought everything was 'cool' with the rest of the band. He made sure everyone knew he would not be able to exist under the Take That regime for another two or three years but he said he would be there until Christmas and thought, with a big tour coming up, that would keep everyone happy for the next six months. He could not have been more wrong.

The Cheshire Territorial Army barracks in Stockport was the unlikely setting for one of the most famous events in UK pop history: the day Robbie Williams left Take That. The boys were there to rehearse for their summer tour promoting their *Nobody Else* album, which was due to start in just two weeks' time. Rob's heart may have still been in a field near Glastonbury but he started to knuckle down and try to learn the dance routines. After a morning practising steps, Rob slipped out for a healthy lunch at McDonalds. On his return it was clear something was up when he had word that the band wanted to see him. They wanted to talk. It was a court-martial. They were clearly unhappy with him dictating at what point he would leave the band. Jason Orange told Rob, 'If you are going, go now so we can get on with it.' Rob reacted just as he always did, just as he did when he was refused entry to a club in Newcastle-under-Lyme. He swaggered. He grabbed a melon from a pile of fruit on the table, declared, 'Is it OK to take this with me?' and with a spring in his step and a smile on his face left. He made straight for his car, with the *de rigueur* rock star blacked-out windows, to be driven home to his mother's house in Newcastle-under-Lyme. He kept up the façade the whole way. This was Robbie Williams. Only when the driver asked what time he wanted to be picked up tomorrow did he tell him, 'You won't be picking me up tomorrow. I'm not coming back. I'm not in the band any more.'

Rob, who, as his real friends know, can be extremely sensitive and vulnerable, waited until he had shut the front door before shedding many tears. Still clutching his melon, he told a concerned Jan that he had lost his job and was out. It was a momentous event in the life of a 21-year-old. For five years he had eaten, slept and breathed Take That but the following day he would have to wake up knowing that he no longer belonged. He confessed to 'feeling abandoned and totally alone'. Later he was able to laugh at the fact that he did not even like melon.

In the mayhem that ensued, it became very difficult to unravel the truth as everyone tried to find an acceptable version of events. Some Take That fans took it really badly. It was reported that a female fan in Berlin had even tried to commit suicide, so distraught was she at the news. Conspiracy theorists had a field day. Technically he was not sacked because this would have been a legal and financial minefield – although the legal ramifications of his departure did enrich the lawyers for several years to come. In many ways he had constructed his own dismissal by revealing a death wish in relation to the group that had made him a household name. His departure, announced the following Monday, even made *News at Ten*.

The following day, Rob issued his own statement and the game of tit-for-tat in the pages of the newspapers began. Rob's utterances tend to be personal, chummy and encouraging of a sympathetic response or off-the-wall and slightly dark. This was a heart-on-the-sleeve, little-boy-lost version: 'At the moment I am very scared and confused. I read the press statements yesterday and feel it is of great importance that I must apologize to everybody who feels let down by a decision for me to leave the band. I still love all the boys and I'm sure there is also a lot of love for me. But things have changed and I need to do something else for my own peace of mind and health.' The key phrase was 'a decision for me to leave'. He did not say 'my' or 'their'. It was left vague and up in the air.

Jan Williams is at her best in a crisis and before Rob could find the time to wallow in self-pity, she was in London talking to lawyers on his behalf. Rob was most angry about missing out on the tour. It would have meant he could have left the band later on a high and from a position of strength. The circumstances of his departure left him in limbo. It was especially galling because Take That were just about to have a big hit in the United States and Robbie Williams was not going to be part of that. In fact, when the album *Nobody Else* was released there a short time later, Rob had already been airbrushed from the cover.

Their summer concerts that year were very well received, with some critics saying that, as a foursome, they gave their best shows yet. All four sang Rob's vocals on 'Everything Changes' and 'Could It Be Magic' as well as two covers that had been earmarked for him, 'Smells Like Teen Spirit' by Nirvana and Pink Floyd's 'Another Brick in the Wall'.

The tour to the Far East, Australia, Japan and the USA was a huge success but things had changed. The fact that

Rob was stealing some of their thunder was getting under their skin and Gary, in particular, was tiring of the boy band format. He wanted a better showcase for his talent and that meant leaving the boys behind. There was also the complex financial situation in which Rob would have to be paid if they continued to perform under the name Take That. Rob wrote to the *Sun* suggesting they should reunite for one last charity concert in order to say goodbye properly to the fans. Nigel Martin-Smith gave the idea short shrift claiming it was a 'cheap trick to get sympathy and public support'.

Take That's demise became official on 13 February 1996, coincidentally Robbie's birthday. At the press conference Gary was asked: 'Have you got a birthday message for Robbie? It's his birthday today.' Gary replied, 'Is it? Oh.' They were contracted to finish two months of promotional work for their new and last single, a cover of the Bee Gees hit 'How Deep Is Your Love'. The Samaritans set up a telephone helpline to offer counselling to distraught girls.

'I'm just having a bit of a blow-out.'

Robbie with Kylie Minogue at the 2000 MTV Europe Music Awards, their raunchy
performance of 'Kids' was a real showstopper

With Jacqui Hamilton-Smith, his first real girlfriend in 1996

With Anna Friel, their relationship only lasted two months but it made great tabloid copy

With Tania Strecker the step-daughter of Robbie's manager, David Enthoven

Robbie and Nicole Appleton. His relationship with Nic has been the
most passionate and volatile of his life

A fundraising walk for UNICEF, for which he has acted as a Goodwill Ambassador since 1998. From left to right: Melanie Blatt, Robbie, Nicole Appleton, Jamie Theakston, Natalie Appleton and her daughter Rachel

Above: On stage with Tom Jones at the 1998 Brit awards, his storming performance
remains one of the highlights of his career

Opposite: With Geri Halliwell and a rather
sizeable entourage on holiday in St Tropez

Performing at the Brits in 1999 when he won the first of his, record-breaking, four Best British Male Solo Artist awards

With the Prince of Wales and Geri Halliwell after she had surprised Charles by singing Happy Birthday in the style of Marilyn Monroe

With best mate Jonathan Wilkes. Jonathan fulfils the roll of brother, best friend and protector for Robbie

Visiting Jonathan in Edinburgh where he was starring in a production of *Godspell*. The two friends always try to support one another's live shows

With his famous Maori 'prayer' tattoo on his left arm, which is 'a prayer protecting myself from myself'

9

Straight or Gay

Rob was very persistent, so Kelly Oakes knew she had to let him down gently. She was a couple of years older and at sixteen more interested in blokes with cars than a fourteen-year-old 'chubby little boy'. But she liked Rob and he gave her flowers and chocolates. He would also send her little notes. One said, simply, 'You are my sunshine.'

Rob's adolescent infatuation with Kelly Oakes reveals the secret romantic side of his nature. Kelly, an athletic blonde, aspired to be a dancer so was in the chorus of almost all Rob's forays into amateur dramatics. She also went to St Margaret Ward and, therefore, was one of the very few people to see both sides of Rob as a youngster. Rob never had a proper girlfriend at school and it is easy to see why. He was brought up in a matriarchal household in which he put his mother Jan on a pedestal, a position she still occupies today. He may also have seen himself, being the only man in the house, as her protector warding off unprepossessing suitors. The other two most important women in his life to date have been his nan and his sister. He admits that he craves love and affection from women, liking nothing more than them putting their arms around him and giving him a hug. That view of women is totally at odds with the mentality of the lads at school, who treated girls of a similar age group with disdain. Rob's dealings with the opposite sex have fluctuated between these two extremes of behaviour.

His problem remains the same now as it was when he first started noticing girls: how can any female measure up to his mum? Zoë Hammond was like a mother in miniature to him. She would cluck around him and make a fuss of him and they never even snogged in ten years despite their obvious affection for one another. As young teenagers, they were at Ritzy's nightclub in Newcastle-under-Lyme when one of his mates asked if there was anything going on between them. 'Her,' said Rob. 'I could never even kiss her.' Zoë recalls, 'I said, "Why, does my breath smell that bad?" and he laughed and says, "Because it would be like kissing my Sally", meaning his sister. After all the years it was so lovely of him to say that. Inwardly I glowed.'

Rob's early excursions into the world of women were pretty unsuccessful. He lost out on Joanna Melvin to Lee Hancock and other crushes, like Kelly Oakes, came to nothing. So he ended up losing his virginity in his bedroom to someone who, according to his friends, he never went out with. He may have enjoyed it at the time but it was utterly meaningless. Giuseppe Romano observes, 'I can't remember him having any birds at school.' Rob did not stand out as a prospective date in those days. The only traditional ingredient of a lonely heart's ad that he had was GSOH (good sense of humour). He could not drive and he was not an ace sportsman impressing everyone with his prowess in the school teams, although he was one of the best at table tennis – not exactly a babe magnet sport. It was only when he could add MOTT (member of Take That) that things started to hot up in the sex stakes for him.

But he was still just a lad and pretty ignorant about the opposite sex. One night he got off with a girl who was a friend of Lee Hancock's then girlfriend. She really fancied him and was more than willing. Lee recalls, 'He took her back to his house at the bottom of Greenbank Road, rat-arsed, grabbed a kebab from the kebab house, shagged her, woke up in the morning, couldn't remember doing it, found all this red on his bed sheets and thought it was the tomato sauce off his kebab.' Rob was a pretty enthusiastic student of sex at this time, however, and one afternoon took a girl back after a lunchtime session in the Ancient Briton and got so carried away in the bathroom that they knocked a load of tiles off the wall.

One of the unfortunate developments for Rob's dealing with the opposite sex during his Take That days was that Nigel Martin-Smith decreed that the boys should eschew having any proper relationships so as not to alienate any prospective girl fans. Very shrewdly, he was making sure that any girl would think she was in with a chance of snaring her favourite member of Take That. The consequence for teenage Rob, with his hormones flying in all directions, was that his sex life became an extension of his 'lads' schoolboy attitude where women were treated as slags and sex was a loveless exercise undertaken in planes, trains, automobiles and lavatories. He certainly had little moral restraint. When a groupie thrust a room number in his hand, he would tuck it away in his pocket, just in case he felt horny later. On one occasion at the Loew's hotel in Monte Carlo he discovered the girl's room was on the same floor as his own, only half a dozen doors away. And so, like a tipsy Milk Tray man, he made his way outside his hotel room window, and, with the water lapping the shore below, crossed the balconies until he found her room, whereupon he tapped on the window – surprise! It was even more of a surprise for the young woman in question because Rob had removed all his clothes before embarking on his adventure. Sometimes he was not that lucky, such as the night when Nigel walked into his hotel room just as he was pulling a topless girl through the window.

In these days of discovery, a one-night stand was a long relationship. Soon the newspapers realized that Rob's sex life was always going to bring great copy and nobody seemed to care much what the other Take That boys were up to. From being an ordinary teenager with fleeting success in the sex department he was a hormonal bull in a china shop able to 'shag anything I wanted to'. The nearest to a real girlfriend was a local girl from Stoke-on-Trent called Rachel who was hoping to become a model. She appeared modelling outfits a few times on Richard and Judy's *This Morning* programme on television but nobody knew she was close to Rob. She was a Rob girl not a Robbie Williams babe. Lee Hancock, who met her with Rob observes, 'They knocked around when he wasn't busy in Take That. She was really nice looking and a nice person as well.'

The less-than-serious conquests of his Take That days and beyond tend to end up in the pages of the tabloid press. Invariably they are lap dancers. Rob's attitude tends to be relaxed about these revelations, providing the girls are quite complimentary about his physical attributes and stamina. One of the changes in the reporting of celebrity sexploits in recent times has been the change of emphasis in that department. Previously, newspapers might delight in alleging that it was all over in two minutes and 'he made me feel cheap'. Nowadays a celebrity is odds on to be given eleven out of ten (even Angus Deayton) because it reduces the likelihood of any litigious comeback and keeps everyone happy. A Robbie Williams fan wants to read that he is the superstud of all time between the sheets. One Bournemouth lap dancer revealed that Robbie had taken her virginity when she was sweet sixteen. She had given him oral pleasure and kept thinking 'bloody hell don't get any bigger'. All good knockabout fun.

As a rough rule of thumb, if the girl telling all calls him Robbie then she is on little more than nodding terms. A real girlfriend will call him Rob. And if he is linked to a celebrity then there is probably an agenda.

In the lyrics of his 1997 hit single 'Old Before I Die', Robbie Williams posed the question, 'Am I straight or gay?' It is a question he has had to answer in almost every interview since the very beginnings of Take That. They were such a camp band that the whispers about their individual sexuality took hold early on. Even today, one of the first questions anyone ever asks about Robbie Williams is: 'Is he gay?' Over the years he has cannily made a joke about it. He plays along with it. Often, one of the biggest mistakes an artist can make is to robustly deny being gay. Jason Donovan made the cardinal error of suing a magazine for alleging he was. He won the case but his career never again achieved the same heights. Overnight he lost his gay fan base, the solid legion of fans he could always count on to buy his records and make them hits. Justin Timberlake, 2003 flavour of the month, was skating on perilously thin ice when, in April, he reportedly slammed down the phone after a DJ asked him live on air if he had ever had a homosexual fling with any other members of 'N Sync. Justin responded, 'Any fan of mine does not want to know a dumbass-question like, "What are your homo activities?" I can't believe I've wasted my time with you.'

Madonna, Kylie and Abba, to name but three, would have achieved nothing like the same success without their position as gay icons. Robbie Williams is another. The pairing of Kylie and Robbie on the 2000 hit 'Kids' was a match made in gay heaven. There is absolutely no evidence to suggest Rob or any of the others in Take That is gay. The rumours where Rob was concerned always involved him and Mark. They were room-mates and best friends within the group. One of the funniest schoolboy interpretations of the song 'Back for Good' goes 'I've got your lipstick, Mark, still on your coffee cup.' Rob continues to tease when the gay question is asked, both in interviews and in the lyrics of his songs. His attitude, since the first time the sexuality question was raised was, 'If everyone thinks we're gay, let them think it. We're not bothered.' He did, however, understand that boy bands were inevitably camp, all hand gestures and flamboyance. Take That's extrovert good-time image was a million miles away from the introspection of indie bands. One of Rob's great heroes, Vic Reeves, might be considered camp in the old-fashioned vaudevillian nature of his stage persona.

Leafing back through the Take That photo album, there are an awful lot of camp beefcake shots of glistening shaved chests. Pride of place goes to a publicity still where they wore gaily-coloured boxer shorts, boxing gloves and butch stares. Gary, who worked hard on his physique at this time, resembled Vanilla Ice's kid brother with a bleached-blond spiky haircut. Almost as provocative was a picture of Gary and Mark smiling sweetly, bare-chested, enjoying a Jacuzzi together. Appealing to the teenage girl market is always a fine line between masculinity and femininity, a subtle balance between sexual promise and unthreatening, cheeky grins. Who could forget George Michael's satin shorts and bleached-blond hairdo when he pranced about in Wham! singing about 'Club Tropicana' – a fantasy figure for a million adolescent girls.

Rob's friends back in Tunstall were not entirely comfortable with the gay association. Coco Colclough recalls one time in the pub when Rob said to him, '"You'll never guess who'd come in the toilets with me." I thought, "Hold on a minute, gay club, what are you telling me here?" And he said, "Jimmy Somerville came over to me and said 'Ooh, I thought you were ever so good.'"' 'Rob, ever an actor, can be quite theatrical and luvvie when the mood takes him. Coco observes, 'You had to get your foot in the door somehow and he didn't mind doing it. It didn't mean he was going to be gay by doing that kind of thing.' Lee Hancock remembers Rob telling him that he had a 'load of gay following'. He observes, 'People who don't know him always ask, "Is he gay?" I have never seen him with any blokes. I know he's been with girls and I could never see Rob as being on the camp side.' Rick Sky believes Rob is just a good actor in these matters: 'There is a lot of mystery to him. He is all things to all people, rather like plasticine. He likes to fuel the gay rumours.' He would almost dare the rumour by openly going to the Queen Nation club in London.

A year after he left Take That he gave an interview to the gay magazine *Attitude* and was specifically asked by the interviewer, Ben Marshall, if he had slept with men during his time in Take That. He replied no 'without the usual sniggers that often make this question so depressing to ask'. But the rumours refuse to go away. Mel B (Scary Spice) once answered a question on children's television about Robbie's relationship with the Spice Girls by declaring, 'Neither Emma, nor Victoria, nor I have gone out with him. Anyway he prefers men.' Then Liam Gallagher taunted Rob about being gay at the 2000 *Q* Awards ceremony. He said the *Q* in his Best Songwriting *Q* Award stood for 'queer', which seemed a little odd as Liam's partner Nicole was once pregnant with Rob's child.

Rob is certainly an attractive and appealing figure to men. He admits to having been propositioned by hundreds of men and takes it as a compliment if a good-looking woman or man tries to chat him up. He has also said many times that he is not turned on by blokes and that they do not 'float my boat'. Somehow that quote only lasts until the next interview. It may be that at some point in the future Robbie Williams may be arrested in a Los Angeles toilet for improper behaviour and the 'I told you so' brigade will be able to feel very pleased with themselves. But at this stage there is no hard evidence that Rob is gay. There is every indication, however, that he has had sexual encounters with more than his fair share of the opposite sex: 'I've shagged for Great Britain.'

Something unexpected happened when Robbie Williams and Take That parted company. The sex appeal left with him. Young female fans might fantasize about their favourite – usually Mark Owen – but it was never a heavy, sexual thing. It was part of the innocent rites of passage. A couple of adolescent girls might take a poster to a Take That concert suggesting lewd behaviour – Rob's particular favourite was 'Rob from Stoke, Give Us a Poke' – but they were more than likely to run a mile if he tried to take them up on it. The slightly, older girl, past the legal age of consent, would, nine times out of ten, pick Rob for a romp. He was a bad boy, not a bland boy.

Rob has had to get used to a public fascination with his sex life. If you spend the night with Rob then you can be on a nice little earner in the future, if you want to go down that road. For his part, Rob seemed to get into the habit of reliving a good bit of his sex life in the pages of the national press.

When he left Take That two young women were quick out of the traps to reveal their nights of passion. A hotel receptionist in Stuttgart claimed he had been up for it five times in one night of unbridled lust. She said he was 'unbelievably passionate' after downing piña coladas, which did not sound like Rob's kind of drink. She also recalled that he had told her how lonely he was and that he had no friends. Then a former model reported that he had bedded her in a hotel in Glasgow, a typical on-the-road rock 'n' roll assignation. She gave Rob eleven out of ten as a lover which, when he read her account, cheered him up immensely. The most amusing thing about her story, however, was that having told all to millions of readers she announced that, 'My mum will probably kill me.'

One of the more unusual stories involved Rob and a mother-of-two more than ten years older than him. Her distraught husband claimed he only knew about their fling when he saw her pictured with him in a newspaper coming out of a trendy bar in London. Soon the headline 'Take That Star Has Taken My Girl' appeared although the reality was that she was part of a group of people who Rob enjoyed a drink with from time to time.

The first well-known face to declare an interest in Rob was Samantha Beckinsale, a star of *London's Burning*, who arrived with him at a Take That end-of-tour party in Manchester. 'I love him to bits,' she declared and Rob wrote a song for her. Rob can afford to buy a girl any present but a song is probably the most personal gift he could give. The song was the haunting 'Baby Girl Window' on *Life Thru a Lens*. Rob, who has a very spiritual attitude towards death, wrote it about her father, the popular comedy actor Richard Beckinsale who had died when she was twelve. Rob imagined that he would be watching proudly over her now.

Rob fell in love for the very first time not long after the shackles of Take That had been cast aside. At first glance, Jacqui Hamilton-Smith was an unlikely girlfriend. He might have been expected to have had a trophy girlfriend, a pop bimbo, an aspiring soap actress or footballer's wife. Instead, Jacqui was a make-up artist working on fashion shoots for magazines and a daughter of a peer of the realm. That always sounded slightly grander than it actually was. Her father Lord Colwyn was a Wimpole Street dentist, who occasionally made the gossip columns because the jazz band in which he played trumpet was in demand at society social occasions. He played at Prince Andrew's twenty-first birthday party and at the Queen's fortieth wedding anniversary celebration. Jacqui, tall, elegant with streaky blonde hair, caught Rob's attention when they met by the way she said the word 'lovely' in a 'dead posh accent'.

Much more importantly, Jacqui, who bears a passing resemblance to Tara Palmer-Tomkinson, was, at twenty-eight, more than six years older than Rob and well equipped to handle the rather immature, rumbustious ex-member of the country's top boy band. The great majority of the important women in Rob's life have been older than him, able to help him through difficult periods, which in his case are almost all of the time.

The world of celebrity is a tiny universe. Rob and Jacqui were introduced by one of her best friends, Patsy Kensit, an old hand at being a rock chick, at a party in London given by record producer Nellee Hooper, who happened to be one of her ex-boyfriends. They shared a good laugh at the party and kept in touch by telephone over the coming weeks before finally meeting up again in Manchester. At a time when Rob was at a low ebb, indulging in far too much drink and drugs, Jacqui was a godsend and she seemed much more interested in him than in telling the world about it all. To her great credit, Jacqui has never spilled the beans on her time with Rob.

Rob accompanied her to the funeral of her grandmother in Cheltenham. Jacqui was brought up in some style in a village in the Cotswolds and after the funeral she and Rob stayed the night at the home of her mother, Lady Hamilton-Smith, and stepfather, John Underwood, who said, 'He struck me as a very pleasant young man.' They popped into the local pub for a drink but, being the country, no one recognized Rob or, at least, nobody admitted to knowing who he was. When the media found out about Rob's first real affair, it substantiated the feeling that he was someone with plenty of mileage left as a celebrity. The rough, working-class pop star and the posh totty is tabloid heaven.

They went on holiday to Barbados and the rest of the world was able to witness their obvious delight in each other's company when the photographs appeared in the *Sun*. The ruse of checking into their hotel under the names of Lord and Lady Tunstall did not fool anyone. Putting aside any cynicism of celebrity pictures, it is abundantly clear that Rob is very happy and pleased to be in Jacqui's company. They rub noses, splash each other in the swimming pool and indulge in smoochy kisses in the natural manner of two young people in love. The rest of the world does not exist for them. For the first time Rob felt able to tell a woman other than his mum that he loved her. Rob found the relationship very liberating after finding it impossible to have relationships in Take That.

Jacqui shared his home for a while but it was at his most troubled time of drink and drugs. Sometimes he would disappear for three or four days with no word of where he was. Sorry, on these occasions, was the easiest word but it quickly proved not enough as Rob showed no signs of wanting to change his ways. He did take her back to Tunstall to meet his nan, who thought she was very pretty and polite. The two of them chatted easily to the old lady while drinking coke in her living room. Betty Williams, who adored her grandson, said, 'Any girl who gets Rob is very lucky.'

Rob and Jacqui stayed together for most of 1996 but it was her bad luck that at a time when she was ready for some stability in her life, Rob was involved in his 'Lost Year', the period post-Take That when his self-esteem was at its lowest and where he had lost track of the important things in life in a fog of drink, drugs and depression. Jacqui pushed very hard for Rob to seek counselling and treatment for his problems. But by the end of the year they were finished as a couple. Jacqui soon started dating Sean Pertwee, the actor son of former Dr Who John Pertwee, and within eighteen months they were engaged. A year later they were married at the House of Lords, a celebrity wedding attended by two people Rob would later feud with – Noel Gallagher and Nellee Hooper.

It might have been different if Rob had been older but Jacqui was ready to settle down and start a family. Ironically, on that holiday in Barbados, she had asked him to marry her. It was Leap Year Day when women are traditionally allowed to request a hand in marriage. She was joking but Rob was convinced that she would have gone through with it if he had accepted. What would have happened to Robbie Williams if he had said yes?

After Jacqui, Rob took up with Anna Friel, a very attractive former soap star and media darling. Both were just coming out of important, longer relationships: Rob with Jacqui and Anna with TV personality Darren Day. They had a laugh together and genuinely enjoyed each other's company but this was a celebrity romance in that it garnered far more column inches than it deserved. The difference between Anna and a number of other young women Rob saw after his break with Jacqui was that she was newsworthy. They made a great 'celebrity couple'. But they were never really a couple at all. She spent most of the two months they were supposed to be together making a film in Ireland. Rob received some terrible publicity while she was away because he was seen partying, going on a seventy-two hour bender and allegedly getting off with a blonde bearing a seahorse tattoo on her breast. The newspapers took the hysterical line of 'How could Rob betray poor Anna?'

Anna was only twenty and, just like Rob, was going out and enjoying herself on location in Dublin (although not on seventy-two hour benders). Rob was self-obsessed at this time. He was taking the huge step of going into rehab for the first time.

'If I hadn't taken drugs and slept with lots of girls when I was in a pop group, then I would be abnormal.'

10

Drink, Drugs and Depression

Drugs have never been good for Rob. The first time he took acid he was with his mates in Shelly's nightclub in Newcastle-under-Lyme. He wound up seeing the devil in the mirror of the gents' toilet, which put him right off.

Robbie Williams and drinking seem to go hand in hand. When he left Take That he became a piss artist: always hammered, falling down and making a spectacle of himself. Alcohol was a fundamental part of the lads' culture he grew up in. His dad liked a pint and so did his mates but Rob had no control. He would have ten pints and then be checking whose round it was. But alcohol was the acceptable face of Rob's problems. A working man could admit to liking a drink but would be unlikely to own up to a massive drug problem. But it was drugs, and one in particular, that scrambled Rob's brain. While the world thought he was just a drunk, he was actually addicted to cocaine.

When he was a teenager in Tunstall there was not enough money around to develop much of a taste for expensive narcotics. The kids at his school would sniff gas or try a bit of blow or the occasional pill but coke was rare. Even after he joined Take That Rob was always broke. He still owes £80 to a local drug dealer who fixed him up with some 'Charlie' one night when he was back home for the weekend. It has not been forgotten. A regular at the pub that was the centre for such exchanges observes, 'If he comes back in he will definitely be asked for the money. It was assumed Robbie Williams was good for it.'

Rob was at the mercy of coke when he found himself in limbo after his departure from Take That. Estimates vary as to his financial worth at that time, from between £1 million to £4 million. And although lawyers would take a large slice of that as he extricated himself from the group's legal spider's web he still had more than enough cash to play hard. His mother Jan did her best to keep an eye on him but there was little she could do when he moved to London in late 1995. It was a different world to his teenage environment of Stoke-on-Trent or from the hundreds of hotel rooms he had stayed in on the road with Take That. He had time on his hands to embrace a new culture, far more sophisticated than the one he knew. He was also very unhappy. Drink, drugs and depression are a filthy cocktail.

Rob had already sampled the pleasures of cocaine while he was in Take That. He tried it for the first time just before he went on stage during their 1993 UK tour. Take That had an anti-drugs image and Rob was expected to support that and advise the group's fans not to do drugs. He admitted taking them, however, and said he could not advise kids not to try them. His growing interest in cocaine was the least publicized reason for his departure. In his High Court case in July 1997 against Nigel Martin- Smith,

the Take That manager's barrister said that Robbie
Williams developed a 'taste for glamorous and flamboyant
company, alcohol and narcotics'. Jan, who could see the
mess her son was making of everything, became a drugs
counsellor so she could understand how best to deal with
him when he turned to her for help.

Rob is hopeless at being by himself. He admits it. The
self-loathing sets in and, as he puts it, he does not trust
himself in his own company. After the demise of Take
That he suffered from chronically low self-esteem. He put
on two stone in weight on a diet of Guinness and kebabs –
although sometimes he would forget the kebabs. His party
trick was lining up five pints of Guinness in a row and
downing all of them in one disgusting, gobbing
movement. He allegedly once drank twenty-five pints of
the black stuff in one day. He would go to the opening of
an envelope and became known as the biggest 'ligger' in
town. He was snorting enough cocaine to keep the
Colombian economy afloat. A record company executive
recalls the 1996 vintage Robbie Williams: 'He was just a fat
schizo – a fucked-up boy.'

Some observers have found it hard to understand why
Rob, so successful so young and with his whole life in front
of him, considered himself such a failure after Take That.
It may have been self-indulgent but it did not make it any
less real. He had been so desperate to be accepted by the
band and the fact that they let him leave was a huge
rejection in his life. Nicole Appleton recalls that one night
when they were sitting on his roof terrace in Notting Hill
he just burst into tears while talking about Take That. Rob
wears his pain on his sleeve but, still, the outside world is
surprised when he is not being a funny guy. Towards the

end of his time in Take That when he appeared on television wearing a T-shirt bearing the slogan 'My Booze Hell', he was declaring his alcoholism to the world – literally wearing his drink problem on his shirt – but no one took him seriously.

Rob's well-worn excuse for his behaviour during the year after he left Take That is that he was cramming all his adolescence into twelve months because he missed out on it during his time in the band. Take That had been his life since he was sixteen. That sounds good but he enjoyed a teenage life involving football, drinking, larking about, girls and fun back in Tunstall. For the great majority that is enough adolescent 'fun'. But Rob has a personality that cannot deal with moderation in any form. It's full-on excess or nothing. He cannot make do with just the one pint or just the one line. He jokingly described it as putting himself 'through the University of Nights Out.' He was able to go to the Met Bar and mix with the showbiz company that he really enjoyed. He became friendly with footballers like David James, Jamie Redknapp and Phil Babb. He socialized with his teenage hero Vic Reeves. Rob would go and stay at Vic's Kent farm and one night he and the comedian famously and very drunkenly serenaded Vic's prize pigs with a version of 'Lady Metroland'. The pigs were deeply unimpressed by the rural karaoke and charged them. He enjoyed drinking sessions with his new best friends Oasis and the Geordie duo PJ and Duncan – now better known as Ant and Dec – who like him were sampling the freedom of London life for the first time. 'Top northern lads,' Rob called them. He joined some of the Oasis entourage on the picket line with striking tube workers, singing 'We Shall Overcome'. Friends back home in Tunstall recall seeing him at the local derby between Stoke and Port Vale when he 'looked elsewhere'. One recalls that he was 'very slow and out of it. You could see how much he had changed.'

When he was making *Life Thru a Lens*, his first album, he famously spent most of the time lying underneath the mixing desk sipping cans of Guinness. He would be drunk before he arrived. His new record label, Chrysalis, would send a taxi to take him from Notting Hill to the studio in Chelsea. He would insist that the taxi driver stop off at one pub after another on the way. Rob would dive inside, have a pint, come out, ready for the next bar. It was a pub crawl by cab. By the time he arrived at the studio he was 'absolutely mullered'. He just let the musicians and his songwriting partner, Guy Chambers and co-producer Steve Abbot, take over. While he was not exactly 'one-take Williams', anything more than four takes of one song was too much for his attention span. Boredom would set in and Rob would resume his position under the mixing desk. He explained, 'When the time came for me to do work again, I had completely forgotten how to stop drinking.'

Rob took heroin on just one occasion. He did not enjoy it and spoke out robustly against the drug, much to the delight of government anti-drugs advisers. He declared, 'Heroin is evil – nobody should go near it. It was the worst experience of my life and I will never do it again.'

Rob's 'lost weekend' lasted until October 1996 when he was persuaded by a concerned Elton John and by his girlfriend Jacqui Hamilton-Smith that he should go to see Beechy Colclough, counsellor to the stars. Beechy, who has treated Elton, Michael Jackson, Kate Moss and Paul Gascoigne, does not believe in treating celebrities any differently from ordinary folk: 'They're just people with addictions.' It was not a cure or even half a cure but it was a start. He paid his fare for the rehab rollercoaster. He saw Beechy every day for a month and said at the time that it had helped him 'immensely'. At least it enabled him to pull himself together enough to be able to finish his first album and, by not drinking for a while, to lose a couple of stone. Rob was lucky in having people who could give him the benefit of their sad experience while he was still such a young man. Sir Elton owned up to twenty years of substance abuse before finally confronting his problems in a US clinic. Coincidentally, he also suffered from waging a continual war with his weight and having a poor self-image – fat boy with glasses and thinning hair. He also had a tricky relationship with his father while adoring his mother. Rob, as always, managed to retain a sense of humour in between his soul searching, observing once that he had left his mother's house on New Year's Eve 1995, saying he was popping out for the night. He returned with the same overnight bag on 1 January 1997, a year and a day later: 'That was some party, Mum,' he shouted as he came through the door.

It was June 1997 when Rob made a major decision that he needed proper rehab and checked himself into the Clouds clinic near Salisbury, deep in the heart of rural Wiltshire. Although he was urged to take that step by his mother and his management, he acknowledges that he alone could actually make that choice. His narcotic abuse had reached the point where he imagined furniture racing around his bed. He admitted, 'I don't have a switch that I can turn on or off in my head. I don't think you can get through frequent drug-taking and then have the sense to take it or leave it.' He arrived at Clouds, drunk and clutching four bottles of Moët in his hands. He had been to a party for the group Sleeper, and after spending most of the night sober, decided that he might as well go to rehab in a blaze of glory.

Clouds is not a half-hearted holiday camp for celebrities recovering from last night's bender. There are no penthouse suites. Rob had to share a dormitory with other addicts but found he quite liked the sense of cameraderie. He had to join the others to help cook and wash up after dinner, never something he much cared for. He was not allowed books (he hardly ever reads a book anyway), magazines or even a radio or television and, at a time when he would normally be enjoying his pop star sleep, he was up for his morning run. Rob responded well to having his life organized in this manner. It encouraged the sense of belonging which has always been so important to him. He had to endure the humbling experience of group therapy, where his status outside the clinic counted for nothing. He was also introduced to the 'programme', the twelve-point plan for life known as the Minnesota Method and which is favoured by Alcoholics Anonymous. Step One is to admit to yourself and others that you are an addict: 'My name is Rob and I am an alcoholic.' Step Two is to believe that a higher power can restore you to sanity. That may or may not be God. Despite being brought up in a Roman Catholic family, Rob is not a churchgoer and admits to being an atheist. He is, however, prepared to accept the existence of a 'force higher than yourself that you have to give in to'.

He stayed in the clinic for six weeks, and emerged fit enough both mentally and physically to promote his first album. He had not mastered all twelve steps, which include making amends to people wronged by your addiction, but he did recognize two important aspects of his problem. Firstly, his addiction had made him very selfish. And, secondly, he should never look further than staying 'clean' for one day. Beechy Colclough observes, 'I think rehab can be harder for celebrities because of the added pressure of being known. They find it difficult to trust anyone when they are getting treated because of what might then get into the papers.'

Rob would sporadically plunge off the wagon over the next couple of years. These binges were always spectacular. He did not become a showbiz hermit. Far from quietly digesting the benefits of Clouds, and perhaps taking secondary therapy, he was Robbie again, presenting *Top of the Pops*. During this first phase of recovery he met and fell in love with Nicole Appleton and got his career back on track. But one of the problems Rob had was recognizing that his cocaine and alcohol addictions could not be separated. He could not have a couple of drinks and think everything was fine because he was not hoovering up several lines of white powder. As Nic later revealed, the first time she and Rob were together they passed out after a marathon drinking session.

One utterly debauched night in Dublin demonstrated his need to go to excess. At an after-show party he was, according to an eyewitness 'off his nut' and 'absolutely crazed'. He woke everybody up by banging on the doors of the hotel rooms looking for drugs. At the same time he had various 'good-time girls' in his room keeping the 'pop star' company. One fellow partygoer recalled, 'He ended up crawling around on the floor of the hotel lobby, dribbling from the mouth. There were these two girls, rough as anything, trying to get him up so they could get him back to his room.' After the 1999 Brit Awards he confessed he was so drunk he did not realize he had won three of the coveted trophies until he awoke the next morning. He included a song called 'Clean' for his first album but spoilt the effect by declaring that he had been drunk when he wrote it.

In September 2000, Rob rolled up to the premiere of the Sex Pistols documentary *The Filth and the Fury* at the Screen on the Green in Islington. It was the start of a night to remember (or forget). Rob was in his best, comic humour when he arrived. A journalist barged up to him to find out why such a poppy person was at a punk premiere. Rob, ever the actor, looked confused: 'I've come to see *Toy Story 2*, me,' he said. The reporter then asked if there would ever be a Take That movie. 'There is one in production,' said Rob, deadpan. 'It will be a bit like *Absolute Beginners*. We're thinking of calling it *Absolute Shit*.' After the film he had a pee up against a wall before hooking up with actor Nick Moran for a trip to the fashionable West End drinking club, Soho House. Rob only popped in for one but ended the night the worse for wear in Stringfellows, minus his clothes.

The most famous, almost cataclysmic night of shame, occurred in Stockholm at the EMI party following the 2000 MTV awards. Rumours were already rife that he was on a downward spiral at the time, after shooting for the video of his single 'Supreme' had to be cut short because Robbie was, as a spokesman said, suffering from severe exhaustion and gastroenteritis. Exhaustion in celebrity circles invariably signals that drink or drugs have got the better of a particular star. Rob travelled to Sweden, however, perhaps against the best advice, and performed a duet with Kylie Minogue at the awards ceremony. At the subsequent party he got into a row with the legendary Nellee Hooper. The millionaire record producer is very much his own man and does not suffer fools. He has his own inner circle, a tight-knit 'crew' of which Robbie Williams was most definitely not a part. A friend explained, 'Nellee has a class and elegance and likes to surround himself with beautiful girls and rich friends from the upper echelons of society like Lucas White and Nat Rothschild. He also likes to be the centre of attention and would not appreciate Robbie if he was in over-the-top mode and behaving like a twat.'

On seeing Rob at the party, Nellee allegedly told him a few home truths. Rob ended up punching him in the face. Nellee, who is a fair bit smaller than Rob, responded by kicking him in the goolies. They then started rolling around on the floor and Rob ripped Nellee's shirt before being hauled off by his bodyguard. Like a good lad who believes a fight is an excellent start to an evening, Rob then proceeded to get hammered on sambuca before being helped to his bed. It was even suggested that he ended the night foaming at the mouth but this was hotly denied the next day by a spokesman for his record company, who claimed he was 'exhausted' and that the whole Nellee incident was a 'simple misunderstanding'. Rob was whisked off to a hotel in Barbados for a good rest. He later admitted that he had been drunk but also said he had flu.

Subsequently and privately, Nellee Hooper wrote to Robbie Williams. It was not to apologize but to express his horror and outrage that a blow-by-blow account of their confrontation had appeared in the newspapers. He hated publicity, almost as much as Rob seemed to court it. That is one of the fascinating aspects of Rob's addiction to drink and drugs. Almost every cough and spit of his problems appear in the media but it has done him no harm whatsoever. Rob is not Machiavellian enough to use his addiction to his advantage in this way but the very best PR opportunities have been made from it. His standing with the general public has not been diminished in any way – in fact the reverse, as Rob has given, and continues to give, interviews on the subject to all and sundry. He has bared his heart and soul to, among others, *The Big Issue*, the *Guardian*, *Top of the Pops*, *Eve*, the *Daily Telegraph*, *Q*, *Select*, *Vox*, the *Face*, *Sky* and *Melody Maker*. That covers most bases.

A record company insider, who has witnessed some of the Rob excesses over the years and understands the role of drugs in music, observes that drugs, and cocaine in particular, continually push back the boundaries of acceptable behaviour. He believes the root of the cocaine problem is in adulation: 'When you are live on stage, singing in front of thousands of people who literally "love" you, it is an incredible high. How can you match that feeling?

'I remember seeing Robbie perform "Angels" on stage at Knebworth. Everyone in the audience was singing along and there was Robbie, microphone outstretched, crying his eyes out. Once you have had all this adulation, where do you go? The whole sex, drugs and rock 'n' roll cliché is actually real. The drugs blur the edges so you feel invincible. I have seen girls at his concerts going in and out of his dressing room to give him blow jobs right up to when he is due to go out on stage. Robbie always wants to push everything as far as can. He loves himself but he just goes too far.'

For someone who has done rehab, Rob seems extraordinarily prone to succumbing to temptation. He is lucky, however, in that he is now surrounded by people who understand the difficulties of recovery. In his current managers, David Enthoven and Tim Clark, he has been fortunate to find two people who have seen it all in the music industry. They are survivors. David, in particular, has a thorough understanding of the support Narcotics Anonymous can provide and he has been a father figure to Rob in a way that his real father Pete Conway cannot be in this particular instance. Pete and Rob forged a relationship in his adult life based around being drinking buddies rather than father and son. They always had a great laugh together over a pint but that was of no help to Rob when trying to confront his problems and perhaps explains, to some extent, why he and his father were estranged for a year and more when Rob went to Los Angeles. His managers, however, understood that there should be no blame attached to falling off the wagon but the important thing was to start afresh the next day. It is something that Jan Williams also appreciates through her work as a drugs counsellor. In the bad old days, he even tried to persuade his mother that it would be a good idea if she tried cocaine so that she knew what it was like. She told him not to be so silly.

Drugs are now banned on Rob's tours and anyone found indulging is summarily dismissed. This is purely to protect Rob. If he succumbs to a drink, he is likely to lose control and demand drugs from all and sundry. It makes sense, therefore, to ensure that no one has anything to give him. In the past, drugs have been too freely available in Rob's space and it is just not that easy to refuse the 'star' anything he wants in order to get him to go on out and perform and pay everyone's wages. At least this brittle area of his life has now been sorted.

No one seems to blame Rob for his weakness. He is metaphorically patted on the head, told he is a good boy really and taken out for a nice walk. Occasionally, Rob slips his lead, although his new life in California appears to have calmed him down. For some time Rob erroneously thought that if he was 'cured' he could go out and just have one drink or perhaps two, be very grown up and sociable and then pop off home. That is not really an option for an addict. He admitted on the *Parkinson* show in April 2001 that he had been trying to get sober for the previous four years and that he kept 'falling off'. The state of affairs has improved no end since he moved to Los Angeles. His chronically addictive personality makes do with playing card and board games hour after hour. And smoking sixty Silk Cut a day.

He also revealed in November 2002, 'I suffer from an illness that's called depression.' The interview in the *Daily Telegraph* with the respected music writer, Chris Heath, also revealed that he had been taking anti-depressant tablets for six months and that the medication was really helping him. The story was followed up in other nationals including the *Sunday Times* on 10 November.

Rob's favourite analogy to illustrate his drink and drugs excess is the book of tokens. He believes you are born with a book of tokens relating to all the important things in life like drink, drugs, sex and love. He 'went off far too early', handing his over willy-nilly until all he has left is a bunch of stubs. He wishes he was like Keith Richards who has 'nicked somebody else's book'. What he needs, of course, are love tokens but you only get a couple of those in your book.

'I popped in for one drink and that was it.'

PART THREE

ROBBIE WILLIAMS

11

The Birth of Robbie Williams

Robbie Williams was about to be dropped by his record label.
It was an open secret in the music business and even the
newspapers were hinting that he was finished. The launch of
his solo career, of which so much had been expected, had
been undermined by the success of Gary Barlow, the
disappointing sales of his first album and by his own
reputation as a party-going Blobby Williams. At EMI's 1997
autumn sales conference he sang a couple of songs before
an invited audience of mainly disinterested media. And then
he sang 'Angels'. A former executive recalls the moment: 'We
were about to drop him. But everyone was saying "Oh my
God! 'Angels' is such a hit!"'

Until that definitive moment in his career, Robbie Williams,
the brand name pop star, did not exist. He has been
resurrected like the proverbial phoenix from the ashes of
his first incarnation as the cheeky lad in Take That and from
his second as the fat-boy ligger of London Town. This was
the third Robbie, the fully fledged, grown-up pop star. And
it was such a surprise. But in the incredibly fickle world of
the music business one great song can change everything.

Everyone seemed so sure that Gary Barlow would make a smooth transition to George Michael-style superstardom while poor old Robbie Williams was just going to flounder around in the water without a lifejacket. Rob was bitter, upset and in a legal minefield that threatened to take most of his Take That cash. Gary was the RCA corporate darling and it would be just a matter of time before his solo career began. The whole saga unfolded like a modern-day version of the tortoise and the hare fable. The hare (Gary) zoomed over the horizon on the way to his first number one while the drugged-up tortoise (Robbie) went round and round in very small circles. Everyone in the music business got it wrong, even those with a proven record of sound pop judgement. Tilly Rutherford, then general manager of PWL, Pete Waterman's label, said just after Robbie had left Take That, 'Gary has got so much talent and he's the only one who can sing.'

Gary's first single 'Forever Love' was released in July 1996 and went straight to number one. It was a slightly dull ballad which sold extremely well but, perhaps, was not to everyone's taste. Rob robustly criticized it at every opportunity. The problems Gary was going to face were not immediately apparent for such an acclaimed singer-songwriter. After all, he had already won four prestigious Ivor Novello Awards for 'Pray' and 'Back for Good'. But he had been the sound and image of Take That, who had been at the very top for three years – a long shelf life for a boy band with a mainly teenage and pre-teenage audience. Rob once crudely remarked that, as a solo performer, he was playing before an audience with pubic hair.

The other major headache for Gary was Robbie Williams. He just refused to lie down and go away. The continual comparison was never going to work to Gary's advantage. While he was giving interviews revealing that he was learning to play tennis and loved *Star Wars*, Rob was falling down drunk, losing it on cocaine, bedding some very tasty young women and livening up breakfast television. Rob was turning into a rock star and Gary? He was forever boring. That turnaround in public perception was still some way off as Gary basked in his initial success whilst Rob appeared so miserable.

His most notable achievement during the first few months of his life after Take That was as a guest presenter on *The Big Breakfast*, the now defunct early morning show on Channel 4. Rob was originally hired to do the star interviews on the Big Bed which had been made famous by Paula Yates. His performance was riveting and often hilarious as he gradually took over the show by the sheer force of his personality. He asked Gary Lineker if, when he was the most famous footballer in the country, he ever dreamt that one day he would be advertising crisps. He tried to enlist the help of actor Stephen Baldwin in fixing him up with his sister-in-law, Kim Basinger. He donned a pair of Mr Spock ears to interview *Star Trek* fans. The viewing figures suggested he had brought in 600,000 extra viewers. At this stage, a career in television for an obviously natural showman and genuinely funny guy seemed a good bet. When he was asked if he might go back and present again in the future, he replied, 'Only if you change the name to *The Big Dinner*.'

Take That officially ceased work on 3 April 1996 following a round of promotional work in Holland for which they were already contracted. On 4 April Gary began work on his first solo album, *Open Road*. He actually had a great deal more to prove than Rob in that everyone assumed he was going to do great things whereas Rob was expected to do little more than a variety turn from time to time. A month later, as usual, Gary was having to answer questions about Robbie Williams. It was a familiar pattern and what it was inadvertently providing for Rob was a huge amount of media coverage, which he would never have had without the publicity machine launched on Gary Barlow's behalf. His observations on Rob were invariably along the same lines: 'I'm very disappointed in the way he has turned out.'

Rob's very public embrace of the sex, drugs and rock 'n' roll lifestyle in the year after his departure from Take That was missing one key ingredient: the rock 'n' roll. There was no music from Robbie Williams because of his contract with RCA, Take That's record company. Two weeks after Take That announced they would be splitting up, Rob was due in the High Court to argue that he should be released from the agreement because of the conflict of interest the company – controlled by BMG – would have trying to represent both his best interests and the other members, who would now be pursuing their solo careers. He withdrew the action before it reached court and left it to his new manager Tim Abbott to broker a deal. His career became effectively frozen for six months while the terms of that deal were sorted out and during negotiations to find another record company to take him on.

Who on earth would want to take on the 'fat schizo'? Abbott ran a company called Proper Management and took over the handling of Robbie early in 1996 after he had split from his first 'solo' manager Kevin Kinsella. In these rudderless days everything Robbie touched seemed to leave legal footprints. Kinsella pursued him for four years for unpaid fees totalling £184,000 before an agreement was finally reached in 2000. After the settlement, Kinsella said, 'When Robbie came to me he was in a bad way and I told him I would sort his career out.'

Rob's legal battles would drag on throughout the rest of the nineties. None of them were particularly significant unless he secured a record deal. A knight in shining armour arrived to rescue Rob from limbo in the shape of a maverick executive at EMI/Chrysalis called J. F. Cecilion, known throughout the record business as JF. A company insider explained, 'He signed Robbie when many in the business wouldn't have touched him. He saw something in Robbie, the naughty rogue, that he wanted to take a chance on. JF fought for Robbie, who has always appreciated that.' The other important figure was Chris Briggs, who was responsible for Rob's A&R at EMI: 'Briggsy was a major force because he made a concerted effort to get Robbie cleaned up.' Briggsy has always been quick to defend his biggest name: 'There's a difference between a prat acting the rock star, and a talented, sensitive person going into meltdown.'

At the end of June, a press conference was called to announce the EMI/Chrysalis deal to the world. Rob was still enjoying his 'lost year', so the whole thing was a considerable gamble. What Rob said at the Royal Lancaster Hotel neatly sums up the importance of the deal: 'I've got a new family now. Thank you JF and everybody at EMI/Chrysalis.' As part of his agreement with BMG, Rob had agreed to a confidentiality clause barring him from revealing its terms or from sounding off any more on the breakdown of his relationship with his former record company bosses. His mother would subsequently sit in on interviews trying to stop her son's mouth from running away with him and, therefore, breaking the terms of that agreement. Rob had to pay BMG to free himself from the contract. Although the figure has never been confirmed it was strongly rumoured to be in the region of £100,000, which is on the low side and perhaps indicative of the fact that Robbie Williams was not considered too valuable a proposition for the future. It was also whispered, but never proven, that the agreement barred Robbie Williams from releasing a solo single before Gary Barlow. The figure Rob was allowed to reveal was the amount he had to pay the lawyers – £400,000.

Rob's first single was to be a cover, his version of the George Michael song 'Freedom', which had been a minor hit in 1990. Rob was celebrating so many areas of liberation with the track: freedom from BMG and his contract; freedom from Take That; freedom from the rules of Nigel Martin-Smith; freedom to party; freedom, in effect, to do whatever he wanted. The song was a statement, if a rather unsubtle one. Rob declared, using a nod to an Oasis lyric, that he was now 'free to do whatever I want and to do whatever I choose'. One of the things he chose to do was to slag off Gary's single declaring it to be 'awful!' He also called him personally 'selfish, greedy, arrogant, thick' and a 'clueless wanker'. He saved his best barb, however, for Jason Orange. When asked how many of Take That would succeed, he responded, 'It just depends what they succeed in. Jason's going to make a brilliant painter and decorator.' Gary was completely bemused by the gratuitous insults flying from Rob's mouth, saying that he just did not understand how he could say the things he did. He thought Robbie had changed a lot in the relatively short time since his departure from Take That.

In the end Rob's solo single came out just eight days after 'Forever Love' hit the top of the charts. Gary's record stayed at the top for just one week, ousted by the Spice Girls' first hit, 'Wannabe', which would outsell almost everything that year. The five-strong girl band also meant 'Freedom' reached no higher than number two, although sales reached 270,000, which was more than respectable. After the massive publicity surrounding both singles from the ex-Take That boys, it was perhaps disappointing that they were swamped by 'girl power'. Would the Spice Girls have made such an impact if Take That were still the idols of the teeny-bop audience? 'Freedom' was never intended for Rob's first album but simply to mark a point in time in his life and career. The fact that it was a George Michael song made it an even more apposite choice because George was a role model for Rob, not as a solo artist, but in the way he had stood up to his record company and upheld his own artistic integrity.

Somewhat surprisingly, shortly after the £1 million three-album deal with EMI had been signed, Rob left Tim Abbott and joined IE Music, based in west London, not far from his new record label. He said he felt it was time to move on and that he wanted 'total artistic freedom in the creative direction of my album'. It was a vital final piece in the jigsaw that led to the creation of Robbie Williams, the biggest entertainer of his generation. Tim Abbott was less than delighted and yet another court case sparked into life. In all, Rob had four different managers in a little over a year if you include Nigel Martin-Smith at Take That. He ended up having to pay a great deal of money to the first three. Abbott filed his proceedings in October 1996 and the case took nearly two years to be settled out of court. He claimed more than £1 million in unpaid commission and finally agreed a sum in compensation, reported to be several hundred thousand pounds. It would have been a messy court case at just the wrong time for EMI. Rob had maintained that he had signed the contract with Proper Management when drunk and without proper advice.

IE Music has been ideal for Rob. The company, based in Shepherds Bush, is run by two ex-public school, country gentlemen types, David Enthoven and Tim Clark. They are in no way flash wide boys on the make but senior and respected figures in the music industry, where they have both been influential for more than thirty years. They are sane and sensible businessmen who have skilfully moved Robbie Williams to the centre of British music. When he first met Rob, David Enthoven thought he resembled a horse that had been abused to the extent that he had lost his faith in himself and in other people. He tried to show him that there was a better place, free from hangers-on who just wanted to be his friend because of what they could get out of it. Enthoven, a witty and urbane old Harrovian, has been a father figure in Rob's life. A friend describes him, 'He dresses a bit like a Californian rock star but the truth is he would not be out of place in a gentleman's club in St James's. He is a very kind man and his staff loves him. He will be as tough as anyone in a business situation but then take you out for an excellent dinner afterwards.' He has great experience in the music business through looking after such legendary acts as King Crimson, Roxy Music, Emerson, Lake and Palmer and T Rex. It was David who came up with the user-friendly name T Rex because he had trouble spelling Tyrannosaurus. But more than that he knew and recognized the dangers of drugs and alcohol in this world because they had almost ruined his own life. As a result he has been a teetotal abstainer for more than fifteen years and can act as a calm mentor for Rob as he comes to terms with his addictions. Like Rob's mother Jan, he is non-judgemental and does not blame Rob for any temporary lapses. Instead, he will be there with a nice cuppa and a pack of playing cards to try and keep Rob occupied and happy. He was the ideal person to guide Rob from Blobby Williams to his new image as Robbie Williams, superstar. His partner Tim Clark handles the marketing and packaging of what can only be described as the Robbie Williams phenomenon. He is the former managing director of Island Records where he signed Bob Marley, Steve Winwood, Free and many others.

Gary Barlow's second song, the more up-tempo 'Love Won't Wait', also went straight to number one in May 1997 but it only stayed nine weeks in the chart, compared with the sixteen for 'Forever Love' and a sign that only the core Take That fans were buying the record. This time Rob was first to the well, bringing out 'Old Before I Die', his first song with his name on it as part of the songwriting credits, a couple of weeks earlier. But like 'Freedom' it peaked at number two. Much would depend on how their first albums were received: Gary's *Open Road* and Rob's *The Show Must Go On*, which would later be renamed *Life Thru a Lens*, a much less corny title although *Life Thru the Bottom of a Beer Bottle* might have been even more apposite. Mark Owen, under new management, also produced his first two solo singles, 'Child' and 'Clementine', with disappointing results. They both only reached number three, leaving the way clear for the main bout – Gary Barlow versus Robbie Williams.

Gary was literally in very good shape for the fight. By the time he started promoting his second single and the album he looked more like a Hollywood action man than the dumpy one from Take That. Both Gary and Rob, the two most driven members of Take That, were also the pair with the worst body image, always concerned about their weight. With hindsight Gary probably should have released his album at the time 'Forever Love' hit the charts but he decided to re-record most of it in the United States, which kept him well away from the public eye. Rob, however, was the new media darling.

One of the first tasks for David Enthoven and Chris Briggs at EMI was to find a musician with whom Rob could write songs. Rob, with Jan's help and influence, is quite shrewd about business. It did not, however, take a financial genius to understand that publishing was where the money was. He had seen the royalties that Gary enjoyed from Take That and he did not want to pass on that particular goldmine. It was not as easy as it looked and Rob would make several false starts before stumbling across the right formula and, more importantly, the right man to help him create it. He first started writing with Owen Morris, the producer of Oasis and friend of Tim Abbott. The partnership foundered when Rob and Abbott parted company, although one guitar-led number, 'Cheap Love

Song', made it to the B-side of one of Rob's early singles 'South of the Border'. He then hooked up with Anthony Genn, the former bass player of Pulp whom Rob had met at Glastonbury in 1995. While Rob danced away on stage with Oasis, Genn took off his clothes during a performance from Elastica and dashed on stage. They wrote seven songs together but none have seen the light of day so far.

Next came an ill-advised trip to Miami to work with two established American songwriters, Desmond Child and Eric Bazilian, who both had impeccable rock credentials working with Bon Jovi and Aerosmith. Rob realized then that American music does not really get 'irony', a key ingredient in the eventual sound of Robbie Williams. He was also uneasy about the materialistic values. He flew back home with several songs but only one, 'Old Before I Die', which he truly liked, although he wanted to re-record it with a more Brit Pop feel. By the end of 1996, Rob had worked with four co-writers and had only two possible tracks to show for it. The first album looked a little ambitious.

Lyrically, Rob could work fast, his poetry coming out in a rapid stream of consciousness. Much of the lyrical content for *Life Thru a Lens* he committed to paper in a week. It was a series of reflections on his life at that point in time, in particular his attitude to stardom and his battle with alcohol and drugs. Rob was introduced to various collaborators but the one he clicked with was Guy Chambers, who had enjoyed a few minor hits in the early nineties with a band called the Lemon Trees. By a happy coincidence, Rob had never heard of the group until his mother's boyfriend at the time mentioned them in passing. When Guy's name came up Rob immediately thought it was a sign. David Enthoven gave Guy two pieces of advice about meeting Rob, which everyone would do well to remember. They were: don't call him Robbie and don't try to be his friend.

Guy first met Rob at the Capital Radio Road Show, when his band was also on the bill. Rob had the shakes, was overweight and looked like death warmed up. Despite that unpromising start the two gelled. When Rob went round to Guy's flat in London he listened to one of his Lemon Trees' songs and loved the melody. With a change in lyrics it was to become 'Lazy Days', Rob's third single. Chris Briggs told *Music Week* that the early demos from Guy and Rob were very encouraging: 'They confirmed we had found a direction. But it had to come naturally.' Guy confessed that he wasn't sure what was going to happen: 'Can we get through this year without him killing himself?'

The beauty of his debut single being a cover was that it gave Rob time to evolve his own sound. He could have come up with anything from the Monkees to Motorhead. Peter Lorraine, then editor of *Top of the Pops* magazine, confirmed that no one had a clue what kind of music Robbie was going to produce. Eventually, when he heard the album, he said, 'Robbie is going to do really well because his music is brilliant. He was always the only one in Take That with any street cred.'

Unfortunately, the album's release barely registered in the charts. The bargain bin selection rather than the best-selling shelves seemed to be its obvious destination – and sooner, rather than later. The hare, aka Gary Barlow, was racing away with sales of *Open Road*. In no time at all it had reached number one status and 350,000 in sales. Then, curiously, it stalled, as if everyone interested in Gary Barlow had gone out and bought it and there was nobody else. *Life Thru a Lens* barely made the top ten albums before disappearing from view. One of the problems, according to Chris Briggs, was that Rob was unable to promote a single taken from the album because of his rehab treatment. 'Lazy Days' peaked at a disappointing number eight. But that was sensational compared to 'South of the Border', written on a platform at Stoke station, which limped to number fourteen at the end of September, selling a paltry 40,000 copies. It was all going horribly wrong – three singles from the album all doing progressively worse. Rob's confidence was shot to pieces as he tried to come to terms with his rehab treatment.

In the first eight weeks of release, *Life Thru a Lens* managed to shift just 33,000 copies before falling out of the charts. It was an absolute crisis for the three-album deal with EMI/Chrysalis. There was little prospect of the second two ever seeing the light of day. And then came 'Angels', a Damascene moment in the story of Robbie Williams. It was an instant classic, albeit firmly in the middle of the road. Even Pete Conway already knew it was a great song. Rob had sung it to him in the car one afternoon. Pete told him it was extra special and went round telling all his mates, 'You wait until "Angels" comes out.' Pete was convinced it was up there with Paul McCartney's 'Yesterday'. In truth, it sounded more like a classic from Elton John, with Rob's voice sounding more mid-Atlantic than before. Some of Elton's great songs, like 'Candle in the Wind' and 'Sorry Seems to Be the Hardest Word' are, however, a little downbeat lyrically. 'Angels' is unusual for such an introspective ballad in that it is unashamedly uplifting and, crucially, can mean something different for everyone. For Rob, it described his feelings about the death of his mother's sister, Auntie Jo, who had died when he was fifteen and, also, of his granddad, Phil Williams, Pete Conway's father. The theme of someone watching over you is one which Rob uses throughout his songwriting. 'Nan's Song' on *Escapology* is a more recent example.

'Angels' was a song about guardian spirits and personal rescue and, as such, rather aptly rescued Rob's career. It could even be said to have begun the career of Robbie Williams as we know him today. The video, almost as importantly, revealed a post-rehab Robbie to the world – strong-featured yet vulnerable, the famous eyes and a new close-cropped haircut with a shaved parting. And the package wrapped up in an impossibly big overcoat that looked as if he had nicked it from army surplus. The jellied buttocks of Take That were light years away.

Life Thru a Lens went straight back in the charts with the pulling power of 'Angels' on its side and ended up selling a million copies and more. Within a year, Robbie Williams would be the biggest selling British artist. Ironically, his next single, 'Let Me Entertain You', had originally been intended for release before 'Angels' but Rob had felt he lacked the confidence to project a song with such a brash title. By the time it finally made the shops in March 1998, all the old swagger had returned. A couple of years later Rob and Jonathan Wilkes were guest presenters on Capital Radio in London and, unsurprisingly, 'Angels' was one of the songs they played. Rob introduced it by saying, 'Shall we play the song that transformed my career from a mere boozing, fat ex-boy band member?'

A year after the final demise of Take That, one bright spark wrote that the current score was 2–0 to Barlow in his Match of the Day with Robbie Williams, thanks to his two number ones against his former bandmate's nil. The current score is 2–5 to Williams, quite a giant-killing act. Gary Barlow, middle-aged man, has a commendably pragmatic attitude to fame: 'In the record industry, literally as soon as your song has gone to the cutting room, it's over and you've got to replace it with something else. I really have had enough of the hysteria. I'm looking forward to having a family, living in the house I've bought and driving the cars I've bought.' And that is exactly what he has done. Rob, however, has so far only scored two out of those particular three goals.

'Just be a dick and people respect you for it.'

12

Nic

Away from the trendy bars and nightspots of Notting Hill, Rob
was determined to show his Canadian-born, pop star
girlfriend a slice of the real, normal British life he adored. He
took her north to visit his mother and some of his old haunts
in Newcastle-under-Lyme and Stoke-on-Trent. In the
evening they went round the corner to the Chinese takeaway,
took a meal back and watched TV with his mates.

Rob's second album, *I've Been Expecting You*, is almost
unbearably poignant if viewed as a memorial to the
destruction of his most important love affair, his
relationship with All Saints singer Nicole Appleton. From
the title itself to tracks including 'No Regrets' and
'Phoenix From the Flames' it is a heartbreaking journey
through the most difficult time of Rob's life. Nic, as
friends call her, even contributes a single line on the
album at the start and end of 'Win Some Lose Some'. We
simply hear her telephone voice declaring, 'Love You
Baby.' And then there is 'Grace', a song about the baby,
Rob's child, which Nic aborted. They were going to call
the baby Grace if it had been a girl.

In May 1997, before he met Nic, Rob was asked in an interview if he ever thought about settling down. He replied that having a family was a major thing in his life and that he had even written a song, the never-released 'If I Ever Have a Son'. He added, 'I want to stop going mad because I want to be a good role model for my kids.'

Nicole Appleton brought out the best in Robert Williams. They were both born in 1974, Nic on 7 October, making her a Libran to Rob's Aquarian. Like him, she came from a broken home. Her parents first split up when she was five and the other famous Appleton sister, Natalie, was seven. They were the two youngest of four daughters. It was a traumatic time because the family were literally split down the middle. Nic went to live in London with her father, a car salesman, and another sister called Lori while Natalie stayed behind in Canada with the eldest, Lee. After two years their mother came to London and they resumed a relatively normal family life but that only lasted a few months before she returned to Canada, this time leaving all four girls in London. It was a very disorientating time, especially when their mother returned yet again within the year and they made the best of it crammed into a small flat in Kilburn.

It became increasingly clear that Nic and Rob were destined to be soul mates, to understand the loneliness and confusion of having their home life divided and of dreaming of a glamorous world of show business as an escape route. She was a superb dancer as a child and passed the audition to attend the recently opened Sylvia Young Theatre School in Camden Town, along with Denise van Outen, who would later also date Robbie Williams, and Emma Bunton, one of the three Spice Girls who did not go out with him. Her sister Nat joined her there but after four years their unhappy mother left once more, this time to live in New York. Both Nic and Nat went with her, part of a relentless merry-go-round as they tried and failed to settle in either London or New York or Florida.

Their new 'stepfather' worked as an entertainments manager for a big hotel. He was almost an American equivalent of Pete Conway. The sisters would be like Butlins redcoats, helping guests with fun activities and then getting drunk in the evenings. If Nic and Nat had lived in Tunstall, they would have been honorary lads, drinking until they threw up or passed out. Nicole was a slower starter than Rob in the music business. She joined Melanie Blatt and Shaznay Lewis in All Saints when she was twenty, the age at which Rob was seriously considering life after the most successful boy band of the time. Rob would be able to understand what Nic was going through when she began having major problems within All Saints. He would also have understood the effort involved in just trying to get that first record deal and how the perception of girl bands was very much the same as for boy bands – usually neither are treated seriously. And just as in Take That, there was meant to be only one talented one in All Saints: Shaznay was their Gary Barlow.

In the beginning Rob and Nic kept their relationship a secret. They met for the first time on a television show when All Saints were performing their most famous song, 'Never Ever', written by Shaznay. Rob was polite and complimentary to Nic about her music. In *Together*, her joint autobiography with sister Nat, she describes how he seemed 'very famous'. It was an insightful observation.

There is nothing nerdy, introspective, geeky or apologetic about Robbie Williams. He is a twenty-four-carat star with the charisma to match. They met again at the rehearsals for the Concert of Hope in aid of the Princess Diana Trust, the first time Rob and Gary Barlow had clapped eyes on each other since the demise of Take That. Gary had lost none of his cheesiness, beckoning everyone over to the piano for a sing-a-long. It was Rob who lit up the room for Nic. He did not seek attention, he demanded it.

One of the intriguing aspects of the Appletons' autobiography is that they reveal so much of their vulnerability and personal insecurities. Nicole Appleton is a celebrity, albeit when she met Rob a very minor one, but she behaves like an uncertain schoolgirl whose knees turn to jelly at the sight of the football captain. She keeps looking over and then looking away quickly. She wants to talk to him but is worried she will be at a disadvantage if he knows she fancies him. She invites him to her birthday party and is ecstatic when he is the first to arrive. She treasures a Polaroid snap they have taken together. And she is secretly upset when she opens the paper and sees he has been out on a date with Denise van Outen. Perhaps, inevitably, considering Rob's history, they got so drunk on Guinness the first night they spent together that they both passed out. A more worrying foretaste of what was to come in their relationship happened when Rob called her in a dreadful state from a house in north London asking for her to come and get him. It was the morning after several nights before and Rob was at his lowest, most vulnerable, guilt-ridden post-euphoria.

In many ways, Rob and Nic found each other at exciting, make-or-break times for them both. Nic and All

Saints were just clutching success for the first time, while Rob was at the crossroads of success and failure with his post-Take That career. His first solo album, *Life Thru a Lens*, was released in October 1997, the same month he attended Nicole Appleton's birthday party. He released his pivotal record, 'Angels', whilst 'Never Ever', All Saints's second release, was creeping relentlessly up the charts.

Nic describes a wonderful scene in Rob's bedroom one Sunday morning just after New Year 1998. His manager rings to give him the new chart position for 'Angels'. He sounds pleased and excited, puts the phone down and announces, '"Never Ever" is number one.' Amazingly it sold 770,000 copies *before* it reached the top, a record. Rob even rang his mother to tell her the good news. Jan always liked Nic.

Rob and Nic's relationship became public property on 2 January 1998, when she was seen by photographers leaving his place in Notting Hill. It was almost certainly a tip-off to the paparazzi that if they hung around outside Robbie Williams's home for a day or two they would spot Nicole Appleton. Or perhaps they were expecting to catch Denise van Outen. Or just any old lap dancer Rob may or may not have spent the New Year with. The next day, the newspapers had their story and Rob and Nic would have to conduct their own private tragedy against a backdrop of superficial media fascination. The heartbreaking irony of both of them telling the press they were looking forward to having kids – after the abortion – makes for painful retrospection.

For a while everything was going well. All Saints were increasingly perceived as an antidote to the Spice Girls, cooler, less noisy and with better music. Rob and Nic were together at the Brit Awards where All Saints won two for 'Never Ever' and he came away with a disappointing zero. He had been nominated for four, his first post-Take That recognition so, although he was his usual life and soul, Nic knew he was very upset. He had, however, stolen the show with his three-song medley with Tom Jones.

The following week, an exclusive interview appeared in the *Sun*, in which she spoke for the first time about their relationship, saying how much he made her laugh, although she warned that they were much too young to be committed yet. Nic was ever present during the filming of a BBC documentary about Rob entitled *Some Mothers Do 'Ave 'Em*. Rob is obviously happy, revelling in the relationship with Nic. He tells the camera that it has given him a lot of security and a lot of love and happiness but that he is learning to cope with the difficult as well as the great times. The difficult times, which he did not chronicle, began in March 1998 when Nic rang from Vancouver to tell him that she was pregnant. Incredibly, considering the goldfish bowl in which they both lived their lives, they managed to keep what unfolded entirely secret.

Rob was absolutely thrilled at the prospect of becoming a father. He started making plans, buying a new flat with enough space to have a room for the baby. He took Nic to Tunstall to see his beloved nan Betty, who was now eighty-three, and who also was happy at her grandson's news. In her book, Nic recalls that Rob put his hand on her belly and told her, 'This baby is saving my life.'

At four months pregnant, Nic had an abortion in New York, with Rob waiting in the next room to support her as best he could. In her version of events, Nic blamed enormous pressure from everyone connected with All Saints. She maintains that she did it for the band – even though Melanie Blatt, who was pregnant at the same time, went ahead and had her baby. It was also implied to her, so she says, that Robbie Williams was bad news. Afterwards, she was consumed with guilt that she had let Rob down.

To this day Nic does not know if and to what extent Rob blamed her for what happened. During the coming months he became more difficult to handle, unable to offer the sympathetic ear she needed over her troubles within All Saints and telling her she should just leave the band. And yet, paradoxically, he would trail along with her on the frequent doctor's appointments she required after the operation. It was as if he had no time for the world of celebrity, of entertainment and of 'Robbie Williams', but he was doing his best to do the right thing within the world of Rob Williams, an ordinary lad from Tunstall who understood the importance of personal loyalty and family.

Rob asked Nic to marry him in June 1998. The newspapers called it a whirlwind romance, unaware that the pair had packed more into six months than many couples do in a lifetime together. More often than not the romantic nature of Rob will win out over the 'love 'em and leave 'em' lad's attitude. He was proud of being in a proper, grown-up relationship and wanted to do everything in the right manner. He proposed on bended knee with an exquisite antique diamond ring proffered from his hand. The slightly less conventional aspect was that it was five in the morning and Rob had been sound asleep in bed when Nic came round to his house, having jetted in from an All Saints visit to Japan. Rob had to get out of bed in order to get down on one knee. Unlike the pregnancy and the abortion, the good news of the engagement was, in true celebrity style, a secret for a couple of seconds. Both of Rob's parents were in London to see him perform an important solo concert at the Royal Albert Hall. They were pleased with his news. If they had not been in London they could have read all about it in the press the following day. Nic was quoted, footballer style, as saying that she was 'over the moon'. Jan, normally so reticent about discussing her son, was just as pleased: 'I am very proud of him and his choice, she is a lovely lady. I was aware the engagement was coming up – they are just so in love and so happy.' More pertinently, perhaps, she added that no date for a wedding had been fixed because they had so much to do in their careers.

The worst thing about celebrity relationships is the absences. Actors, actresses and rock stars meet each other at celebrity parties, enjoy a 'whirlwind romance' and then say cheerio for a week, or a month or six months while they go off on tour or start filming in the Peruvian jungle. It is very hard to deal with. Kylie Minogue's great love affair with Michael Hutchence went up in smoke when they were at opposite ends of the globe, pursuing their careers. Rob's friend Patsy Kensit once described how even something as trivial as your partner saying hello in the wrong tone of voice could send you into agonies of doubt if you were thousands of miles apart. Rob and Nic were apart a great deal in the summer of 1998 as All Saints flew all over the world promoting their first album and Rob started work on his second in London. He was also struggling to come to terms with a traumatic event in his life – the death of his beloved nan.

Nic and Rob split up for the first time by telephone, after she had been away for a week. He was at home in Notting Hill and she was in a hotel room in Rio de Janeiro. There was a message from Rob waiting for her when she checked in. He just told her to call but, proving the veracity of Patsy Kensit's observation, she knew something was not right. In her version of the conversation, he told her they should end their relationship, claiming they were apart too much. Reading between the lines, it was Rob the small boy wanting some attention and affection. He hates being by himself and, probably, just wanted her to say she was dropping everything to return home and give him a cuddle. Celebrity life is just not like that.

The newspapers claimed that it was Nic who had called things off and that Rob was distraught. He certainly looked very down when he was pictured leaving the Groucho Club in Soho at 2.30 a.m., after earlier attending the reopening of the Heaven nightclub and then a party at the Café de Paris. He told reporters that he hoped he could sort things out with Nicole, who meant the world to him. Jan Williams appeared just as disappointed as her son: 'I can't believe they have split. It was a match made in heaven and I pray they make up.' Rob promptly flew off to the Spanish resort of Puerto Banús to drown his sorrows with wine and women, at least that is how the newspapers saw it. Jan was again quoted at her supportive best saying that he was upset because of the Nicole situation: 'He's looking on the positive side and wouldn't jeopardize his music career. He always tells me if he has got any problems.'

There is no reason to disbelieve Nicole Appleton's recollection of their first break-up, something she said she never understood. There is a curiously repetitive theme in the press coverage of Rob's relationships, in that he is almost always the one who is dumped. A relationship of this intensity was completely new to him and he undoubtedly acted impetuously, his constant craving for attention and approval getting the better of him. His addiction to drugs had left him with a predilection to loiter in the darker recesses of his mind. In his relationship with Nic, he could really have done with lightening up. Within days of her returning to the UK, they went out for dinner, got completely drunk and were seen stumbling around, with Rob, wearing a football shirt, giving Nic a piggyback. He proposed again at the end of August and she accepted.

Their respective careers, at first glance, could not have been going better. 'Bootie Call' was the third All Saints number one of the year when it topped the charts on 12 September. One week later it was replaced by Robbie Williams's first number one, 'Millennium', from the *I've Been Expecting You* album. They both, however, had ongoing problems. Rob was doing his best with his addiction treatment and Nic would go along to AA meetings to support him. She, meanwhile, continued to be unhappy within the band, feeling that she and Nat were the poorer relations of Shaznay and Melanie. It also did not help when Melanie had a baby girl, Lilyella. Nic recorded a song she had written with the help of Rob and Guy Chambers called 'Love Is Where I'm From' but it failed to obtain a release, much to her disappointment. They broke up again just after All Saints had switched on the Christmas lights in Regent Street. Once again, Rob seemed to suggest it out of the blue, with no rhyme or reason. And, once again, he regretted it almost immediately. The old romantic in him took over and he bought her 1000 red roses.

Their final reconciliation lasted a mere two weeks, when a wild Christmas drinking session by Rob spelt the end. In a theatrical confrontation, Nic says she told Rob that if he walked out the door he needn't come back. He left and that was basically that. His bender went from bad to worse and he passed out in the lobby of a hotel, where a cruel passer-by covered him in shaving foam and toothpaste and then called the papers to witness his humiliation. It was the end of a dreadfully sad, tortuous year for both of them. It would not be completely accurate to describe Rob and Nic as star-crossed lovers because most of their bad luck they brought on themselves.

Once again, the ups and more frequently the downs of their relationship were public property. At the Brit Awards in February 1999, they found themselves the centre of attention simply because they were not sitting with one another. Rob was nominated for an unprecedented six awards and this time he picked up three. He went with his family and she was escorted by Huey Morgan of the Fun Lovin' Criminals.

Nic was subsequently quoted in a Sunday paper as saying that Rob was a mess in his personal life. She drew attention to his inability to forget he was Robbie Williams when he was out of the spotlight. That was a bit unfair because Rob did try to be ordinary and natural but hardly anyone would let him. When he took Nicole out for a Chinese meal in Stoke-on-Trent, he was continually hassled by people who recognized him. They could hardly be blamed for being excited at seeing a star ordering sweet and sour but it forced him to retreat into a shrinking world. On one occasion, when he went to the airport to meet Nic, a man wanted Rob to speak to his girlfriend on his mobile phone. When he declined – this was private time – the man told his girlfriend, 'Wanker won't speak to you!' One can imagine that the chump in question has dined out ever since on the story and that, in his opinion, Robbie Williams is a wanker. The distinction between the public and the private Rob continued to blur when he started talking about Nic to his audience at a concert in Newcastle-upon-Tyne, saying how much he missed her. Usually superstars do not share their private lives with their fans the way Rob does.

The Brits ceremony was not the last time they saw each other or went out together but the Christmas break-up was, for Nic at least, a form of closure. She still telephoned him for advice and a sympathetic ear. But at the Cannes Film Festival in March she met Liam Gallagher. Intriguingly, her relationship with Liam developed along similar lines to the one she had just shared with Rob. They, too, spent much of their spare time drinking, he gave her support in her ongoing strife within All Saints and they also had to deal with an early pregnancy. Crucially, this time she was determined to keep the baby and was strong enough to do so. Looking at the two relationships there are so many similarities it does beg the question of what would have happened if she had become involved with Liam first and had then met Rob. Her relationship with Liam has become so homely. While Rob lives a solitary existence in a gated community in Los Angeles, Liam is watching TV with his kids, eating roast dinners, having a few beers and enjoying the love of the woman in his life, Nicole Appleton. You, Rob, leave with nothing.

After All Saints finally split and the lawyers moved in, Nic and Nat wrote their autobiography, which came out at the same time as their solo record career was launched in the summer of 2002. Most shockingly, Nic revealed all the deeply personal details about her relationship with Rob and their aborted child. It was a brave decision to be so open about what, in celebrity terms, is a very negative experience. Many women in showbusiness have abortions in order to protect their careers but very few admit it, let alone talk it through from beginning to end. Perhaps Nic needed to cleanse herself of the details in order to put All Saints and Rob behind her and move forward with a new career and family. Many were amazed that she could be so insensitive to Rob's personal feelings although he, too, has never been slow to air his dirty linen in public. It all depends on whether he considers Nic to be part of the story of Rob or of Robbie. It was such an eye-opener for the public that Robbie Williams, the cheeky chappie, had been through such an ordeal.

Although brutally frank, Nicole Appleton is nice about Rob. She is not bitter. She did not hear from him when her baby was born and they are no longer in touch. Nic loves cats and Rob once bought her a kitten from Harrods as a present and as a companion for the two she already had. She called her Kid.

'I was really sad for both of us.'

13

Beauty in Sadness

> When he was on holiday with Jonathan Wilkes in the south of
> France, Rob wrote a truly awful song called 'Where's Your
> Saviour Now?' Frustrated, he closed his eyes and prayed:
> 'John Lennon, if you're there, send us a song.' He then
> proceeded to write 'Better Man' in under an hour.

In 1998, *Life Thru a Lens* and the follow-up album, *I've Been
Expecting You*, sold a combined total in the UK of 2.32
million copies, making Robbie Williams the biggest selling
artist of the year. *Life Thru a Lens* seethed and bubbled
with anger and frustration and revealed for the first time
a key ingredient of the Robbie Williams musical package:
the quality of the lyrics. The music distanced him
immediately from boy bands and the sound of Take That,
Gary Barlow's sound. Instead, the album continued a
tradition of Brit Pop popularized by Oasis and Blur in the
earlier nineties. It would have been easy to dismiss Robbie
Williams as a boy band member with ideas above his
station if the album had not been such a good debut.
Almost every review, while noting the musical pedigree of
Guy Chambers, paid special attention to the lyrics. Who

else could rhyme 'needy' with 'inbreedy'? The most amusing review came in *Melody Maker*, which, while scoring the album eight out of ten, made the observation that 'Angels' was the record's nadir, describing it as a 'slimy pre-Oasis ballad'.

By the time *I've Been Expecting You* had been digested, a clearer picture of where Robbie Williams would be in the musical market place could be discerned. The music sounded like a magpie had been let loose on the Radio 2 playlist. 'Let Me Entertain You' tipped its hat at mid-seventies Elton John camp rock – 'Pinball Wizard', 'Saturday Night's Alright for Fighting' – with a nod to Alice Cooper's 'School's Out'. 'No Regrets' was unashamedly Pet Shop Boys to the extent that Neil Tennant was even persuaded to provide backing vocals. Rob brazenly phoned him up and said he had written a new Pet Shop Boys-style tune. 'Millennium' sampled the famous James Bond theme from *You Only Live Twice*. 'She's the One' was actually an old track by World Party, the group with which Guy Chambers had cut his musical teeth in the early nineties. Rob's lyrics raised this musical pot pourri above the ordinary. 'Millennium' may have conjured an initial image of Sean Connery in a tuxedo but on second hearing the lyrics include references to liposuction, detox and overdose at Christmas – hardly topics for the British Secret Service. They were very personal, self-aware and, best of all, ironic. There is nothing bland in his self-portrait, 'Strong', which begins the second album. Rob is revealed as a natural poet. He must have died from embarrassment in Take That when he sang lead vocals on 'I Found Heaven' (on the wings of love)'. The new Robbie Williams would have found heaven in a pint of mild.

When the albums were released in the USA in 1999, they were packaged together under the title *The Ego Has Landed*. The reviews in America were encouraging and not at all disparaging of the music as too British or idiosyncratic, the two excuses often trotted out to explain Rob's relative lack of success across the Atlantic. One reviewer observed, 'This kid is a seventies variety show looking for a place to happen.' Another commented that the tracks were brimming with cleverness and raffish charm. The most ironic observation was that Robbie Williams was the drinking man's George Michael. Up until then, it was always Gary Barlow's name that was mentioned in the same breath as George's.

One reviewer in San Francisco wrote, 'Like many great pop singers Robbie Williams knows how to uncover the beauty in sadness.' Nothing better encapsulates that than 'One of God's Better People', a deeply personal tribute to his mother in which he admits the hurt he must cause her by continually losing himself. It is a song about love at a time when Rob said he did not know how to write one. When he talked about *Life Thru a Lens* for *Smash Hits*, he revealed that he had sung it to her down the phone and she had broken down in tears.

Rob was getting his old swagger back after the battering of his 'lost year'. The success of *Life Thru a Lens* gave him the confidence that he had hit on a winning formula – the Robbie Williams formula: a cheeky, sarcastic, funny, sensitive showman. He declared after reading his album's reviews, 'I love listening to good music and I can't stop playing my album!' He could get away with such conceit because of the twinkle in his eye. All the smart wisecracks and wistful words would, of course, have counted for nothing if the music had not been so well crafted.

I've Been Expecting You had a much slicker feel to it than *Life*. Rob and Guy Chambers had settled in to a better writing rhythm and, perhaps crucially, Rob was sober more of the time. Instead of hauling himself out from underneath the mixing desk he was contributing from a vertical position. By the time of *I've Been Expecting You*, Rob's voice had grown immeasurably stronger from the anaemic warbling of 'Everything Changes'. Even the best opera singers need training and Rob's voice was now maturing from Beaujolais Nouveau to decent claret. It was a powerful mixture of Elton John and Liam Gallagher, with a soupçon of his dad thrown in for good measure.

The *New Musical Express* gave the album an encouraging review and encapsulated the image of Robbie Williams brilliantly: 'a bovine sex god, rehab fuck-up, cabaret clown and UNICEF ambassador'. The record was so difficult to dislike. Robbie Williams was proving to be a pop star (not a rock star) that was hard to fault. He was still hung up on the desire to be Oasis, and Liam in particular, but that was waning and would be consigned firmly to the dust when he fell out with the Gallaghers. The *Daily Telegraph* summed it up: 'Robbie and his showbiz mates the Gallagher brothers have one thing in common; all their songs are naggingly reminiscent of classic tracks that you can't quite put your finger on.' Both 'Millennium' and 'She's the One' went to the top of the UK singles chart.

Guy Chambers was now rejoicing in the grandiose position of 'musical director', which sounded the sort of title you might give yourself if you were involved in the production of *Oliver!* at the Queen's Theatre, Burslem. The North Staffordshire Amateur Operatic and Dramatic Society had a 'musical director'. Unintentionally, that gave the game away about the 'new' Robbie Williams. He was putting on a show, the whole thing was a big entertainment, a musical entitled *West Stoke Story*, in which a working-class lad with a comic for a dad, who loves his mum, achieves fame and fortune, only to throw it all away when he gets led astray by a bad lot, rediscovers himself as a star and becomes 'a better man'. What's Andrew Lloyd Webber's number?

Seeking the influences of Robbie Williams in the songs of the Beatles, Elton John and Oasis is fun but his heart is strictly Cole Porter, sung by Frank Sinatra – witty lyrics that roll around on the tongue for a bit before emerging into a catchy popular song. The public lapped it up and so did the record industry. Rob was nominated for six Brits in 1999. His music was far from bland and forgettable but it was as a showman and entertainer that he flourished and the character Robbie Williams could really come into its own.

Sing When You're Winning built on the success of the first two albums. In some ways it's a celebration of that success. The formula of self-revealing, self-healing lyrics grafted on to decent melodies is the same as before. There is a hint that Robbie Williams is too pleased with himself: from the sleeve's pictures of Rob celebrating in a football shirt, being carried shoulder-high by other players, all of whom are Rob, to the hidden track at the end of the album. On *Life Thru a Lens* there was one hidden track – the vitriolic attack on his old teacher; *I've Been Expecting You* had two. But twenty-two minutes and twenty-five seconds of pregnant pause elapses after the last track of *Sing When You're Winning* before Rob's voice chips in, 'No, I'm not doing one on this album.' The critic John Aizlewood amusingly suggested that a more apt title would have been *Sing When You're Whining*.

Rob has achieved both continuity and stability in his recordings. Guy Chambers, the diffident old hand who lit the flame of Rob's musical ambitions, has been a constant thread. During their first songwriting session they wrote four songs together. Rob would be extremely irritated if he believed anyone thought his was the minor contribution to the Robbie Williams songbook. Of almost equal importance was co-producer Steve Power, brought into the mix by Guy. A Liverpudlian like Guy, Steve had moved to London in the mid-eighties and worked as an engineer at Battery Studios on hits like 'World Shut Your Mouth' by Julian Cope and 'Because of You' by Dexy's Midnight Runners. His breakthrough as a mainstream producer occurred when he masterminded Babylon Zoo's 1996 number one 'Spaceman', which was then the fastest selling debut single of all time. Then he produced Babybird's 'You're Gorgeous', another huge hit. He candidly admits that they were both records that everyone hated (perfect training for 'Rock DJ').

Steve is well known in the business as a perfectionist. He will spend three days on a vocal take to 'make Rob sound like God'. He is adept at constructing the sound so that a song, 'Angels' for instance, can reach its maximum potential. He needed to be patient because both Guy and Rob were easily bored, eager to get on with the next song. They would write songs like a conveyor belt and had thirty-five for the first album by the time Steve was involved. He quickly helped them chop that down to a dozen or so possible tracks. He was as responsible as Guy for moulding the sound that so surprised those expecting Robbie

Williams to be son of Take That. Rob's well-documented difficulties at the time of recording *Life Thru a Lens* made it extremely difficult for Guy and Steve to get the record they wanted out. Steve explained it in football parlance that Rob was like an out-of-form striker, unaware of his capabilities, but that changed as his confidence grew. As Rob improved his personal standing so the music improved. Where Guy Chambers arranged, Steve Power mixed. He is the third ear of the Williams/Chambers team. It was Steve, for instance, who picked out the demos of 'Strong' and 'No Regrets'. He revealed, 'Guy didn't think "Strong" was very good.' Together they won Producer of the Year at the 1998 International Managers Forum. They shared the award and, most of the time, they share the priceless ability to handle Rob at his most mercurial.

Guy Chambers is refreshingly frank about his songwriting with Rob. He admits that they 'plunder' the best bits of modern, popular music. Sometimes that proved a little unwise, as when they had to pay a six-figure sum to a New York publishing firm. They had taken a verse without permission from an obscure 1973 song by the quirky American folk singer, Loudon Wainwright III, 'I Am the Way (New York Town)', and inserted it, more or less intact, into the verse of 'Jesus in a Camper Van', which was on the *I've Been Expecting You* album and the US release *The Ego Has Landed*. It was the seventh track on Rob's second album but if you order the CD today it has disappeared into the Bermuda Triangle of recordings. Instead, a completely different song entitled 'It's Only Us' occupies the seventh position. Guy has observed that, while Rob would not claim to be the most original artist in the world, there is a strong argument to say he is the most entertaining. He is also one of the most professional.

Sing When You're Winning did boast a track that moulds all the finest components of Robbie Williams: 'Better Man', which would have made a far better single than the vacuous 'Rock DJ', although that song which sampled Barry White was a huge show-stopping number one. Even Rob described it as a bit of rubbish. 'Better Man', however, is a ballad in the 'Angels' mode but this time a plea for love that endorsed the view that Rob could deliver beauty in sadness. Rob says he was inspired to write the song by John Lennon.

'Robbie Williams' may be a creation to perform these songs but it is Rob who writes the words. There is even a small homage to his Tunstall life in the title 'Knutsford City Limits', which was also the name of a song by his teenage favourites the Macc Lads.

This third album and the accompanying tour, which spawned the book *Somebody Someday* and the film *Nobody Someday*, were the culmination of the branding of Robbie Williams. He was like a ubiquitous soft drink, but was the brand now strong enough to withstand consumer fatigue or did it have to develop, repackage and reinvent in the manner which has kept Madonna at the top for twenty years?

The persona of Robbie Williams is seen at its finest on tour: the showman has landed. It is such a professional job. A music fan who has seen him live ten times says, 'He has never been shit – even if he was feeling shit.' Two years after his departure from Take That he was live on stage in the UK singing 'Back for Good' but not in any shape or form that Take That fans would have recognized. It all started out harmlessly enough but degenerated into a Sid Vicious-style pogo dancing frenzy. It was totally unexpected but the corruption of the boy band classic was typically Robbie, almost shocking. The banners in the crowd had a sense of Take That déjà-vu as well: 'Rob – We Want Your Knob' and 'Point Your Erection In My Direction' were rhymes the lad himself would have been proud of. It was still very much a teenage audience that Rob played for in 1997.

Rob seemed genuinely surprised at the reception. Everyone knew the words to everything. 'I've wanted to do this for two fucking years,' he exclaimed in the style that has become a familiar one in the past six years. Rob engages the audience. He talks to them, lets them know how he is feeling. When his biggest hit 'Angels' is showcased, Rob does not sing it. He holds out the microphone to the crowd, to indulge in their favourite karaoke number. He is probably condemned to having 'Angels' as his encore for evermore. He has tears in his eyes. There is nothing to compare to this. A record executive observes, 'He gets such an incredible high out of performing. How can you follow it?'

In August 1998, he headlined the V98 pop festival in Leeds at a time when he was at his most confident. He was halfway through introducing a song when he was interrupted by the band yelling at him that he was on the wrong song. 'Am I introducing the wrong song?' he enquired politely and proceeded to check the playlist. Then he turned to engage the audience in the way other less charismatic artists can only dream of and said, 'You're missing "Life Thru a Lens". That one's shit anyway.' And belted out 'Millennium' instead, which would be his first number one the following month.

At Slane Castle, Dublin, in August 1999, he performed before an audience of 82,768, which was about 82,700 more than saw him perform those few years before at Flicks in Huddersfield as the uncertain fifth member of Take That. His set ended with a storming version of the Clash anthem, 'Should I Stay or Should I Go'. Ironically, the Clash topped the charts when this classic record was re-released in 1991, the same year Rob's recording career began. Rob admitted afterwards that the sheer size of the occasion almost caused him to have a nervous breakdown, especially as it was broadcast live on television. That, however, did not stop him flashing his bottom for several million viewers.

A year later and Queen's camp classic, 'Fat Bottomed Girls', blasted out from the speakers as fans took their seats at the London Arena in Docklands for a show promoting the new album, *Sing When You're Winning*. Rob is a great admirer of Queen, and Freddie Mercury in particular, incorporating some of that masterful entertainer's mannerisms into his own stage act. Rob began with 'Let Me Entertain You', of course, and then proceeded to gallop through a mammoth set of seventeen songs, including eight tracks from the new album. All the Robbie trademarks were on show: the cheeky grin, the heartfelt look that can melt a female heart at thirty paces, the football shirt that declares he's just a lad. There was a feeling that at any carefree moment he might take all his clothes off. There was no set, just a video backdrop, proving that Rob needs no props or diversions to hold centre stage. The encore was masterful:

'My Way' (the Sinatra version, cigarette in hand just like his dad, not the Sid Vicious mutilation), 'Millennium', 'Angels' (sung by the crowd naturally, cigarette lighters in the air) and the very silly 'Rock DJ'. The album was relatively new but already songs like 'Supreme' and 'Knutsford City Limits' sounded so familiar.

Before he left the stage Rob shouted, 'Are you going to go home happy tonight?'

The irony is that the audience probably went home a great deal happier than the performer they had queued for many hours to see. Incredible as it may seem to all those people applauding a genuine megastar showman, he can be racked with doubt about his worth as a performer. That had become a particular curse in the months leading to him moving to Los Angeles at the end of 2001. Jonathan Wilkes's mother Eileen says it had become so bad he wouldn't go on stage in Ireland without her son in the wings to support him: 'It was a low time. Robert was on such a downer. He lost his confidence and just felt he wasn't good enough.'

'Every year I'm getting more addicted to applause.'

14

Have You Met Tom Jones?

It was a Vegas moment. Tom Jones was pausing between songs and addressed his adoring audience: 'I would like to introduce you now to a young man from Great Britain who has got so much talent I think he is going to take over from me. Mr Robbie Williams.' The spotlight shone out on a table as a delighted young man rose and took their applause with a nonchalant grin. It was Rob.

Rob's love of the great songs and singers of a previous generation did not begin – or end – with his next album, *Swing When You're Winning*. That number one album was the culmination of a lifetime of devotion to Sinatra and his great contemporaries. In *Somebody Someday*, Mark McCrum's evocative account of Rob's life on the road, he describes how, before he goes on stage, Rob kisses in turn photographs of Sinatra, Dean Martin, Sammy Davis Junior and Muhammad Ali. The first three knew how to swing and the great boxer knew how to win.

There can scarcely be anyone living in the Stoke-on-Trent area who has not heard Rob's version of 'Mack the Knife'. For years, it was his favourite song to perform at karaoke or at parties. He had first heard his father sing it at a holiday camp, a typical space filler between jokes for a crooning comedian. They always seem to sing in a curiously unnatural American twang and Pete is no exception. Eric Tams, who heard father and son perform together when Rob was a lad, recalls, 'Pete used to sing a lot of the songs on the *Swing* album. He used to stand there and he would get a fag out and sing them all while he smoked. When Rob did them I heard Pete singing as well. Pete's got more of an American drawl. He listened to the records and Rob listened to his dad.' Eric heard Rob perform at the open mike night at the Sneyd Arms in Tunstall, after he had had one too many, during his Take That days. 'He came off and said, "Don't you dare ask me to get up there again!" He was a bit over the top with the drink.'

The many musicals Rob was in as a boy served as an ideal training ground for projecting a song. 'Mack the Knife', from *The Threepenny Opera*, is a song which lends itself to some acting. Rob's karaoke interpretation of the song owed as much to his theatrical talents as to his vocal ones. Zoë Hammond observes, 'It suited him to do something where he could really play up and act.' She also recalls that he already loved Frank Sinatra when they were acting together as children: 'That wasn't just a thing that happened as he grew up. He loved him even when he was a little lad. I knew he grew up on that sort of thing. If we were rehearsing, he would stand at the piano and lean across like they did in those old black and white films. He would move about as though he was taking that era off. When I saw him do the concert of *Swing When You're Winning* on the telly, I said to my mum, "God, it's dead freaky", because it just took me back to watching him when he was podgy and little. He was brilliant.' On learning of Rob's plan to record an album of Sinatra songs, his collaborator Guy Chambers was impressed enough to observe that it was as if he was born to do it.

Frank Sinatra was peerless in his ability to interpret a song. He had no equal in finding fresh nuances in lines as hackneyed as moon and June or love and marriage. The sneering killjoys in the music criticism business took great delight in denouncing Rob's musical tribute as impoverished fare, which was mean-spirited and totally missed the point. *Swing When You're Winning* was not a Sinatra copy, nor a Dean Martin or Sammy Davis one. It was a celebration of their style, which brought their music to several million younger listeners who had probably never heard of these greats. The kids that bought Gareth Gates's version of 'Unchained Melody' are unlikely to have heard the Robson and Jerome version let alone the definitive Righteous Brothers recording (not forgetting Jimmy Young's!). If it's more than five years old it will only be cherished by sentimentalists.

When it came to music, however, Rob's first love was Showaddywaddy. He wanted to be Dave Bartram, the lead singer of the fifties throwback group, whose cheery renditions of American rock 'n' roll standards were all over the charts like a rash during the first eight years of Rob's life. Showaddywaddy, complete with brothel creepers and nipped-in suits, would dress the part. They were the first group he went to see live in concert, when, aged seven, his mother took him to the Queen's Theatre in Burslem. He thought it was fantastic and was very disappointed when Jan said he could not have a teddy-boy outfit for his birthday on the grounds that he would soon grow too big for it. His other great small boy favourite was John Travolta. He sang as Travolta during his first 'international' performance at the age of four at the Pontin Continental in Torremolinos and *Grease* is still his favourite film twenty-five years later. Olivia Newton-John's character of Sandy is the cinematic encapsulation of his perfect woman. She is sweet, innocent and caring but able to transform herself into something totally hot and naughty if provoked. Some of the swagger Travolta employed, both in this film as Danny and earlier as Tony in *Saturday Night Fever,* seemed to have infused themselves into the mannerisms of Robbie Williams.

To those who did not know that Rob had been brought up on a diet of the great singers, *Swing When You're Winning* would have been an amazing choice. He might have done a tribute to Elvis, which would have been less surprising. Or he could have re-recorded Pink Floyd's *The Wall*, the first album he ever bought as a lad. At a pinch he could have been Dean Martin. He was one of the few performers who could match the drunken stage persona of Deano. The impetus for *Swing* came from Rob being asked to record the Sinatra classic 'Have You Met Miss Jones' for the soundtrack of the film, *Bridget Jones' Diary*. When the film proved to be big box-office in the USA, he was invited to sing it on Jay Leno's *Tonight Show*, which is filmed in Los Angeles. His performance was well received and he formulated the idea of doing a swing album dedicated to Frank, Dean and Sammy. It was unexpected to say the least because everyone had assumed he would take it easy after his world tour promoting his third album *Sing When You're Winning*.

Rob has his own rat pack. It is not a group of impressively famous people falling over their egos. It is his own inner group of important people who give him the impetus to function day by day. They are Jonathan Wilkes, David Enthoven and Josie Cliff, who is his personal assistant and about the same age as her employer. Mark McCrum, who wrote *Somebody Someday*, described her as 'scarily switched on'. They give him the stability to make the smooth transition from Robbie Williams to Rob. They bridge the gap between home and work. David is the father figure, Jonathan the brother and Josie the mother/sister making sure he has clean socks and fresh milk in the fridge. Obviously, things have changed since Rob has moved to Los Angeles. Jonathan, for instance, now has his own home and David has a business to run. But they are fiercely loyal to a man who has surprisingly few real friends. Jonathan's mother Eileen Wilkes observes, 'Robert can be very wary when he first meets people.'

Rob has always loved the Tom Jones classic 'Delilah', believing it to be the all-time best song to get you out of bed on a Sunday morning when suffering from a Saturday night hangover. The only problem for a Port Vale lad like Rob is that 'Delilah' is a favourite terraces' anthem of arch rivals, Stoke City. He used to study old footage from the sixties and seventies of Tom performing his hits and seek to emulate him. When they finally appeared on stage together at the Brit Awards ceremony of 1998, it was as if they had been performing together for years. Rob could not believe his good fortune in finally getting to duet with Tom. The song 'Man Machine' on the *I've Been Expecting*

You album was allegedly inspired by Tom, although it's hard to imagine that from the lyrics.

Their Brits duet of songs from the film *The Full Monty* was the best thing to have happened to that tired awards show in years. Rob was prancing about the stage in black leather and Cuban heels having the time of his life. He began with a version of the Cockney Rebel classic, 'Come Up and See Me'. Then Jones the Voice arrived to sing the film's biggest hit, 'You Can Leave Your Hat On', which featured Rob dancing like a clockwork toy that had been overwound. It was a tongue-in-cheek *tour de force*. Tom gave Rob substance and in return Rob made Tom appear up to the minute. It is a formula the Welsh Star has since milked to the limit in collaborations with Wyclef Jean, Catatonia and the Stereophonics. It did wonders for Rob's confidence when Tom told him he thought he was a great singer. The duet had been so well received that Rob put it out as the B side of his next single, 'Let Me Entertain You', which was released the following month.

The performance was almost as big news for Tom as it was for Rob. His stock soared and *Reload*, his album of duets, produced coincidentally by Steve Power, was a huge hit. Rob joined him to record 'Are You Gonna Go My Way', a Lenny Kravitz song. Rob was understandably nervous about joining the great man in the same vocal booth, so he did what he has always done. He revealed how he handled it in a phone-in with fans: 'I thought "I know I'll do an impression of him", so I did and I think I pulled it off.' The first time Rob had sung the complete song was their first run-through. After they had finished, Tom announced, 'That's it then. Shall we go to the pub?'

By a twist of fate, Rob has followed Tom's example by making Los Angles his main home. They have become firm friends, although Tom is obviously old enough to be Rob's father. When Rob went round to Tom's Bel Air mansion, the Welshman's long-suffering wife, Maureen, who has steadfastly shunned the limelight for forty years, refused to come downstairs because she was too shy to meet a star of the magnitude of Robbie Williams. She had to be coaxed and cajoled before she agreed to meet such an important celebrity.

> **'Those five minutes eleven seconds on stage with Tom Jones were the happiest I've ever been in my life.'**

15

Jonty

Pete Conway had not spoken to his son for more than a year. Rob had gone to Los Angeles and they had lost touch amid rumours of a rift. Then, by chance, Pete was travelling from London to Stoke by train when he recognized the tall, good-looking boy at the buffet counter. 'How's that son of mine doing?' he asked Jonathan Wilkes. Smiling, Jonathan replied, 'Why don't you speak to him?' and there and then dialled Rob's private number. 'Hello mate, I've got your dad here,' he said before passing the phone to Pete. Father and son were a bit guarded for a few minutes but then started cracking jokes just like the old days.

Jonathan Wilkes is one of the enigmas in Rob's life. He is scarcely afforded a personality of his own by media observers of the star's life, too easily dismissed as Robbie Williams's best pal or flatmate. The friends have reacted to unfounded whispers that there is more to their relationship than just 'mates' with knockabout good humour, a total lack of outrage and a fierce loyalty to each other. Their duet on the *Swing When You're Winning* album encapsulated their public personae. They chose to do 'Me and My Shadow' but punctuated the classic Frank Sinatra and Sammy Davis Junior. treatment with some cheeky ad libs about Stoke-on-Trent and being gay. The sleeve notes jokingly suggest they sing the song together in the shower at home. They are cocking a snook at those with their noses pressed against the glass scrutinizing their every move.

Their relationship is, however, a vitally important one in Rob's life. It is Jonty, as family and friends know him, who transcends the chameleon compartments of Rob's personality. He is the footballing, drinking, singing, acting, golfing, pinball-playing mate who understands what it is like to be a lad who grew up in Stoke-on-Trent. Far from being a chancer hanging on to the coat-tails of a famous friend, Jonathan has been the rock offering Rob support when he was down and nearly out.

They are not related, although many people believe them to be. They were never neighbours, nor did they go to the same school, belong to the same golf club or 'grow up together'. Their mothers, Jan Williams and Eileen Wilkes, met by chance on holiday in Majorca and hit it off immediately. Little Jonty was four and Robert, as he was always introduced, was nearly five years older. Both boys had elder sisters – Kay Wilkes, who they were always a little frightened of, was Rob's age – as well as lively mums who liked getting out and having a laugh together and dads who were larger-than-life characters who could light up any room they were in. Graham Wilkes, Jonty's father, has come through his share of adversity. His travel agency went bust when he was just thirty-nine – Jonty was eight – and a subsequent heart attack led to some troubling years for the Wilkes family. He has since bounced back and is a well-known face in the world of entertainment and sport in the Potteries through his role as a professional toastmaster. His signed photograph hangs on the wall of a Tunstall curry house, a sure sign of local celebrity.

When Jan and Eileen returned home from Majorca they decided to keep in touch, sharing a common enthusiasm for musicals and the theatre, an interest that would bring their sons together. Rob and Jonty first appeared together on stage as members of the chorus of children in *Hans Christian Andersen* not long after they met. For once, Rob did not have to worry about being accepted. Jonty was his young acolyte who hung on his every word. So much so, that during a performance at the Theatre Royal in Hanley, Rob persuaded his young chum that there was a change in the script that night and they should lift up their night-shirts and reveal their bottoms to the audience. The cheeky ingredient, so important to the Robbie Williams image, is a quality he was born with. He has never been slow to flash his bum – or any other part of his anatomy – if he thinks it will get a reaction.

Zoë Hammond, who met Rob for the first time in *Hans Christian Andersen*, remembers Jonty as a little 'lard-arse', which means 'cry baby' in the local slang: 'He couldn't take anything as a kid. You'd only have to say to Jonathan, "Why have you come in then?" and he'd be squealing. And he'd make it quite clear to everybody around him that he didn't like what you had said. He was a bit of a creep at times but he was very small.' Even Eileen Wilkes admits her son could 'always cry easily and turn the taps on'. That is why one of the favourite childhood turns of the boys was doing a Laurel and Hardy double act for their families. Rob, bigger and chubbier, would be fat Ollie, while Jonty, small and skinny, would be Stan, contorting his face into the comedian's famous blubbing expression.

Rob, such a brilliant mimic and a genuinely funny boy, gave Jonty the confidence to perform himself, even if in those days he was very young and not much good. Jonathan himself admits that when he was a little kid Rob was like his big brother. He was also a role model, the boy who Jonathan aspired to be. They did not, however, live in each other's pockets as children. While Rob lived in Tunstall and went to St Margaret Ward High School, Jonathan was five miles away in Endon, attending the Hillside School. But like all good friends they could always pick up where they left off. 'They had a natural rapport,' observes Eileen Wilkes. 'They used to laugh all the time, even if they hadn't seen each other for weeks, or months at a time.'

The Williams and Wilkes families cemented their friendship by joining up in the school holidays to go caravanning or, sometimes, skiing. 'If there was a talent competition where we were, then the boys were always the first up,' recalls Eileen. 'They both had great confidence to play to a crowd.' There was no doubt who was the more talented. Rob was an accomplished entertainer as a boy, while Jonty had a voice like a foghorn. 'You couldn't compare the two. I'm not being horrible but Jonathan wasn't a patch on Rob,' says Zoë Hammond. 'But there was an age gap and I do remember that Jonathan really loved the theatre.' The difference in their ages never seemed to affect their friendship: 'They were definitely mates even though Jonathan was younger.'

When he was with Jonathan, Rob was less likely to get up to mischief, preferring a game of Monopoly to causing

At the Sotheby's auction for his Give it Sum charity in aid of Comic Relief, April 2001
. . . 'these are the pants I shagged Geri in'

Above: Robbie's clearly overjoyed to be picking up an MTV Europe Music award in Spain, 1998

Right: Supporting Chris Briggs after he had received a British Music Roll of Honour Award in 2001, 'Briggsy' has been an invaluable help to Robbie at EMI/Chrysalis

Collecting his Brit award for Best British Male Solo Artist for the third time in 2002, via satellite. The speech he made raised quite a few eyebrows

Kilts again, this time on stage in Sydney, Australia during his hugely successful *Sing When You're Winning* tour

The Ego Lands on *Later with Jools Holland*

With Rachel Hunter on their way to an evening's bowling in Los Angeles

Marilyn Manson, Ozzy Osbourne and Robbie, after Ozzy received a star on the Hollywood Walk of Fame, in April 2002

Outside an AA meeting in Los Angeles

Walking his dogs in LA is Robbie's favourite way to relax

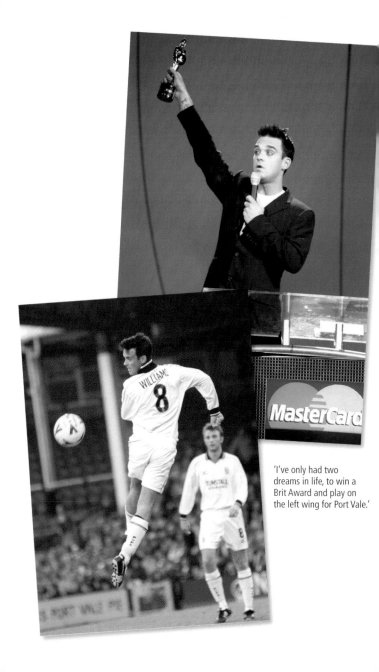

'I've only had two dreams in life, to win a Brit Award and play on the left wing for Port Vale.'

trouble in Tunstall Park. Eileen Wilkes's explanation for a friendship that was unaffected by the difference in their ages is that her son has always been 'more grown up for his age and Robert not so grown up'. That view would be reinforced when the friends started living together in London a few years later. In the meantime, they joined their mothers in Olde Time Music Hall and Jonathan had a very small role in *Oliver!*, which proved to be such an important production in the development of Robbie Williams the performer.

Jonathan shared Rob's aversion to schoolwork, preferring playing football and supporting Port Vale. Jonty lived and breathed football. He was even Vale's mascot for one game. There is no greater honour for a young fan than to walk out on to his team's pitch dressed in the squad colours, surrounded by his heroes. For a while, it looked as if the course of the friends' two lives would diverge irrevocably. While Rob's ambitions for stardom were taking shape in Take That, Jonathan was on the threshold of a career as a professional footballer. He was captain of Stoke-on-Trent Schoolboys and, at one time, was on the books of their beloved Vale. More promisingly, Jonathan was taken on by Everton as an adolescent defender when he was spotted by a scout while playing alongside his father Graham in a local lads and dads team. Twice a week, he would make the journey to Merseyside to rub shoulders with other young hopefuls, including Francis Jeffers, who has made the grade at Arsenal, Danny Cadamarteri, now with Bradford City, and Michael Branch, who subsequently played for Wolves. None of the three have, perhaps, done as well as might have been expected from their early promise.

The highlight of Jonathan's footballing life was when he played against Liverpool, which featured a certain Michael Owen in their boys' team. Sadly, the Everton lads were trounced 4–0, with the England striker of the future scoring all four. Guess who was meant to be marking Owen? Despite that setback Jonathan was absolutely certain that his future revolved around the 'beautiful game'.

'Football was my life,' he admitted. 'It was all I knew.'

Alas, his hopes were dashed by his lack of size. One of the chief Everton backroom boys told him when he was fifteen: 'You're not going to be good enough for Everton son, you're too small.'

Jonathan was devastated and quickly became disillusioned with the football scene. He tried a week at lowly Chester FC but was totally disinterested. A couple of other offers from Wrexham and Crewe came in but barely raised a shrug of the shoulders. After being so close to a career with a top club, nothing else seemed worth getting out of bed for. While Rob's career was at its Take That zenith, his old pal from Stoke-on-Trent felt at rock bottom, just turned sixteen with no academic qualifications to speak of, no prospects and no idea what to do.

He did exactly what Rob would have done under the circumstances: he went on a six-month spree of drinking bitter, putting on loads of weight and feeling rebellious. The one bright point in this teenage torment came when he had his tonsils out. His mother Eileen recalls, 'Miraculously he could sing afterwards. He really got into the singing lark.' Jonty discovered that when he went up to do karaoke, it no longer cleared the pub. He also tried his hand at a few jokes and a bit of banter and discovered he liked being an entertainer. He even produced a demo of a song cheerily entitled 'You Are Always Going to Be Alone'. He pulled himself together, confident that he could 'sing and make people laugh'. He also, according to Eileen, started 'sleeping in a grobag', which resulted in his height spurting upwards to over six feet. His present height of 6ft 3ins makes the Everton rejection seem slightly comical now.

It was his father Graham who managed to kick-start Jonathan's showbusiness career. He was impressed by his son's blossoming talent. Graham was in Blackpool on business when a local impresario, Amanda Thompson, asked if he knew of anyone who could sing for the Star Bar on the Pleasure Beach. Graham cannily said he might know of someone but did not let on it was Jonathan he had in mind. Instead he said, 'I'll see if I can get hold of him.' Together, father and son returned to Blackpool and Jonathan sang some numbers but was under strict instructions to let Graham do any negotiating. Amanda offered £200 a week but Graham demanded and secured £250 a week plus lodging and food and then asked, 'Who's going to do his washing?' Eventually the deal was clinched but Amanda insisted that because Jonathan was only seventeen she would need a guardian's signature to ratify the contract. 'Hand it over then,' said Graham. 'I'm his dad.' Amanda glared at him and said, 'You bastard!'

And that is how Jonathan Wilkes became the youngest headliner in Blackpool doing an exhausting twenty-nine songs a night, seven days a week. His show business break had absolutely nothing to do with Robbie Williams, although Rob would take every opportunity to visit his pal so that he could spend the day on the famous Blackpool rides. Jonathan was seventeen when he started in Blackpool and only twenty when his three-year contract came to an end. It was the making of him. *Jonathan Wilkes and the Space Girls* became one of the most popular shows in town and, for the teenager, surrounded by a bevy of girl dancers and with good money in his pocket, it was as if he had died and gone to heaven.

Blackpool is a quintessential English institution, cheesier than a pound of stilton. Jonathan found himself getting noticed in this world of Variety with a capital V. He was a million miles away from the cool youth culture of mid-nineties Britain. While Rob aspired to a legitimate 'Glastonbury' music scene, his mate was appearing in charity shows alongside the Grumbleweeds, Schnorbitz, Frank Carson and Joe Longthorne. Jonathan was just seventeen when he was a prize-winner in the Cameron Mackintosh Young Entertainer of the Year competition. He had impressed the judges with his Tom Jones-style rendition of the Prince song 'Kiss'. The irony is that Jonathan was living the sort of career which was Rob's heritage – the mainstream cabaret style of Pete Conway. He was fast becoming an accomplished performer: 'I had to sing the same bloody songs every night and try and make them believable to an audience which was the toughest in the world.' He may not have been breaking into the consciousness of Take That fans but Jonathan Wilkes was a huge favourite among the Lancashire granny set.

Jonathan's ambitions stretched further than Blackpool Tower and so he jumped at the opportunity to present a television programme called *The Hype* for the former digital channel BBC Choice. It would mean moving down to London. When he mentioned it to Rob, his friend did not hesitate to invite him to live with him in Notting Hill in what Graham Wilkes describes as a lads' paradise: 'They had pinball, table football and the biggest television you have ever seen.' Pride of place was a platinum pool table which Rob bought in a swanky shop in New York. Rob had popped in wearing jeans and the shop assistant assumed incorrectly that it was well out of his price bracket, at a quarter of a million dollars. 'I'll take it,' said Rob casually handing over his credit card, much to everyone's amazement.

During this early period of Men Behaving Badly, the roles of the two friends subtly changed. Jonathan was no longer the snotty kid described by Robbie as a 'little twat'. Instead, he became the big brother and protector. 'There may be an age gap but it would always be Jonathan, looking out for Robert, who would say at the end of the evening, "Let's go mate,"' observes Eileen Wilkes. It was Jonathan, at the time of Rob's worst drink and drugs excesses, who would be desperately trying to stop hangers-on providing his friend with supplies.

The special bond of being the only person – apart from, perhaps, Jan Williams – who could say to Rob, 'Oi, you're being a bit of a prick here', brought the two friends incredibly close. When Jonathan had a bad car accident while he was doing a pantomime in Scotland, Rob rang him up on the hour, every hour, to cheer him up, telling jokes and dusting off his Frank Spencer voice. In the eyes of the army of Robbie Williams's fans, Jonathan Wilkes was officially the 'best friend'. Inevitably, thoughts turned to a career in pop music for Jonathan. His father had found him new management and a deal soon followed with

Innocent Records, an imprint of Virgin and label of Billie Piper and Martine McCutcheon.

Rob was delighted at the thought of sharing his world with his buddy. He declared, 'It will be like Popstar Towers at our house.' They already used to have songwriting competitions in which they would give themselves five minutes to cobble together a smash hit. During one such game at a villa in the south of France, Jonathan wrote one called 'Dave's House', which was pencilled in for his first album. It all seemed a little too easy. The general public, not realizing that Jonathan had already served a tough apprenticeship, could be forgiven for thinking he was a young man enjoying the privilege of success thanks to his friendship with the nation's favourite pop star.

Jonathan could hardly complain when Robbie Williams was the number one topic of any interview he gave on the release of his first single, 'Just Another Day', a song he wrote himself when he was 'having a really bad day'. It was released amid a blaze of serious media interest – seventy-five interviews in two weeks – but entered the charts at a profoundly disappointing number twenty-four which, considering how the charts work these days, is absolutely nowhere. The howls of derision began, which was very problematic as an album, *Borrowed Wings*, was finished and a second single co-written with Canadian rock star, Bryan Adams, was ready to go. The single reached number one in Dubai, Sweden and Germany but that was not enough to prevent Innocent, who had spent £1 million trying to muscle the song into the UK top three, from putting the album 'on hold'. It is still in limbo and the prospect of an early release looks grim. A five-album deal bit the dust and Jonathan was officially dropped by the record company.

Why did it flop? Like most failures, it was a combination of factors. The timing was bad. It was released the same week as *Popstars* winners Hear'Say's debut single, 'Pure and Simple' which sold a million. Hear'Say absolutely hogged it. And Shaggy also moved vast quantities of 'It Wasn't Me', leaving very little spare sales for anyone else. It can happen to the best of them. When Kylie released 'Some Kind of Bliss' in September 1997 great things were expected of it. But Elton John's 'Candle in the Wind 1997' sold so outrageously there were only a few crumbs left for other releases. Kylie charted at number twenty-two. There was also almost certainly a built-in resentment factor against Jonathan because of his connection to Robbie.

Jonathan was very proud of the album. He had written and recorded it while still presenting on television. Rob contributed two songs, one unintentionally. Jonathan won 'Sexed Up' from him as a side bet during a game of pool. Rob would eventually take it back for *Escapology*, claiming that he would write him another one. He did, however, do Jonathan an enormous favour by persuading him to perform the duet of 'Me and My Shadow' and, just as importantly, go on stage at the Royal Albert Hall and sing it before a live audience. It revealed that Jonathan could genuinely sing and was an accomplished performer in his own right. He also showed he was the master of the cheesy showbiz remark when he declared, '"Me and My Shadow" is the perfect best-mate song.' The one-off concert of the album was a fantastic success and the sales of both video and album have provided Jonathan with a tidy nest egg and helped him finance his new £600,000 house in Chiswick, round the corner from his friends, Ant and Dec.

The Albert Hall was not the first time they appeared on stage together in a duet. When Jonathan was performing the Robbie Williams song 'She's the One' during a concert in Brighton, the man himself unexpectedly came on stage and casually asked, 'Do you want a hand mate?' Jonathan, who was as surprised as the audience, replied, 'I could do with one, mate.' On another occasion, when Jonathan was in panto, a gorilla unexpectedly came on stage. It was Rob hijacking the event.

From a career point of view, the best thing Jonathan could do was to put some distance between himself and Robbie Williams. Fortuitously, the first lull in his career came when Rob was preparing to spend the majority of his time in Los Angeles. Eventually, realizing that the pop business was as fickle as football, he accepted a leading role in a touring revival of the seventies musical *Godspell*. He alternated the parts of Jesus and Judas with former *Neighbours* star Daniel Macpherson. Almost seamlessly, he moved on to a thirtieth anniversary revival of the classic *Rocky Horror Show*, playing Dr Frank N. Furter and singing the famous 'Sweet Transvestite' show-stopper from the musical.

Needless to say, Rob was there on the first night at the Churchill Theatre in Bromley, barracking his best pal from the audience – 'Don't think you're coming round my house looking like that!' – and informing the press that it was not the first time he had seen him in suspender belt and mask. At least the presence of Robbie Williams, as well as Ant and Dec, Cat Deeley and Edith Bowman, ensured nationwide coverage for a provincial opening. Jonathan had to struggle through with a chronically sore throat, so it was no bad thing that Rob, accompanied by

Rachel Hunter, was there to take everyone's mind off the show. As the tour went on, Jonathan's performance grew in stature and the local reviews from Bradford to Woking were ecstatic, especially in his home town of Stoke-on-Trent. Eileen Wilkes was there to cheer on her son: 'It was like a rock concert with everyone standing up. My mum, who is eighty, thought it was wonderful and said, "Jonathan has given me an extra ten years on my life. He knows everything about women, doesn't he?"'

Jonathan's immediate future looks very rosy. His father is convinced that in five years' time he will be a household name: 'He loves live theatre and hopefully there will be a musical written for him. He will be a Des O'Connor type.' Jonathan is already on the way to realising his father's ambition for him. He is the new host for the television show *You've Been Framed* in which he oozes cheesiness as if to the manor born – perfect for this Saturday night ratings winner. He is also taking on the John Travolta role in a new stage production of *Grease*.

His ongoing friendship with Rob looks equally assured. He is the voice of normality, the good guy part of his friend's conscience. He is very middle of the road and an ordinary guy. His favourite album is *James Taylor's Greatest Hits* and he prefers Ribena to Guinness. He shares his new house in Chiswick with his fiancée Nikki Wheeler, a dancer he met five years ago on *The Hype*, and the chances are they will have a low-key, *Hello!*-free wedding in the near future. He shares Rob's affection for Stoke-on-Trent; the pair of them still order oat cakes from the High Lane Oat Cake Shop to be sent to them in London. And if Jonathan takes Rob round to his parents' house, Eileen will tell him, 'Put the kettle on Robert.' It is a valuable dose of normality for a superstar surrounded, inevitably, by superficial yes men. In return, Rob will always put himself out for his best friend and the Wilkes family. At Eileen Wilkes's fortieth birthday party at The Place in Hanley, Rob took time off from Take That to turn up and take his turn on the karaoke – he did 'Mack the Knife', of course. Lee Hancock, who had never heard the song before, recalls, 'It was absolutely fantastic.' When Jonathan's sister Kay was married at Eccleshall Castle in Staffordshire, Rob flew in especially from the States. And he sang 'Angels'. When he reached the famous last line, 'I'm loving angels instead', he changed it to 'I'm loving Kaysie instead.'

'They weren't street corner boys.'

16

The Illustrated Man

Rob, his mother and his sister had joined the Wilkes family for dinner at their favourite local curry house, the Kashmir Garden, in the High Street. Halfway through dinner, Rob took off his sweater to reveal for the first time the now famous Maori tattoo that adorns his upper left arm. 'Oh Robert,' sighed his mother. 'Why do you mark your beautiful body?' Rob grinned and said, 'Don't worry Mum, when I'm sixty I'll still have a beautiful bird on my arm.'

Rob never had a reputation for being a sharply-dressed man. At Burslem Golf Club his sweatshirt was legendary. His playing partner Tim Peers recalls, 'It was a hideous thing, white with a sort of skiing scene on the front with lots of pine trees. He wore it all the time.' He was scruffy at school, even before he took part in the notorious lads' sweating competitions. He would always be nicely turned out when in the company of his mother and certainly wore more ties before he joined Take That than he ever did subsequently. Rob was square with a capital S and, as a pop star, clothes have never been the most important part of his image. Old habits die hard and he wore a hideous

black and white V-neck net jumper for the cover shots of
Life Thru a Lens. He looked like the master of ceremonies
for a low-budget game show. Perversely, he looked more
elegant wearing a tie while playing the part of a James
Bond-type smoothie for the sleeve of *I've Been Expecting
You.*

His hair has not been much better. It's been downhill
since his first day at senior school, when he had blond
streaks in it, a legacy from a stage role. His skinhead look
for 'Angels' was well-timed but his Los Angeles Mohican
was after the sell-by date – David Beckham had already
ditched it. Then when he came back to the UK to
promote his single 'Come Undone' in April 2003, he had
little wispy blond streaks at the front of his hair, which
commentators thought made him resemble a penguin. As
a fashion icon, Rob could do with taking a few pointers
from David Beckham. The one area where Rob has
achieved a certain individuality and style recognition –
and even matched Becks – is in respect of his tattoos. He
seems to have hundreds of them. And since he moved to
Los Angeles, where there is so little to actually do, the
Shamrock Parlor on Sunset has become a home away
from home.

Tattoo originates from *ta-tau*, a Polynesian word
meaning mark. Captain Cook came across the body art in
Tahiti in 1769 and noted it in his journal, adding that it
was a common practice amongst both sexes. Marking the
skin is frowned upon in the Bible and, with the advent of
Christianity, was banned in Europe until Captain Cook's
discovery. As a form of body art and self-expression,
tattoos have only achieved widespread popularity relatively
recently. Tattoos have joined piercing as an accessible

form of fashion statement for young people. The days are long gone when tattoos were confined to sailors with a Popeye anchor on one forearm and 'Mum' on the other.

Rob has suffered for his art because the method of raising the skin with needles can be extremely painful. He was able to warn Nicole Kidman of the agony involved when she told him she was thinking of having a tattoo on her ankle. He told her a design close to a bone was the most painful because the skin was stretched so tightly there. Rob has an addictive personality, so one of anything is not enough. He already has nine or ten tattoos of all shapes and sizes dotted around his body.

One thing Rob has been careful about is having anything etched indelibly into his skin that may embarrass him later. Patsy Kensit and Liam Gallagher are a prime example of this folly of passion. When they split acrimoniously, they were left with unpleasant and unwanted reminders of their former partner every time they took a shower. Patsy spent £6000 having 'Liam' removed from her ankle. Liam covered 'Patsy' on his right arm with a lightning bolt and the letters TCB – standing for Taking Care of Business. Pamela Anderson had to change 'Tommy', in honour of her husband Tommy Lee, to 'Mommy'. The funniest mistake, however, was Courtney Love's shamrock, which she had tattooed on her ankle as a tribute to her Irish ancestry. She had it removed when she discovered she was, in fact, Jewish.

Rob's first tattoo was also Irish influenced, a Celtic cross on his upper left thigh. He had it done when he was in Take That, a small act of defiance against the regime he found so oppressive. He confided in Jim and Joan Peers ('Mr and Mrs Peers' as he always called them, even when he was famous) when he popped in to see them one weekend. He said, 'I've had a tattoo done and I daren't tell me mum.' Rob is proud of his Irish roots and wears a temporary tattoo of the Irish flag whenever he plays a concert in the Republic.

His most famous tattoo is the Maori 'prayer', which dances around the top of his left arm and then licks around his back like a flame. He had it done in Amsterdam in 1998 not long after 'Angels' and rehab had given him a new sense of identity. Although Rob likes to joke that the drawing means, 'I hope it's chips', the actual explanation is that it is a prayer. He explained, 'It's a prayer protecting myself from myself.' He had intended for the tattoo to wind its way down his entire body as a personal security blanket but he thought better of it, having spent seven hours with tears in his eyes for the starter session.

On his opposite arm is a rather serious-looking lion, not fierce, just stern. The lion is a symbol of strength. Coincidentally, in May 2003, Rob signed to provide the voice of Linus, one of the lion characters in a BBC drama called *Pride*. The previous year he had been the voice of Dougal for a movie version of the *Magic Roundabout*. Fortunately, he is not concealing a tattoo of the famous shaggy dog. He had a phrase tattooed for the first time a little while later: 'Born to be Mild', an ironic distortion of the seminal hit from the film *Easy Rider* 'Born to be Wild'. The words sweep below the lion like a pennant motto. Above the lion he has 'Elvis Grant Me Serenity', an important phrase in Rob's life. It is part of the essential ritual he conducts before each live concert: a tribute to the king of rock 'n' roll, which Rob uses to empower himself before going on stage.

Everyone from his entourage, from David Enthoven to the musicians, make-up and wardrobe, bodyguards and drivers, must link hands with Rob – usually in a corridor backstage – and take part in the energy-giving half-prayer, half-chant. It is a little like the 'Haka', the famous rugby chant of the New Zealand All Blacks, except nobody jumps in the air at the end of it. The majority of performers have some sort of pep talk which becomes part of their performing routine. This is Rob's. He is the master of ceremonies, the lay preacher leading his congregation: 'Elvis grant me the serenity to accept the things I cannot change; the courage to change the things I can; and the wisdom to know the difference.' At the conclusion the whole group shouts out, 'Thank you very much.' Rob is an atheist but, in this context, Elvis is suspiciously like a euphemism for a higher being.

On his right wrist he has the name 'Jack', matched on his left wrist by 'Farrell'. Jack Farrell was his maternal grandfather. On his forearms are two newer tattoos, both in honour of Jan Williams. One says 'mother', and the other 'I love u'. Rob's least effective tattoo, which he had done on a night out with Jonathan Wilkes but now does not care for, is in the shape of a necklace around the upper part of his chest, which he had shaved for the process. It spells out 'chacun à son goût', which means 'each to his own taste', but sounds more like something you would order in a charcuterie. Much more stylish is the musical stave across the base of his back. It is marked 'chorus' in the key of 'G' and is the notation for 'All You Need is Love', the famous Beatles hit of 1967 (did he need copyright approval to reproduce it?). Rob revealed it for the first time on a bitterly cold day in Paris, at the end of

December 2002, when he flew in to the French capital for a secret gig showcasing songs from *Escapology*. He spoilt the effect by wearing an old white jumper with large, bright blue stars, which had been a Christmas present seven years before. He topped off the outfit with a black woolly hat with a skull and crossbones on the front. Like David Beckham, Rob has a piece of headgear for every occasion. When he was in Take That, he wore a different cap or hat practically every time they had their picture taken. He has always favoured hats or T-shirts with slogans on them.

Rob's most surprising and cryptic tattoo is the numbers '1023' on the topside of his wrist. It is a tribute to his close friendship with Jonathan Wilkes. 10 stands for the letter J and 23 for the letter W. Jonathan, who has never gone in for tattoos, has '1823' etched on his wrist, representing the letters RW for Rob. In April 2003 Rob unveiled a new tattoo, a loopy letter B behind his left ear, which he says is a tribute to his nan Betty. He has been spotted in the Shamrock since then. Surprisingly, Rob has yet to decorate his much-bared bottom, a popular place for a tattoo as it is a relatively painless area in which to have the needle-work. He was rumoured to have been planning to have an acknowledgement of Rachel Hunter marked there before they split up. But he has no track record of having any girlfriends honoured in this fashion. He is more likely to have High Lane Oat Cakes tattooed on his rump. Or Port Vale FC.

'I want the letter W on each bum cheek so when I bend over it says WOW.'

17

A Little More Conversation

The young blonde in high heels and figure-hugging dress, perched on the bar stool in the Holborn club, looked fabulous but Rob appeared not to have noticed her. He was busy chatting and laughing with a group at a table. Eventually, he got up, went over to where she was sitting, whispered a few words in her ear and went back to his company. 'What did he say?' asked the woman next to her. 'He just said "Come home with me," but I've got a boyfriend.' The woman exclaimed, 'But it's Robbie!' A minute or two passed before Rob got up, said his goodbyes and, without glancing over, strode out the door. Five seconds later, the blonde picked up her bag and tottered after him.

Rob remains one of the most sought after bachelors in the world, the heady mix of celebrity and money which glossy magazines find so attractive when they compile their lists of most desirable men. One music business veteran, who has seen many stars rise and fall, observes, 'Rob could shag any girl he wants to.' That may be so but Rob memorably described the hollowness of such encounters as having a wank in someone else's body. Rob might be able to sleep with any girl but he cannot make her fall in love with him or fall in love with her himself. He has used up two of his love tokens so far, on Jacqui Hamilton-Smith and Nicole Appleton. The former was young love, his first encounter with those feelings; the second was quite tragic in the way it unravelled.

The world's press sits like vultures on a dead tree ready to pick over the bones of any Robbie Williams entanglement. As long as he remains unattached, the newspapers can enjoy the lurid revelations of girls who may or may not have slept with him. Occasionally, Rob minds, as he revealed to his audience at a *Top of the Pops* special. He said, 'Did you see that girl in the *News of the World*? As if I would sleep with her – she was dog rough!' In any case, it is more fun if his alleged dalliance is with someone as famous as Kylie Minogue or Nicole Kidman. He first met Kylie in the early nineties when he was in Take That and she was the jewel in the crown of Stock, Aitken and Waterman. They were showbiz mates. Rob thought she was tiny and said he wanted to wrap her up very carefully in cotton wool. He hoped she would say hello if she saw him walking down the street. Kylie nominated Rob on more than one occasion as her favourite member of Take That. She was not a fan of boy bands but thought Robbie Williams stood out: 'I always knew he was going to be a star. He's such a natural.'

In 2000, EMI had the bright idea of putting Robbie Williams and Kylie Minogue together. Rob was their biggest artist, while Kylie was on the verge of one of the great comebacks in popular music. After her spectacular success in the early part of the nineties, she had been in independent wilderness until taken on by Parlophone, like Chrysalis a subsidiary label of EMI. The important thing was to reposition her in the market place as a mainstream artist. An alliance with Robbie Williams would give her timely street cred. Her gay following had remained loyal and her supremely kitsch appearance at the Sydney Olympics reminded a worldwide audience that she was still a top-grade entertainer. But it was not yet cool or chic to admit to liking Kylie Minogue. Rob could help change that.

He readily agreed to contribute some songs for her comeback album, *Light Years*. He wrote three with Guy Chambers: the highly camp 'Your Disco Needs You'; a smooth mellow track called 'Loveboat' – because Kylie asked him for a song with that title – and 'Kids', which became their joint single release. Kylie put it on *Light Years* and Rob included the track on *Sing When You're Winning*. The lyrics to 'Kids' are typical Robbie Williams, mischievous and tongue in cheek. Only he could come up with a rap rhyming sodomy with Billy Connolly. 'Kids' was a superb, bass-driven dance track, although Rob seemed to be struggling with a high-pitched falsetto for most of the song.

The Robbie–Kylie alliance was good business, although surprisingly kept off the number one spot by U2's 'Beautiful Day'. They were perfect musical partners. He introduced her to a whole new generation of girl fans, who saw her next to Robbie and wanted to be her. He also augmented her position at the pinnacle of the gay market. Kylie's gay fans were not going to be alienated by Robbie Williams, who also enjoyed a loyal following built up from the early days of Take That. They made each other appear sexy and naughty at the same time.

Kylie and Rob had great performing chemistry. That was evident when she was the guest on the *Top of the Pops* special in August 2000. It was even more apparent when she joined him on stage in Manchester to perform 'Kids'. Rob had no idea what Kylie was going to wear when she came out to join him. It was a tiny silver slip of a costume and left very little to the imagination. Kylie recalls, 'For a second he completely lost it. He was sweating and I loved it.'

Those stage sparks were reserved for their professional life, although heavy-handed hints that there might be something more in the air surfaced to fuel some record sales. Privately, Rob enjoyed Kylie's company. A record company insider recalls, 'He would follow her around and she was like "Robbie you stink" but I think she ended up quite liking him really.' It would have been a show business fairytale if they had got together but Kylie had a steady boyfriend, James Gooding, and there was never any romance. That did not stop Rob enquiring publicly, 'Do you reckon she'd shag me?'

The UK chart number ones of 2000 provide a fascinating backdrop to genuine and alleged Rob dalliances. As well as Kylie, the following very eligible young women made it to the top of the charts: Geri Halliwell, Melanie C (two solo number ones), Nicole Appleton (as part of All Saints), Andrea Corr (lead singer of the Corrs) and Billie Piper. They all had one thing in common, real or imaginary romance with a certain lad from Tunstall. If they had all been true, then Rob would have been the first male artist to have 'had' six number ones in a year.

Melanie C was linked with Rob a couple of months before he started dating Nic Appleton. They stayed together at a luxury hotel near Dublin and were seen shopping together in the Irish capital. It was the autumn of 1997 and the Spice Girls were the pop phenomenon of the year, while Rob was not doing so well prior to the release of 'Angels'. Like many busy celebrities they spent more time on the telephone to each other thousands of miles apart than sitting down in a quiet bistro to tell one another about the day they had just had. It was just a fling, although Rob has joked since about being in the Spice Girls, two of them anyway. Melanie maintains that Rob ditched her in favour of Nic, although the ex-All Saint did not mention her in her autobiography. Funnily enough, Melanie does feature in the book *Together*, not in the context of Robbie Williams but as a friend of Natalie Appleton, who touchingly describes her as having a 'generous heart'.

When she was asked directly if she had slept with Rob, Melanie replied, 'Might have done.' That sounds like a yes. Melanie C and Rob do have three other things in common – they sign their own contracts; they have had to deal with a great deal of innuendo and whispering about their sexuality; and they have had periodic problems with their weight and body image. Rob later claimed he slept with Geri Halliwell during their friendship – something she firmly denied.

Rob had just split from Nic Appleton when he met the elfin Andrea Corr backstage at the Brits in February 1999. The Corrs were a phenomenally successful group of three sisters and one brother whose harmonized, middle of the road pop was very fashionable at the time. Their *Talk on Corners* album was one of the few to outsell Rob's *Life Thru a Lens* and *I've Been Expecting You* in 1998. They were

pictured together shopping in Dublin – he must know the
shops there very well by now – and also went out a couple
of times to bars. Rob lost his temper with a photographer
who trailed them one afternoon to a pub outside Dublin.
They may have tested the water to see if there was a
prospect of a relationship but Rob was on the rebound
and he also had a concert tour of the USA to worry about.
It was pretty much a non-starter although, ever the
romantic, he did send a massive bunch of red roses, which
failed to do the trick.

Billie Piper was the youngest ever female artist to go
straight to number one when she topped the charts in July
1998 with 'Because We Want To'. Then she was just Billie,
a 15-year-old Swindon girl bringing a fresh-faced
innocence to the charts before the sleazier nymphet
image of Britney Spears took over. Billie was a number one
artist before Robbie Williams, beating him by two months.
She also had three successive number ones before her
career stalled, coincidentally at the time she met Rob. He
was the ideal person to give her advice – she was only just
eighteen – about the destructive elements of teenage fame
in the music business, although she appears to possess less
self-interest than the young Robert Williams. They were
introduced to each other by Jonathan Wilkes and the
three were seen out in one of Rob's local pubs in Notting
Hill.

The *News of the World* quoted a 'friend' who claimed
that the couple had 'great sex' together. Neither Billie nor
Rob commented on this. They certainly only saw each
other a few times because by December she had embarked
on a romance with multi-millionaire broadcaster Chris
Evans who wooed her with a Ferrari filled with red roses.

They subsequently married. That must be where Rob's been going wrong: he sends the roses but forgets the Ferrari.

Rob could have made it seven chart toppers from 2000 if he had taken a shine to the tall and languid Sophie Ellis-Bextor. The opposite was true. She turned down a chance to be his support act on tour and Rob was far from impressed, saying he would make her cry when he saw her, only half-jokingly. He told a writer for the *Sunday Times* that she had a face like a satellite dish and 'my nan's ankles'.

Away from the charts a number of young women popped in and out of his life. The only one who actually meant something to Rob was Tania Strecker, presenter of *Naked Elvis*, a late night, offbeat quiz show on Channel 4. She was a well-connected girl in the same mould as Jacqui Hamilton-Smith. She is absolutely stunning with legs that Rob described as 'going on and on . . . and on'. She was also the first of his real girlfriends to have a child, a 3-year-old daughter, Mia. Rob does not find children a problem at all – in fact, quite the opposite. They were together in the early part of 2000, when they spent Millennium night in St Moritz and a month later he escorted her to the Brits.

Tania, who had dated Madonna's husband Guy Ritchie, is the stepdaughter of Rob's manager David Enthoven and had known him since the mid-nineties. She had seen for herself the private Rob, before she began a closer friendship with him. She is the only woman to receive a glowing mention in *Somebody Someday*, the book of Robbie Williams on tour in 2000. He admits that he had not had a proper relationship for two years – since Nic Appleton – but does say that Tania was the last person he 'walked' out with. He complimented her as being a 'nice person'. It would have been much more surprising, however, if he had been rude about his manager's family.

Geri Halliwell and Rob were a perfect match, their lives taking such similar courses. Like Rob, Geri had been one fifth of the most successful band in the UK. She too had been isolated and the first to leave, thereby having first crack at solo fame. She understood fame and that the all-consuming thirst for it was like being chained to a lunatic. For a time they were inseparable but now they are embroiled in a petty and bitchy feud.

Geri is from a working-class background in Watford but always had the conviction that she was meant to live a different life. She lived in a fantasy world, admitting later that she was sure she was adopted and her real mother was a princess. The death of her father six months before she joined the Spice Girls had a profound effect on her, focusing her ambition even more acutely: 'I became almost militant about my life after a period of dark depression.' During a fly-on-the-wall documentary filmed in 1994, before the Spice Girls were famous, Geri is seen pointing at her rollerblades. She says, 'Rollerblading – Robbie out of Take That does that. One day we will go skating together.' It would be six years before she achieved that ambition. She also revealed in the documentary, *Raw Spice*, that she perceived herself as the Queen of Pop. Perhaps she saw an alliance with Rob as a royal marriage. In another twist of coincidence, when Geri was about to leave the Spice Girls, Melanie C asked her if she was 'doing a Robbie' on them.

After she left the Spice Girls, Geri had to reinvent herself much as Rob had done after leaving Take That.

She jettisoned Ginger Spice, busty red-head in a Union
Jack dress, and became a sleek, classy blonde, a number
one solo artist and a UN Goodwill Ambassador. The
'romance' between Geri and Rob has divided opinion
between those that think it just a promotional stunt
dreamt up by their record company – they are both with
EMI – and those that think it real love. The truth is
probably somewhere between the two. The hysterical
media coverage of their year-long friendship did raise
their profile at useful moments but it was a real
relationship. After all, they did not *have* to go on holiday
together on several occasions. Geri has constantly denied
that she and Rob slept together, although not everyone
believes that. A record company insider reveals, 'Geri and
Robbie were brought together by the label. They are both
following a path but they were shagging. But Geri can be
a bit demonic. In fact she is as mad as a fucking hatter.'

Geri and Rob found that they really did hit it off in the
middle of 2000 when they first got together, not long after
he split from Tania Strecker. Geri fulfilled the number one
function for any woman in Rob's life: she mothered him.
She had a metaphoric arm around him, giving him
security. Jonathan Wilkes, who was sharing Rob's home in
Notting Hill, described Geri, most revealingly, as their big
sister. The pair had met when Geri was still in the Spice
Girls and Rob was one of the few men linked to Melanie
C. They had both sung at the fiftieth birthday party for the
Prince of Wales but nobody suspected anything until Geri
was spotted leaving Rob's home in the small hours.

Their first holiday together in St Tropez was paparazzi
paradise. They were pictured frolicking by the poolside
like a couple of big kids. It did not escape the notice of

cynics that Rob's third album, *Sing When You're Winning*, was out at the end of the month and Geri's first autobiography, *If Only*, had just been published in paperback. The front page of the *Sun* declared, 'Robbie and Geri: It's Love'. It was certainly good business as the first single from the album, 'Rock DJ', went straight to the top of the charts.

They took different flights to Nice but rendezvoused at a villa down the coast that Geri had rented for a couple of weeks. There were plenty of photo opportunities for the photographers, who fortunately were in prime position right from the start. Soon after arriving, Rob joined Geri at the pool, she in toned body-revealing bikini, him wearing checked Bermuda shorts. They chatted, swam and dived and played with Geri's beloved shih-tzu, Harry. Then they were off on a scooter tour of the area. Much was made of Geri wrapping her arms around his chest as a gesture of love, although it was more likely fear at being his pillion passenger. Geri's red bikini photographed beautifully when she went jet-skiing. The whole jaunt made an excellent photo spread in *OK!* magazine, although her other guests at the villa stayed well away from the photographer's lens. They even had time to have a row in a local restaurant, when Geri allegedly was upset at Rob apparently paying too much attention to Claire, the wife of hypnotist Paul McKenna. Rob left early after he and Geri exchanged some witty repartee, which involved liberal use of the f-word. Geri was reported as ending the night throwing up in the ladies' loo. It was, perhaps, an early indication that Geri could be just as much of a handful as Rob.

Unlike Geri's whirlwind 'romance' with Chris Evans, which lasted about a week at the time of the release of her number one record 'Lift Me Up', an unexpected and genuine affection sprang up between Geri and Rob. In her book, *Just for the Record*, Geri writes that they were perfect playmates for each other. They also offered mutual support. He was particularly supportive when she admitted to being at her lowest ebb with her eating disorder. At a time when Rob also needed crutches, Geri was strong and supportive. They spent a low-key New Year, at Rob's suggestion, with friends in the Swiss ski resort of Gstaad, having a laugh together and obviously enjoying each other's company. They went ice-skating with Rob gallantly preventing Geri from falling over. He was pretty nifty on skates having had tuition from former Olympic champion Robin Cousins when he was filming the video for his number one 'She's the One', which was set on an ice rink.

She was helping to keep him sane during one of his worst crises over drink and drugs. The famous incident in Stockholm when Rob allegedly collapsed foaming at the mouth had taken place the previous month. After New Year, they flew to Los Angeles where Rob was trying to keep away from the temptations of the fleshpots of Notting Hill. She went with him to AA meetings, waiting patiently outside to see him home. She would spend hours chatting to the girlfriends and wives of the addicts inside. Friends thought Geri saw herself as a guardian angel to Rob. They were still obviously on the best of terms at the Brits in February 2001, when Geri presented Rob with the Best British Male Solo Artist award. She said, 'This winner is healthy, talented and, according to press reports, giving me one. So it's about time I returned the favour and gave him one – the winner is Robbie Williams.' It was an amusing riposte to Rob's joke that he was in the Spice Girls: 'I've been in two of them.' After the Brits, Geri joined Rob and Jonathan for tea at their place, chatting while they played the card game Uno, then Rob's latest obsession. His number one record 'Eternity' was reportedly written in her honour.

The change in their relationship seems to have coincided with Rob revealing, with deliberate indiscretion, that they were friends who enjoyed 'the occasional shag'. When he auctioned off his pants, with a picture of a tiger embroidered on the crotch, he announced, 'These are the pants I shagged Geri in.' Geri thought it a typical lad's silly boast and, as part of a robust denial, let him know that she found it upsetting. After this, Rob is barely mentioned again in her autobiography. He does not feature at all in the last chapter of her life in Los Angeles in 2003, even though he is living in the same city. They did fall out but a more likely source of confrontation was that they are both strong-willed, used to getting their own way and liable to fluctuate wildly between euphoric highs and dismal lows.

Analysing Rob's experiences with the opposite sex reveals a 30-year-old, amazingly eligible multi-millionaire who has found very few women with whom he can share a conversation. Ever since the creation of Robbie Williams confirmed his superstar status he has suffered from living in ever-decreasing circles where the opportunity of meeting people who are not celebrities themselves grows relentlessly smaller. There is a slim chance that he might meet someone while out walking his dogs but, now he lives in Los Angeles, she will probably work on a daytime soap.

There will always be available lap dancers but he is unlikely to find Mrs Williams hiding behind a thong in Stringfellows or Spearmint Rhino. His hit rate of one-night stands may be impressive but not necessarily any better than an average lad in Stoke-on-Trent out for a few jars and a good time on a Friday or Saturday night. He probably has to work at it for another twenty years to match the figures set by Bill Wyman and Mick Jagger.

A Robbie Williams romance is entirely different from a proper Rob relationship. It might appear that everything in his life is conducted in public but that is just Robbie. Rob is never going to reveal something as private as Nic Appleton's pregnancy. He is happy, as Robbie, to tease everyone about his friendship with Kylie, when there is a record to promote. Nothing illustrates this double existence better than the hot romance he was rumoured to be having with Nicole Kidman just as their duet, 'Somethin' Stupid', was released for Christmas 2001. It was a PR dream with bookmakers offering as little as 16–1 that they would wed in the New Year of 2002. There was a better chance of Rob flying to the moon. Still it was light entertainment and very Hollywood: the king of pop and the elegant film star.

After her enormous success with the film *Moulin Rouge*, in which she sang, Rob met Nicole in Los Angeles and persuaded her to record a duet with him for the *Swing When You're Winning* album, his tribute to the great crooners and, in particular, Frank Sinatra. 'Somethin' Stupid' had been a number one for Frank and his daughter Nancy in 1967. The Kidman/Williams version more than does justice to a classic song. The video was even better. Shot in a bedroom, it was sensual and sexy with Rob and Nicole entwined in steamy embraces. It was like Cary Grant and Grace Kelly with a touch more Tabasco.

The pair were very complimentary about each other. Rob said he was worried when they met that he would behave like an idiot or try to lick her face. But they had chatted and he had a 'real blast' with her. Nicole agreed that it was fun, that Robbie was very talented and that she was seriously thinking of getting a tattoo on her ankle. One of Rob's endearing characteristics is that he can be a little star-struck at times. He was mesmerized by the Kidman scent, three parts vanilla and one part musk. For her part, Nicole was just as nervous recording a song with a famous pop star. In the end, the recording took little more than an hour.

Nicole flew into London for a cosy chat with Michael Parkinson for his show, *Parkinson*, and Rob courteously acted as her host. He took her go-karting, bought her an expensive dinner before a visit to the blackjack tables where she had to lend him £100. The gossip frenzy began on the night of the *Parkinson* recording. Nicole, wearing a smart black suit, white shirt and tie, went straight from filming back to the Dorchester Hotel at 9.30, where, five minutes later, Rob arrived. He was wearing tracksuit bottoms and a cricket jumper and went straight up to her suite. It was apparently the second night in a row he had visited her. He was clocked by the *News of the World* leaving at 2.55 a.m. precisely. They had enjoyed room service together, bottled beer for her and soft drinks for him. When he left, he was smiling and chatting on a mobile phone. A spokeswoman for Robbie reportedly confirmed that he spent the night in Nicole's room. He hardly 'spent the night', which in pop star terms had only just begun.

The spokeswoman added, 'They are friends and they were hanging out', which was a lot nearer the truth.

The device of putting two stars together to promote a film or a record is becoming such a cliché. The whole thing degenerated into farce when two blonde, ex-lap dancers from Spearmint Rhino claimed they had enjoyed a threesome with Rob just hours before his first visit to the Dorchester and that he was an 'astonishing' lover. They had apparently met Rob when they delivered junk mail to his house. Nicole Kidman? The romping ex-lap dancers? Where does the truth lie? The truth is that it really does not matter because it was just great fun and nobody got hurt. 'Somethin' Stupid' sold a million and was the Christmas number one, as was the album *Swing When You're Winning*, a great double for Robbie Williams who has not been spotted any time since in Nicole Kidman's hotel room. They did have a laugh together, though. Rob may be arrogant at times but he is not a no-conversation, self-preening bore.

Unreported but far more relevant to the real Rob was his encounter with an attractive girl he picked up one night after spotting her in a London club. She was thrilled to be getting off with a star like Robbie Williams and was expecting to tell her friends the next day of her fantastic night of passion. But when they arrived at his house, instead of sweeping her up in his arms, he just wanted to talk.

'Pretty girls are just passing faces.'

18

The Feudster

Rob was not happy with guitarist Bernard Butler, whom he had read had called him Bob Monkhouse's bastard offspring. So when he saw him at a recording studio where he was picking up Nic Appleton, he went over to confront him. He asked, 'Are you Bernard Butler?' 'Yeah,' came the reply. 'You are a fucking c—t!' said Rob.

Rob was a huge fan of Oasis. The Gallagher brothers represented everything he aspired to in music and pretty much everything Take That were not. They were true Manchester lads with edge and bottle, not prancing about like refugees from Copacabana Beach. He espoused them with almost childlike enthusiasm in those heady days of Glastonbury and beyond. He even described himself as the Artful Dodger to Noel Gallagher's Fagin. Rob gave every indication that Liam Gallagher was a hero, a role model, a drinking buddy and the man he wanted to be. He could, naturally, do a brilliant impersonation of the Mancunian headcase. Now, just a few years later, Liam lives with Nicole Appleton, the woman Rob wanted to marry and start a family with. Nic aborted Rob's child but five years later she and Liam have a baby son, Gene, and the happy, domestic life that Rob yearns for. If that were not enough of a Greek tragedy, Liam split from Patsy Kensit, a friend of Rob's and the person who introduced him to his first serious girlfriend, Jacqui Hamilton-Smith. Beneath the veneer of a public spat between Robbie Williams and Oasis, Rob is very hurt. A friend of Nicole's confirmed, 'He thinks her romance with the man he regards as his arch enemy is the ultimate betrayal.'

The suggestion that everything was not as friendly as people thought between Rob and the Gallaghers was in the air at the start of 1998. Rob insisted he had not fallen out with the boys, although he did boast that his live shows were superior and that people were leaving his concerts saying they had a better time than at Oasis. It probably started off as nothing more than a spot of professional jealousy. The shambolic, unthreatening character in the latter days of Take That bore no relation to the multiple Brit-winning, number one machine that Rob became – probably the only serious British rival to Oasis. The catalyst for the public falling-out was the Gallagher brothers punching below the belt as far as Rob was concerned by making less than flattering references to his weight. Liam referred to Rob in 1999 as 'Robbie tubby-arsed Williams' and declared that his music was 'rubbish'. Liam is a charismatic rock star but he is never going to win a war of words with someone as razor-sharp in this department as Rob. Liam is a name-caller, an unsubtle insulter. Rob bounced back with a classic, 'I knew I could write poetry but I also knew I only knew three chords. And those three chords can't last for ever . . . unless you're Oasis.'

Rob finds it impossible to let things lie. In his Robbie Williams persona he will air all his dirty laundry in public. He can always be relied upon to give an opinion about anything – if he is in character. The Gallagher brothers really got under his skin because they were picking on him as if he were the fat boy in the playground whom nobody liked. It was time for Noel Gallagher to join the fun. When Radio 1 listeners asked Oasis to record Rob's classic 'Angels' for a special session, Noel refused point blank, adding that Liam would have to 'sing it with fifty meat pies in his mouth'. He followed that up in an interview in *heat* magazine in which he called Robbie, 'the fat dancer from Take That'. Rob could not believe it and reacted to it all, in his own words, like a 13-year-old. He sent round a wreath of white roses and lilies to the showbiz desk of the *Sun* with a note which read: 'To Noel Gallagher, RIP. Heard your latest album, with deepest sympathy, Robbie Williams.' Rob had bought a bootleg copy of the album, *Standing on the Shoulder of Giants*, in Camden Market and, after listening to it, declared, 'Noel's run out of other people's ideas.' The great thing about Robbie Williams in these circumstances is that he is genuinely witty.

Liam responded by threatening that if he ever saw Rob in a club in London, 'I'm going to break his fucking nose.' He also maintained that the new Oasis record was 'the best fucking album out this year, better than anything Fatty will ever do'. Rob was determined to give as good as he got. He dusted off his talent for impersonation by mimicking Liam's monkey walk and facial expressions before telling reporters, 'So he's going to beat me up, is he? I'm just not angry enough to hit him. It's not my career going down the drain. But if he hits me, I suppose I'll have to defend myself.'

At this stage, however, the public slanging match became silly with the suggestion from Rob at the Brit Awards that he and Liam should settle their difference in a boxing match. William Hill offered odds (Robbie Williams 1–2, Liam Gallagher 6–4), while Lloyd Honeyghan, former world boxing champion, said he would add the feuding pair to a bill at the Elephant and Castle Leisure Centre in south London. The idea was that the bout could raise £200,000 for charity. Rob entered into the spirit by saying he was definitely up for it and that it was nice to see Liam so angry. Great knockabout fun and some free publicity for the boxing and bookmaking fraternity.

Unsurprisingly, it was called off by Liam, who said it would be childish and pathetic and, in future, he would let the music do the talking.

The war of words between Liam and Rob could be treated with a degree of caution if it were not for the Appleton factor. This sort of thing is meat and drink to pop columns with pages to fill, while record companies love the free exposure it gives to new releases. The intriguing thing is that it has been getting steadily worse and distinctly more personal. Liam overstepped the boundary of celebrity etiquette when he publicly stated that Robbie was queer at a *Q* Awards party. Rob left abruptly, saying that Liam was 'fucking out of order'. By this time Liam and Nicole were very much an item, soon to make an announcement that she was expecting his baby. A week later Rob took a somewhat puerile revenge on stage at the London Arena by taunting Liam about his sex life with Nicole. He told the audience, 'Nic is my old bird. I have had her as well, mate. I bet you go to bed every night scratching your head, thinking "Is he better than me?"'

The feud is likely to simmer as long as Nicole Appleton and Liam Gallagher remain together. For the moment, there is a truce. In an effort to close the situation, at least in public, Rob was conciliatory on a Radio 1 interview. He said, 'At the beginning of it all it was quite a laugh and then it just became too destructive. I wish them both the best of luck and I hope Nicky keeps safe and the baby does fine.' When Liam and Nicole's baby Gene was born she expected Rob to call or send some message but she heard nothing. In her autobiography *Together*, which she wrote with her sister Natalie, she concedes that the thought of Gene must hurt Rob and that she wished she could speak to him but that they had no contact. When Rob was at school, girls would flit between the boys. Everyone was young and it was not the end of the world if Joanna Melvin preferred Lee Hancock to Robert Williams. Lee and Rob could still be best mates. But this was different. This was adult, life-changing circumstance. How could he be friendly with a man who has everything he wanted for himself?

The world got the message that Rob and Geri Halliwell were no longer on good terms when Geri ended up on the cutting-room floor of the documentary *Nobody Someday*, the film of the best-selling book of his life on tour. He famously described her to journalist and friend Adrian Deevoy as a 'demonic little girl playing with dolls and a tea set'. Rob thought she had become a different person once

her career took off again after her departure from the
Spice Girls. He even refused to be in the studio for
Parkinson at the same time as Geri. He recorded his songs
in the afternoon and had long gone before Geri arrived
for an interview in the evening.

Geri Halliwell is a fascinating celebrity, who, like Robbie
Williams, seems to want to share every thought she has
with the whole world. They have many similarities which
Rob almost certainly hates. Geri has had a fixation with
her weight and body image; she loves dogs; she worries
about her personal security; she has many gay friends; she
lives in Notting Hill and Los Angeles; she seems unable to
hold down a serious relationship with the opposite sex;
she wants children and a family life; she is close to her
mother and she has dragged herself up by sheer
determination and will. Probably the only thing they don't
have in common is irony. No wonder their friendship
could not last.

Rob certainly bears a grudge. Eileen Wilkes, who has
known 'Robert' for twenty years, observes, 'If people
attack Robert, he will get back at them.' No one is
immune from the Williams anger. He seems to find it
cathartic. If this were an *X File*, he would be a disc jockey
who gained great magical powers from slagging people off
on air. When he has turned against someone that would
appear to be it for life. Courtney Taylor of the Dandy
Warhols was critical of Robbie Williams in print. The
response was, 'You smell like poo and the girls don't like
you.' Sometimes the perceived slight may be relatively
minor or a major, life-altering one like that between him
and the former Take That manager Nigel Martin-Smith,
who Rob has cast as Voldemort to his Harry Potter. If Rob

was not a famous man, he would be like the great majority, getting something out of his system with his mates over a pint in the pub. He would be like one of Harry Enfield's 'Self Righteous Brothers': 'If that Gary Barlow walked into this pub now, I'd say "Oi, Barlow! You may be a world famous singer-songwriter who wrote 'Back for Good' but—"'

But Rob is famous and almost anything he says at a concert or in an interview finds its way into print. It imbues him with great powers because it allows him the last word. His tirade on *Life Thru a Lens* against the teacher who thought he would never amount to anything is quite unsettling in its bitterness and fury. The spark that sets him off is often a form of rejection. His need for acceptance and approval is so overwhelming that he is deeply hurt by something a more level-headed person might shrug off. That can partially explain the complete overreaction to his 'rejection' by Take That. The sense of hurt and frustration is so great it can, as Nic Appleton witnessed, reduce him to tears years after.

At first, his resentment was aimed at the other four members of the band. It was as if the lads in Tunstall Park had told him to run away and find his own game of football. In particular Gary Barlow, the skipper, came in for some football terrace abuse. The press lapped up the slanging match with Gary but, in reality, it was more competitive than anything else, a desire to prove that he, Robbie Williams, could do just as well, if not better. The feud with Gary Barlow was also good publicity for Robbie Williams, like the time he took back Gary's album *Open Road* to the record store where he had bought it and declared, 'This is crap. I want my £14.99 back.' In any case,

Rob was disappointed to lose touch with Mark Owen, who, for a time, had been a close friend. The real vitriol from the Take That saga was aimed at Nigel Martin-Smith, who Rob felt had confined him to a prison during his time with the band and had subsequently threatened his future in the courts. Nigel did not improve his standing with Rob by criticizing Jan Williams and her involvement in his career.

At the famous 'Freedom' press conference to launch his solo career in June 1996, one year after the break, Rob said, 'I'd like to meet up with the manager in a fork lift truck, souped up to go about 150 miles per hour non stop with no brakes!' A month later in the gay magazine *Attitude*, there was no doubting Rob's own attitude to his former manager: 'I don't even have words for that c—t,' he declared, which was not strictly true as he has never been short of words about him unless restricted by a legal agreement. He told *Stern* magazine that Take That had been a 'devil's pact'. He added, 'He [Nigel] gave you fame and riches, you gave him your soul and 25 per cent of the takings.'

The legal process involving Nigel was a long-drawn-out saga, with his former manager winning a case for unpaid commission on Robbie Williams's royalties. The cold logic of the law was against him. Some estimates put the final figure he had to pay Nigel as high as £1 million. Rob has found it virtually impossible to effect closure with Take That. He is far more successful now than Take That ever were. But, amazingly, as recently as November 2002 Take That was still on Rob's mind. He told an invited audience at Pinewood Studios where he was recording the BBC 1 special, *The Robbie Williams Show*, 'I want to apologize because when I left I said some really bad things; it's the truth I said some really bad things about the band. And I just want to say I'm really, sincerely sorry – we're only young once.' He then launched into 'No Regrets'. It remains to be seen whether that is the last word on the subject.

Rob's falling out with his collaborator Guy Chambers was shocking. They had been so successful together, a partnership to rival the greatest in pop history. Williams and Chambers had produced five number one, million-selling albums together. Even on *Swing When You're Winning*, for which they only contributed one original song, Chambers acted as producer. In pop music terms they need not be embarrassed about being included in a list which begins Lennon/McCartney, Jagger/Richards and Elton John and Bernie Taupin. And yet something was missing. 'Williams and Chambers' has never had a Lieber and Stoller ring to it. Guy Chambers was just the hired help, a guiding hand to help cast the new image of Robbie Williams. They were not a partnership forged at school in Stoke-on-Trent, drinking in Tunstall Park or playing pool in the Ancient Briton. There was nothing Hollywood about it. Mick Jagger met Keith Richards at Wentworth Junior County Primary School, Dartford, when they were seven. It was more than fifty-two years ago. Williams/Chambers is strictly a business arrangement. Guy was short-listed for the position of Robbie Williams's musical guru and secured the position after interview.

Out of the blue, Rob sacked Guy as his songwriting partner in October 2002. Just two years earlier the dedication of the *Sing When You're Winning* album read, 'To Guy Chambers who is as much Robbie as I am.' And, if that had failed to make the point strongly enough, Rob called him a 'musical genius', whom he was lucky to have in his life.

What a difference two years make. The falling-out is reportedly over Guy's unwillingness to sign an exclusivity agreement with Rob. The change in their relationship neatly coincided with Rob signing his new deal with EMI and, although details of that agreement are secret, it does not require a huge leap of imagination to conclude they are connected. This had all the hallmarks of a financial tiff. Guy was said to want to concentrate on new projects, in particular a girl band called the Licks, managed by his brother, Dylan Chambers. Rob's spokesman issued a statement: 'Robbie Williams wishes Guy Chambers the best of luck with his band the Licks.' Guy's spokesman said, 'Guy has decided to work with other people and on other projects. He feels he cannot commit to working exclusively with Robbie.' Guy described the sacking as brutal and too upsetting to think about.

Guy and Rob are very different people who came together and gelled perfectly under the umbrella of Robbie Williams. Guy is a family man from Liverpool, ten years older than Rob, who lives quietly in London. He will be in his forties before Robbie Williams releases another album. He is also devoted to his music and completely shuns the limelight. When the dust settles on this tiff there may well be a reconciliation. A mutual friend revealed earlier this year: 'You have got to move and experiment, which is what Rob is doing, but, between you and me, Guy Chambers is back on the scene.' When Guy married in 1999, Rob sang 'Angels' at his wedding and he doesn't do that for just anybody.

The biggest feud in Rob's life is the one he is conducting with Robbie Williams. He has even threatened to kill off his alter ego and start again. Robbie Williams, he once said, is just an identity he puts on to go to work. Rob, the lad, was born to act. Right from childhood he was a performer, entertaining fellow children, trying to impress adults and trying to make his parents proud of him. Robbie is an extension of that ability to play a role. Rob described him as 'a character he's worked'. That is why he will not answer to 'Robbie' if someone calls out to him in the street. Nor will he give an autograph to someone when he is not on duty as Robbie. He is Rob when he closes his front door, chats to his mother, plays table tennis with his dad, checks the Port Vale results or waits patiently while his girlfriend has an abortion in the next room. He is no more Robbie Williams in private than Rowan Atkinson is Mr Bean or Pierce Brosnan is James Bond. That is their work. Can you imagine Harry Hill settling down to watch television in the evening wearing an enormous white shirt collar and Max Wall shoes? Or Kylie Minogue loading the dishwasher in a minuscule pair of gold hot pants?

Rob explains it himself using his hero and now friend, Vic Reeves, as an example. Rob and Jim (Vic's real name is Jim Moir) were at the races one day when a man came up and said, 'Vic, when's your new show coming on?' Jim suddenly became the zany television comedian and replied, 'Hey, it'll be on in a couple of months.' Rob was deeply impressed at how he could change from Jim, family man with a farm, to Vic almost at will. He is able to do the same with Rob and Robbie.

Rob, as his childhood friends reveal, is a mixture of sensitivity and cheeky fun. He is also polite and kind.

Robbie is a mouthy rascal and a showman. The difficulty for Rob is when he and his alter ego merge into one, the ventriloquist taken over by the dummy. Rob, a lad from Tunstall, can be greatly hurt by criticism whether from a teacher, a fellow pop star or someone he passes in the street. Robbie is a mouthpiece for him to fight back. Rob faced a crisis after his departure from Take That because his image as the cheeky boy of the nation's most popular band was instantly taken away from him. He floundered around in a drink and drugs haze until he invented Robbie Williams, a complex superstar. Perhaps, rehab and therapy have allowed Rob to separate himself from Robbie.

It is Rob who sits down and writes witty, intelligent lyrics that reflect his inner feelings about life, love and the people around him. It is Robbie Williams who performs the songs they become. EMI have paid a fortune for the whole package of Robbie Williams, so the character is safe for the moment. Rob would like Robbie Williams to be a cool rock star but for the time being at least he will have to make do with being the king of pop.

'Robbie Williams is a persona I can take on or off.'

19

Show Me the Money

Rob has always appreciated the value of money. When he
got his first (small) pay packet from Take That he went straight
round to his nan's house in Newfield Street, picked up her
electricity bill and told her he would be taking care of it as a
thank you for all the times she had lent him a quid.

While living in Los Angeles, Rob was filling the pages of
the newspapers less frequently. There was a relationship
with Rachel Hunter to keep the glossy magazines happy
but nothing really meaty. That all changed at a press
conference at EMI's west London offices on 2 October
2002. Wearing a Mötley Crüe singlet, which showed off his
tattoos, Rob told the assembled media, 'My mum told me
it would be really uncouth of me to talk about money . . .
but I'm rich beyond my wildest dreams!' From the mouth
that launched a thousand quips it was one of the best. The
£80 million deal was immediately hailed as the biggest in
British recording history.

Rob's previous contract with EMI had expired earlier
in the year and there was talk in the press that he was
unhappy with the way he had been promoted in the

USA. His managers were open to offers in an auction for his considerable record-selling ability. It all seemed a bit like the football transfer market. Would Rob stay with EMI (Manchester United) or go to Sony (Real Madrid)? The reality was that EMI was never going to let him go. A record business insider explains, 'Chris Briggs was with Guy Chambers in LA for two months working on Rob's new album, *Escapology*. Rob was never going anywhere else. Chris Briggs worked out the *Escapology* deal. Tim and David wound it up. EMI were over a barrel because they don't really have any other artists, other than Kylie and Coldplay. David and Tim pushed a very hard deal.'

EMI knew they had to keep Robbie Williams at all costs: 'He paid the salaries of everyone at EMI for years. He could afford to be a bit arrogant at record company parties because he knew how important he was. These days he is liable to be understated and clean cut with his AA mates around him. They are quite hard, you know.'

The whole timing and strategy of Rob's record deal was quite brilliant. It placed Rob centre stage of the whole music industry one month before his fifth album, *Escapology*, came out. The music press was wondering if he could still command such devotion now that he had apparently deserted the country to live in the United States. The £80 million figure seemed to be one picked at random to dwarf all previous deals and give the impression that the greatest star in the country was among us and about to give us the privilege of a new recording. It worked 'beyond the wildest dreams' of any record company executive. Despite only being released in November *Escapology* racked up 2 million sales to make it the best-selling album of 2002 – in two months! Never, it appeared, had £80 million been so well spent.

But was it actually £80 million? Those details will never be made public but the wisdom in the record industry was that there was a signing fee (perhaps £20 million) and the rest was a projected figure of what the deal would be worth over the next four albums. The *Financial Times* thought EMI had a 25 per cent stake in a new company which Rob was setting up. This was not a deal that concentrated on CDs pushed over the counter at HMV. This was an investment in Robbie Williams the brand: the culmination of everything he had worked for since the desolate day when had left Take That clutching a melon and his shattered pride. David Beckham has discovered that in football, there is much more to his value than just being able to take a sweet free kick. In terms of marketing and merchandising he is a precious commodity. It is the same for Robbie Williams. The music industry is changing and the deal with Rob reflects it. EMI will share in the money made from touring and merchandising as well as in publishing and record sales. Robbie Williams is like a limited company absorbed into a larger one. In those terms, it is far easier to see how the split with Guy Chambers came about through his apparent unwillingness to sign an exclusivity deal. If you are a director of BT, you couldn't really do some work for Orange on the side. The preservation of Robbie Williams the brand is rather like safeguarding Harry Potter – nothing can be seen to undermine its identity. The music industry has been chugging along like a hippy commune far too long, with people drifting around with abandon. Robbie Williams/EMI is a deal of the future.

Escapology seemed like a 'long-awaited' album even if it was only one year since *Swing When You're Winning* had topped the charts. Rob was now living in Los Angeles, an exiled superstar. Would he be a new Robbie Williams, a mellow man from Hollywood? Or would it be the old cheeky lad from Stoke-on-Trent, full of witty one-liners and dark humour. Or would he have become so introspective and miserably self-aware that Leonard Cohen would have told him to cheer up? The answer, unsurprisingly, is that it was all of these and none of them. Rob was quite fortunate in that anything was going to be completely different from *Swing*, which was really a one-off. Rob's progress, or lack of it, with *Escapology* should be analysed in respect of his third solo album, *Sing When You're Winning*, which was such a perfect embodiment of the Robbie Williams brand.

Rob says he thought of the title for the new album when he was out driving in the Hollywood Hills one day and he started thinking about Houdini, the most famous escapologist of all time. Tiresomely, it was suggested it was a thinly veiled reference to his escape from Take That. If you want to go down that road it is far more likely that it was an escape from his life in Britain, which was making him so miserable. The album cover is a breathtaking homage to Houdini, with Rob suspended by his feet above the Los Angeles skyline as if in mid-bungee jump. The most noticeable aspect of *Escapology* – besides the one-word title – is that critics only identify one track, 'Monsoon', as having an Oasis influence. Having so successfully ditched the boy band sound when he began life as Robbie Williams, solo star, Rob now has the dilemma of being too often compared with Oasis.

The problem for Robbie Williams as a musical artist is that there are too many discernible influences – Queen, Elton John, George Michael, John Lennon, Oasis and more. Perhaps it's all part of a masterplan to crack the USA: collect all the great British stars that have ever made it big in the States, take a little piece of their sound and put it into a giant jigsaw. Hey presto, you have a sound guaranteed to appeal to every possible audience in the United States.

It may be fun to spot the influence but, at the same time, it does devalue the musical content and leave the listener clutching once more at the lyrics as something familiar to hang on to. The lyrics to *Escapology* do not disappoint. The very first track, 'How Peculiar', was almost an elongated ad lib, with no formal lyrics written down before recording, so it became like a stream of consciousness, with Rob allowing a train of thought about a crush he once had on someone to prompt the song. 'How Peculiar' sounds very much like the old Robbie Williams and would not have been out of place on *Sing When You're Winning*. It is a false impression of what is to come. The very next track, 'Feel', was the most talked-of song on the album, not just because it was the first single. It is a mature, silky production of a gentle song, with a universal sentiment of someone searching for love. Rob is very proud of 'Feel' and called it a 'beautiful' song. There is a small suspicion that it would have made a big hit for Barbra Streisand but it was very inoffensive. Dominic Mohan of the *Sun* described it as sheer genius. The most successful songs on *Escapology* are infused with melancholy with a twist. None-more so than 'Come Undone', the second UK single from the album, and a retrospective look at the drugs and alcohol troubles that have beset him. To some extent he is blaming his environment, the England he has now left behind. When he sings of being a son, it is of England, not of long-suffering Jan Williams!

The reviewers singled out two tracks above the rest, although it's all very subjective. The first was 'Revolution', which featured a duet with gospel singer Rosa Stone, and was another song about loss of hope and love. The second was 'Nan's Song', the simple, acoustic ballad that is a tribute to Betty Williams and closes the album. As the first song Rob has written completely by himself, it points the way to the future sound of Robbie Williams. One critic wrote, 'It is from the heart and he wears it on his sleeve.' Rob's nan was still alive when he wrote 'Angels' but the sentiment is very much the same, the idea of someone watching over him and taking care of him. Rob played the guitar live for the first time while performing the song at his BBC showcase for the album, which was filmed at Pinewood Studios. He could not help making a veiled reference to the falling-out with Guy Chambers: 'There's been a redundancy at our place and I've had to start playing this thing.'

Rob, benefiting from a much quieter and even-paced life in Los Angeles, took a much greater responsibility for the final sound, something he previously found a chore. Perhaps this is a portent for the future. In the past he has been the singer who does a few tracks and then leaves everyone to get on with it. Rob recorded the vocals for *Escapology* minus his clothes because he claims he finds it very liberating. He was very involved in the video for the album, aware of the importance of image at this stage of his career. He also further endorsed the opinion that Robbie Williams is now a brand product with the production of a new logo, which he drew on the back of a cigarette packet. Like all the best logos it is very simple, a circle with RW across the middle, and a star at the top of the R instead of the hole. It actually looks like a brand of cigarettes, which is, perhaps, what gave him the idea. The three outstanding tracks on *Escapology*, by common consent, 'Feel', 'Revolution' and 'Nan's Song', are probably the three least 'Robbie Williams' tracks on the album. They don't have the cheeky chappie stamp on them. Rob is closing in on thirty and taking the music far more seriously than before, when it was just oxygen for his Robbie Williams persona. It will be interesting to see how many un-Robbie tracks there are on his next album.

The success of *Escapology* is already a fantastic return for EMI. Some naive commentators have cast doubt on the deal's long-term value because of the relative failure of two singles from the album. A source, however, explained, 'Singles are just a promotional tool these days to sell albums and concert tickets. They are a complete loss leader. You could have a top ten single one week and be dropped by your record company the next.' Nobody is going to drop an artist who can sell 2 million albums in two months. That assertion was backed up by EMI Chief Executive Tony Wadsworth: 'Signing an artist like Robbie Williams is a lot less risky than most of our business. In the last five years he has sold 20 million albums around the world.' Even if sales for *Escapology* had been disappointing, EMI would still have been able to recoup a sizeable chunk of their initial investment by speedily releasing *The Best of Robbie Williams* for Christmas 2003.

On the back of the general euphoria over the £80 million deal, Rob announced his 2003 summer tour. The response to this as well was beyond his wildest dreams. The

121,000 tickets for the first of his two nights at Knebworth sold out in just thirty minutes on the morning they went on sale. The second night was sold out by mid-afternoon and a third show was added to accommodate the ticket frenzy. With a nice twist of irony, Rob sold out the two nights beating by two hours the previous record set by Oasis. The 'fat dancer from Take That' shifted 650,000 tickets for twenty nights across Europe in a day, raking in an estimated £22,750,000 in receipts, highlighting the riches a major tour can bring. Under the terms of the new deal, a good proportion of these receipts will be going to EMI, a spectacular return on their investment. And the company could also expect a cut of the merchandising many of the 650,000 fans were going to buy.

For once, a record company spokeswoman was positively garrulous, delighted no doubt not to have to give a 'no comment' to a story of sex, drugs and rock 'n' roll. She said, 'At Knebworth alone Rob will play to 350,000 fans in three nights, that is the equivalent of 4,270 jam-packed double-decker buses.' If Rob was nervous when he played Slane Castle in front of 80,000 what torment must he have faced at Knebworth?

The *Sunday Times* 'Rich List' of 2003 estimated Rob's personal fortune at £68 million. That placed him at equal 504th, a highly commendable £8 million ahead of George Michael and £18 million ahead of David and Victoria Beckham. He was also, by some way, the youngest of the fifty richest music millionaires. It may not have been enough to give Paul McCartney (£760 million) any jealousy-fuelled sleepless nights but it was still an awful lot of cash for someone who once said his principal enjoyment in life was playing backgammon.

Rob had insisted on certain clauses in his new contract, which would improve the 'brand' over the next few years. With the future in mind, Rob insisted his management team pay particular attention to DVD and the internet as part of the modernization of the music industry. Much was also made of his insistence on a commitment from EMI that they would invest in a big promotional push in the USA. Although Rob was breaking all European records, it was small beer compared to the fantastic riches Paul McCartney, the Rolling Stones and U2 continued to reap from their sell-out US tours.

Like all artists who have yet to crack it in the United States, Rob says he is not bothered about it. Kylie Minogue is another who professes indifference to American success. And yet a nod from Jay Leno will have them in make-up like a shot. From the very beginning Rob has tried very hard for a breakthrough as a solo artist, promoting his albums and performing at all manner of venues. In 1999, his old friend Tim Peers was in New York when he heard Rob was performing at a small hall in Chinatown called the Bang Bang Room. He was disappointed to find it was sold out but went along on the off-chance. He was standing outside the back when a huge limousine pulled up and out stepped Rob: 'I shouted over to him "Rob" and he turned round, came running over and gave me a hug. He took me into the VIP area which was great. His mum and his sister were both there with him.' Rob played this small New York venue the same year as he played before 80,000 people at Slane Castle in Ireland, which gives the lie to the idea he is not bothered about making an effort in the USA. *The Ego Has Landed* garnered good reviews, with critics in the main predicting that he would translate his success across the 'pond'. But he didn't make the phenomenal breakthrough that he had achieved in the UK. The 'Angels' factor did not happen in the USA. His journalist friend Adrian Deevoy reported that Rob blamed Capitol Records, the American partner of EMI, for treating him with indifference. The suggestion was that Rob was too English. A record company executive observed, 'The States does not get irony. Not being big in the States has really got under Robbie's skin. The problem he has is that EMI do not have much clout over there.' Take That biographer Rick Sky confirms, 'It is very important for him to crack the States. It was a key factor in the new deal. He wanted EMI to promise to make it for him in the US.'

The fact remains that very few British artists have made it big in the States since the Beatles took the American music scene by the scruff of the neck. Craig David's style of light R&B has given him a platinum album but, in general, British artists would be struggling to make the top fifty most popular. The dinosaurs of rock are forever popular and can sell out any stadium, but the relatively newer acts like Robbie, and even Oasis, are far from household names. Rob has questioned whether he wants to spend another three years touring arenas in the USA, especially as he does not need the cash. When you are playing in front of 100,000 fans at Knebworth the idea of returning to the Bang Bang Club must seem particularly unappealing.

Rob has always felt a little guilty about splashing his money around. He once took delivery of a new, vivid red Ferrari but sent it back to the showroom because he felt guilty about owning such a status symbol. He then changed his mind and had it delivered back again. He has never passed a driving test, which made it even more of an indulgence. In Los Angeles he lives in a gated community, which means he can whizz around the private roads in his black E-Type Jaguar but he cannot go out on to the freeway. Rob loves the thrill of speed and finds go-karting particularly exhilarating. He makes his way around London, however, on a Honda Shadow scooter, a fashionable retro-design bike much favoured by celebrities.

Even before the EMI deal, he was extremely wealthy with reports estimating that he made more than £20 million in 2001 alone. He was said to have earned £450,000 in one night for his triumphant *Swing* concert at the Royal Albert Hall. Rob does give more than a little something back, however. In April 2001, an auction at Sotheby's raised £221,044 for his Give It Sum charity as part of the Comic Relief appeal. The items, auctioned by Lenny Henry, for the 'Bid It Sum' sale included the guitar from the 'Let Me Entertain You' video (£6500), his DJ console (£7500), bed (slightly damaged) (£13,000) and his tiger pants (£2200). Rob showed up for the sale of the final item, his handwritten copy of the lyrics for 'Angels', which went for £27,000, prompting him to plunge into the audience to give the successful bidder a hug.

Rob is a great supporter of Comic Relief and never fails to contribute to Red Nose Day. He was the narrator of the award-winning *Robbie the Reindeer*, which raised money for the appeal, and sang a special version of 'Come Fly With Me' for the animated film. Besides his ongoing interest in the Donna Louise Trust, he has signed up as a potential bone marrow donor for the Anthony Nolan Bone Marrow Trust, which was formed to try to help save the lives of leukaemia sufferers. He is a patron of the Jeans for Genes Appeal, when once a year in October everyone is encouraged to swap their suits for jeans and donate £1 to the appeal. Rob is also a big supporter of Great Ormond Street Hospital and even spent one Christmas Eve there visiting the sick children. He has also travelled abroad for UNICEF since the late Ian Dury first suggested he get involved in 1998. He joined Dury for a trip to Sri Lanka to witness children being immunized against polio in a war zone. He has also been to Mozambique to highlight the appalling problems that country is having with the spread of HIV/Aids among children.

As with most famous celebrities, his most tangible assets are his various houses. His current property portfolio includes a selection of several million-pound properties; two in London, one in Los Angeles and one in Staffordshire. Pride of place belongs to his main house in Holland Park, west London. It is an unashamed example of palatial pop star luxury, although more grown up than his previous homes. It is still a lad's paradise of massive televisions and platinum pool table. Rob can watch a state of the art TV whenever he enjoys a soak in the bath, takes a shower or uses the toilet. The town house in a quiet residential street apparently cost Rob £3 million and he spent a further £2 million on refurbishment, including converting the entire first floor into one master bedroom. He also spent £15,000 on a giant outdoor hot tub which could accommodate five people and which needed to be winched into position by crane. Pride of place in the hallway is given to a set of Andy Warhol original prints of

Muhammad Ali, one of Rob's heroes. The four portraits making up the set were a bargain at £25,000.

In true rock star fashion he is never there, having made his home for the time being in Los Angeles.

'I'm going to count it all now.'

20

LA Story

Now that Rob was living in Los Angeles, it had been ages since Eileen Wilkes had seen him. On a visit to the UK, he popped home with her son Jonathan and she was pleased at how well he was looking. 'You look great,' she told him. He smiled and told her, 'I have never felt so well. I am looking after myself.'

Rob worries about his personal safety. It is not something he likes to advertise too much but he has had to get used to having bodyguards around as part of his daily life. In his Take That days he would run for safety when he was a given a hard time by Stoke City fans. But they were pussycats compared to the fanatical 'fans' of Robbie Williams hell-bent on pursuing their idol. It was manageable when they were young girls sitting on the wall outside the house in Greenbank Road. He would see them only at weekends or if he was taking a break to spend time with his mother. But, after Stuttgart, Rob's confidence was shattered. He was appearing in concert at the city's Hans-Martin Schleyer Hall on 21 February 2001, when a crazed fan dashed on to the stage while he was singing 'Supreme' and pushed him off because he believed he was not the real Robbie Williams at all but an impostor. Apparently he thought the real Robbie was elsewhere. Rob fell five feet into the area normally occupied by a photographer or two taking pictures. Security came to his rescue and hauled his attacker off him.

Rob was much shaken but, to everyone's surprise, he did not storm off and play the wounded martyr. Instead he got back on to the stage and asked the audience if they were OK. When they shouted, 'Yeah!' he responded, 'Well so am I. And I'm not going to let any fucker get on stage and stop you having a good time.' He powered his way through the rest of the concert before deciding that he wanted to get out of Stuttgart immediately. Although everyone was impressed by Rob's mature reaction on the night, the unspoken question that hung in the air was, 'What if the attacker had been brandishing a knife?' The unfortunate aspect of this assault was the element of surprise and Rob didn't see him until it was too late. Fans have run on to stages before and usually the artist can deal with it – Keith Richards used to whack fans with his guitar if they came too close – but Rob, who is not a little fellow, had no chance to react. Jonathan Wilkes said he spoke to Rob straight after it happened: 'It shook me up and it shook him up. He was shocked and scared.'

Safety for performers, whether entertainers or sportsmen, has had a dramatic rethink since the infamous stabbing of Monica Seles during a tennis match. Rob could no longer afford to take any chances with someone ringing his doorbell in the middle of the night or rushing up to him with an autograph book. Rob had full-time bodyguards before Stuttgart but the level of protection was substantially increased afterwards. When the *Sing* tour ended, he could not settle back to his life in London, where he was feeling increasingly depressed and imprisoned. He would open his bedroom curtains to be greeted by a telephoto lens and a group of pointing girl fans, usually Italian. His life had become like *Groundhog Day*, a ghastly repetition of the worst day in your life. He could not go to the pub or a local café without so much hassle that all he wanted to do was go back and watch the History Channel on his giant TV. He started to occupy the celebrity netherland, only being seen out among other celebrities. His erstwhile friend Geri Halliwell could not have helped because her security fears since her home was burgled are well documented. Rob even made plans to have high walls and iron gates built around his new London home, as well as closed-circuit television and dog patrols.

When he first became famous, Rob thrived on still being able to be himself, to have a laugh with his mates back home, to play football and tell jokes. But fame was now becoming intrusive and his best mate Jonathan Wilkes could not always be there to offer the support and company which Rob needed so much. Jonathan was in a settled relationship and had his own career path. Rob had not had a proper girlfriend since Tania Strecker and that had only lasted three months. There seemed little chance of new friendships developing within the celebrity goldfish bowl where his every move was forensically examined and which bred a climate of mistrust.

At the end of 2001 Rob badly needed to change his life. So he went to LA.

Initially, Rob was going to spend six months in the Californian sunshine, with the blessing of his management, to recharge his batteries after his exhausting schedule. Mark McCrum reported that the singer was keen to dispense with the pressures of being Robbie Williams, at least temporarily. Rob, he said, was looking forward to the anonymity of Los Angeles and living a relatively normal existence for a while. Hollywood seemed an odd destination for a dose of normality. But LA has so many celebrities per square mile that it is used to them. If Rob had gone to a mountain retreat in Peru, you could guarantee that he would have become a one-man tourist destination. But here in the decaf society of Hollywood he could be seen standing in line to buy a latte at the Malibu branch of Starbucks and nobody raised an eyebrow.

Rob had already begun to build up one or two real friendships throughout 2001, most notably with Ashley Hamilton, the 25-year-old son of perma-tan actor George Hamilton and the very glamorous Alana Hamilton. More famously, he had been the stepson of Rod Stewart, who had been the father of the house while Ashley had been growing up. Ashley is a real child of celebrity LA. When they first became friends he had already been married and divorced twice even though he was several years younger than Rob. He knew his first wife, Shannen Doherty, star of *Beverly Hills 90210*, for a mere two weeks before they wed. The marriage lasted five months. His second, to another actress, Angie Everhart, reportedly foundered when she accepted the gift of a Porsche from Sylvester Stallone. The acting highlight of his career to date was a six-week stint on *Sunset Beach* before he left the show abruptly in unexplained circumstances. He once appeared in *People* magazine's list of the fifty Most Beautiful People in the World.

Ashley and Rob met at an AA meeting, which is hardly surprising because in Los Angeles NA and AA groups are, to some extent, social gatherings. One of the first things Rob does in any city now is check out where the nearest meetings are. The most famous in LA is the Red Hut on Robertson but there are others in Malibu and Hollywood where, on any given day, he might bump into Lara Flynn Boyle, Robert Downey Jr or Matt Perry. While they were close friends, Geri Halliwell would go along to meetings with Rob. Not everyone at these meetings is going to be an addict; some are just there to make connections and others are journalists looking for a bit of juicy gossip. But there is a much better chance for Rob to make real friends at a meeting than there is at a singles bar on Sunset Strip. Ashley is also a bit of a tattoo fiend and introduced him to the Shamrock Parlor. Speaking of their friendship, Ashley joked, 'He is so cool. We have a lot in common. In fact, if we were gay we would be the perfect couple', which is just the sort of remark that Rob himself might have made. Rob was happy to help Ashley with his ambition to break into the music business. They worked on some songs together and one of them, 'Wimmin', a typically raucous Robbie track, was released in the UK in May 2003.

His other mate who eased him into Los Angeles is rocker-turned-screenwriter Sacha Gervasi, who used to be in the band Bush, one of the few of British origin to have succeeded in the USA in recent times. He knew all about the difficulties of making it in the American music world and was also familiar with the LA scene. Rob has never lost his interest in listening to other artists. He may not be such a collector of records as Gary Barlow, who would buy thirty a month, but Rob was constantly surrounded by sound. He installed a state-of-the-art Bang & Olufsen sound system in every room of his West London home and planned to do the same with the house he ended up buying in LA. One of the first concerts Rob went to in LA was to watch heavy rock legends Aerosmith at the Forum. Aerosmith enjoy huge status in the United States and so provided Rob with an early indication that in LA he would not be the centre of attention every minute of the day. Photographer Fraser Harrison, who was at the gig, recalls, 'He was walking around backstage very aimlessly. He hadn't been drinking at all and was just sipping from a can of Coke. He was in a good and relaxed mood. I think he was getting used to being seen out in public over here, although nobody really recognized who he was.' Sacha introduced Rob to the smaller, less public places to listen to bands.

Despite the easygoing attitude to celebrity in LA, Rob still relied on his personal protection that came with him when he moved into the Sunset Marquis Hotel to begin his exile. He stayed there for several months before renting, for $15,000 a month, a Tudor-style house in Beverly Hills, complete with compulsory swimming pool, which belonged to the comedian Dan Ackroyd. He could have bought a small house in Tunstall for the price of a short let. Rob was gradually easing himself into the LA lifestyle. But there was no point in spending a million or two on buying a house if he was really only going to stay six months. Routine is very important to Rob, perhaps because of his addictions. His routine in London consisted of staying in bed until lunchtime but nobody does that in Los Angeles. Rob gets up early, grabs a coffee and chats to new friends before heading off to Crunch Gym on Sunset. This is not a gym for the man or woman with a fuller figure but one where the bodies beautiful of this world tone and preen themselves. A frosted-glass panel separates the men's showers from the lobby so many a masculine silhouette can be admired from reception. That is not going to worry Rob whose naked form has been seen by thousands of people.

The British community in Los Angeles, rather like in other major cities around the world, still has the feel of the colonies about it. Everyone may wear shorts and swimsuits instead of tuxedos and cocktail dresses but the principle of (non-alcoholic) drinks before dinner is basically the same. The current king and queen of the British community are Sharon and Ozzy Osbourne. They have welcomed Rob into their world with great warmth and friendship. Their television series *The Osbournes* has turned them into arguably the biggest British stars in the USA. Rob can only dream of that sort of American fame. Television really is the quickest and most certain way of achieving celebrity, as our home-grown reality TV shows like *Big Brother* and *Pop Idol* have proved. Rob could do a lot worse than trying to fix up a regular guest spot on the next series of *The Osbournes*. He could be the cheeky friend from Britain. It would be the sort of promotion that money cannot buy. There is a huge billboard in a prime position on Sunset Boulevard, which was filled with a poster of the front image of *Escapology* – the dramatic picture of Rob tied by his feet above the LA skyline. It has not made any marked difference to what have been very disappointing sales figures for the album, which barely made a ripple in the US album charts. The effect would have been far greater if it had been a poster for *The Osbournes* with 'special guest star Robbie Williams'.

One of the factors for the success of *The Osbournes*, which is easy to overlook amid all the hype and bad language, is that veteran rocker Ozzy has a massive American following because, as the former lead singer of Black Sabbath, he has been one of the giants of Heavy Metal for more than thirty years. He has certainly had more than his fair share of those books of booze and drugs vouchers that Rob described. Robbie joined Ozzy when he received a star on the Hollywood Walk of Fame on Sunset Boulevard. Journalist Cliff Renfrew, who was there, recalls, 'Robbie was roundly booed by the crowd when he was introduced. It was really because they didn't have a clue who he was.' Ozzy and Rob can relate because of their mutual problems with drink and drugs over the years. And, despite his rock 'n' roll history, Ozzy is quite a family man, which Rob admires.

Sharon Osbourne is hugely popular with the British community in LA. She is down to earth, pragmatic and cares deeply about her family – just like Jan Williams. Rob thoroughly enjoys his trips over to the Osbourne mansion for his Sunday roast. Cliff Renfrew observes, 'Sharon is like a second mother to Rob over here.' As a gesture of family friendship Rob invited Kelly Osbourne, Sharon and Ozzy's teenage daughter, to be his support act for his twenty-one date European tour in the summer of 2003. Kelly, whose own pop career is just beginning as a bolshie young woman in the Pink mould, could not buy the exposure that puts a new artist in front of several hundred thousand people. Rob was also able to relate to the problems of Jack Osbourne, the teenage son who ended up in rehab in the spring of 2003. Jack is a classic case of too much too young, rather like Rob in Take That. Jack's bad behaviour, however, seems very tame compared to Rob's debauched excess. One friend explained, 'Jack is only seventeen and he is just trying to find himself.' Sharon Osbourne was in tears after she visited Jack at the clinic in Pasadena. The best person to give her advice, of course, is Jan, drugs counsellor and mother to errant pop star.

Through his friendship with Ashley Hamilton, Rob met Rod Stewart's daughter Kimberley Stewart, Ashley's half-sister. They were thought at one time to be enjoying a romance but, basically, they were part of the same circle of friends and would go out to dinner and socialize with Ashley and his girlfriend, Sara Foster, a model. Poor Rod must have thought Rob was the Stewart family stalker, especially when he met the veteran rock star's estranged wife Rachel Hunter. Rachel provided Rob with something he badly wanted, an instant family. Rachel was very nearly the perfect woman for Rob in that she embraced the two most important elements he looked for in a member of the opposite sex: she was a loving mother and she was a lad's goddess who regularly appeared in the masculine bible, the *Sports Illustrated* annual swimsuit issue.

Rachel was a middle-class girl from Auckland in New Zealand and, like Rob, her parents split up while she was still a child. Her blonde good looks and long legs led almost inevitably to a modelling career, which she began when she was seventeen. Although she was becoming a

well-known face in magazines, her celebrity was assured
when she married Rod Stewart in 1990. She was twenty-one
and he was forty-five. The age gap did not seem to matter
as the couple became a fixture of the Hollywood A-list and
had two children – Renee, named after the Four Tops'
classic, 'Don't Walk Away Renee', and Liam. The age
difference seemed to matter a great deal more at the
beginning of 1999, when the couple split just as Rachel hit
the watershed age of thirty. It seemed she wanted to
achieve more in her life than just being regarded as Mrs
Rod Stewart. Rod was said to be devastated by the break-up
but has since found a new statuesque, blonde companion.
Rachel, however, has drifted, being linked with various
Hollywood names including Bruce Willis. She has also
made no secret of seeking therapy to help her cope with
being a single parent.

The romance between Rachel and Rob came out of
nowhere and has prompted a great deal of speculation as
to its authenticity. They started becoming friendly in the
spring of 2002. Just how 'hot and heavy' this friendship
actually became is open to doubt. At first, there were the
usual denials that anything was going on but the pair were
trailed by a photographer to a bowling alley in an
unfashionable area of Studio City. The Los Angeles
picture agency, Fame, had been following the couple for
a month in the hope of getting the right set of pictures.
They showed the couple happy, relaxed and affectionate.
The pictures were sold all around the world for a
rumoured $250,000.

The genuineness of their intimacy was questioned
when a series of raunchy shots of the couple appeared
in the *News of the World*. They were pictured romping,

semi-naked, next to a secluded hotel swimming pool. According to an eyewitness: 'They were pretty steamed up.' Rachel took her bikini top off and, at one stage, Rob let his towel slip to the ground so that he was naked. The moment the pictures appeared everybody started shouting foul and claiming that it was all a set-up. It was alleged that the location was actually the back garden of the house where Rob was staying, a place no photographer would have had access to without permission. Rob was accused of selling photographs of a 'fake sex romp'. Renowned PR Max Clifford commented, 'If you're not very careful you end up like Geri Halliwell or Anthea Turner'.

These pictures may well have been a set-up, certainly Los Angeles observers believed them to be, but celebrities stunt things up for the cameras all the time. It did not prove they were not having a relationship. Cliff Renfrew observes, 'They did hang out together as friends. I think some kind of relationship did occur but there was definitely a big publicity element as well.'

The problem for Rob, in this instance, was one of credibility. He went to LA to get away from it all, claiming he wanted to be anonymous. That ambition looked threadbare if he was setting things up to keep his name in the spotlight. The Rachel affair did keep Rob in the newspapers during his quiet year. Neither of them, however, were big enough names in America to garner much publicity there. Really, Rob needed to pull a girlfriend like Britney Spears out of the hat, an alliance which, both during and after, afforded limitless publicity for Justin Timberlake until he eventually eclipsed her own celebrity. Rob was briefly linked with Christina Aguilera, who has had two number one singles in 2003 and is potentially much more interesting to the newspapers than the bland Miss Hunter.

Reports as early as the summer of 2002 were suggesting all was not well with the couple. It was Rachel, however, who was with him when he went to watch the first night of Jonathan Wilkes in *The Rocky Horror Show* in Bromley. Rob was in his best Robbie form when asked where Rachel was. 'Rachel who?' he replied deadpan. They left quietly together via an underground car park.

Rachel's mother, Janeen, met Rob on a visit to LA from her home in New Zealand and thought he was lovely and that they made a happy couple. Even Rod Stewart was quoted as giving his approval to the relationship: 'He's a good guy and I like him because he's a good footballer too.' Rod had an album to promote and there were whispers that privately he was not jumping for joy over the affair. For his part, Rob admitted that he was commitment-phobic, which did not bode quite so well.

Rob and Rachel were not seen much at the renowned celebrity haunts around Beverly Hills, preferring a quieter friendship revolving around coffee shops, nights in watching a movie with Rachel's children or the odd trip to support the LA Lakers basketball team, which is a sport Rob quite likes if there is no football. This homely, comfortable existence was soon to be disrupted, however, by the classic celebrity problem – separation. Rachel was left behind while Rob was promoting *Escapology*. She was seen spending a weekend partying in Las Vegas amid speculation that she was involved with someone else, a musician called Wes Scantlin. Rob and Rachel did spend a family Christmas together and he bought her a Mini

Cooper car. He had previously bought her a scooter when the two had visited London.

The rumours persisted that all was not well and, two days before Valentine's Day and the day before Rob's birthday, he and Rachel officially split up, a decision they reached over dinner. The press had a field day with stories of Rachel dumping Rob. He was strangely silent about it all, allowing Rachel and her spokesman to speak to the press about it. Based on past experiences, his reaction suggests Rob likes Rachel, that she hasn't done or said anything to upset him and that the chances are they will remain on reasonable terms in the future. Rachel and Rob's relationship does not have the makings of a feud. She graciously gave a world exclusive to *Hello!* magazine where, over nine pages of photographs, she confirmed the split: 'We are, and always will remain, the greatest of friends. I will always absolutely adore him. He is a very special guy to me. There is no one else involved.' A spokeswoman for Rachel added that it was difficult to maintain a relationship when they were both so busy and often in different countries – absolutely true.

The break-up with Rachel appears to have caused little disruption in Rob's life. He has moved forward a great deal in Los Angeles, where he can be Rob more and 'Robbie Williams' less. He now has a beautiful $5 million home in a secure estate off Mulholland Drive. In the States this is known as a 'gated community', which means people cannot just wander into the area. Instead, they have to pass security at the entrance. Guards also undertake regular patrols around the estate – all designed to make Rob feel a lot safer than he ever did in London. The houses are linked by a network of private roads, which means Rob has been able to drive without having the worry of passing his test. His pride and joy is a black E-type Jaguar convertible which cost £75,000. He also has a cream-coloured Cadillac. Rob has also been seen having driving lessons from his chauffeur, who lives at Rob's mansion and is a permanent bodyguard as well as a driver. Occasionally, Rachel Hunter was seen driving Rob around but most of the time it is the chauffeur behind the wheel. The man, who is about the same age as Rob, is more companion than hired help. On one visit to the Earth Café, Rob bought some new age pebbles with 'peace' and 'love' written on them, which he gave to his driver, apparently as a gift.

Jonathan Wilkes has been out to visit as often as he can. Eileen Wilkes says he loves it in Los Angeles, just as much as Rob. He may yet follow his great friend and make his home out there. Rob's father Pete has been for visits, any rift well healed now. They are able to enjoy each other's company as friends. And Jan is a frequent guest. She stays in a cottage which can be reached by a flight of steps from Rob's mansion. His small circle of friends is loyal and discreet and he still has the back-up if needed from David Enthoven and Josie Cliff. David made the observation not long after Rob went to LA that he was in the early stages of recovery from his drink and drugs problems. His earlier treatment in 1997 was little more than dipping a toe in the water. Should he have any relapses in LA, the chances are we will not hear of them. He has three dogs which he walks every day: an Alsatian called Rudy, a wolfhound known as Sid and a Labrador-pit bull terrier cross that answers to the name of Sam. If one happened across this heavily tattooed young man walking three large dogs in

Tunstall Park, one would be forgiven for making a run for it. Until Rob finds a new girlfriend, the only picture of him in LA is going to be one of him walking his dogs. The support system for Rob in California is very strong but he does still have to venture out to fulfil his obligations as Robbie Williams, British superstar. If he had wanted to hide away, he would not have signed a new deal with EMI and agreed to a summer of touring with all the stress and temptation that has brought him in the past. Entertainment remains in his blood, just as it does with his dad.

Football also remains in his blood. He has trained with the Hollywood United team, a group of ex-pats who play in an organized league. One squad member observed, 'They are a good standard. Rob wasn't good enough to make the team but he was still not that bad.' Rob was introduced to the team by a new friend, Billy Duffy, former bass guitarist with the Cult. As a publicity stunt Rob had enrolled on-line as a clergyman so, as the Revd Robert Williams, he was able to marry Billy and his girlfriend in the grounds of the Sunset Marquis Hotel. The pictures made the glossy magazines around the world, so it was a ruse that worked.

Whether Rob views Los Angeles as his personal home, a temporary tax haven or a stage in his long-term recovery, remains to be seen. He told a talk show over there that he was looking for Mrs Williams. A serious relationship might well determine where he settles in the long term. He even said he might have to return to Stoke-on-Trent to find the right woman for him. His childhood leading lady, Zoë Hammond, believes Rob is still looking for love above everything else: 'He needs a love which is genuine and proper, not full of diamonds and bullshit. He'll find happiness because he's the wrong one not to but he has to get his head right. I don't blame him one bit for living the life but I know that when he does settle down, it will be with somebody dead right. He'll just think "Fuck it, this is what I should be doing . . .""

'I don't want to be unfamous.'

Afterthought

Jan Williams looked like she had been taken by surprise. She was dressed casually in trousers and sloppy top when from the stage her son called her out to take a bow – in front of 121,000 people. She gave the impression of someone who had been given a sharp shove from the wings as she trotted out into the spotlight to be greeted by a massive, deafening wall of sound. And then she was gone, back into the shadows where she remains the rock in Rob's life.

The public acknowledgement of his mother on the first night of Knebworth, his biggest concert ever and the culmination of his career so far, captured the essence of why Robbie Williams has transformed from boy band prankster and fat druggie into a national treasure. He wears his vulnerability like a tattoo on his forehead and we love him for it. He epitomises cheesy cool, a quintessentially British quality, and so can get away with bringing his mum to the biggest pop concert of the year.

He did not forget Jonathan Wilkes either. It was the night of 1 August, Jonty's twenty-fifth birthday, and so he too was given his moment on stage to be introduced as Rob's 'best friend'. No duets, not even a quick refrain of 'Me and My Shadow'. Instead there was a deafening chorus of 'Happy Birthday' even though the majority of the delirious crowd probably did not have a clue who he was.

Rob needed his mother and his pal around him to face the nerve-racking ordeal of Knebworth but nobody could have prepared him for the reality of the sheer scale of the crowd for whom he was performing. He first glimpsed the fans from his helicopter as he flew in while Irish band, Ash, was playing on stage. An enormous cheer went up when it was announced that Robbie had arrived. The feeling of anticipation grew during a magnificent set by Moby. As the sun went down, barely a square foot of grass was left available at the site as a sea of people tried to find a vantage point. The reality was that relatively few could actually see the stage, having to make do with a giant screen – but, unusually, it didn't really matter.

And then Robbie appeared suspended upside down from a rope just as he is pictured on the front cover of the *Escapology* album. When, with dextrous technology, he was set the right way up his face filled the screen. He looked utterly and completely astonished, scarcely able to believe what he was seeing. All those people!

Robbie was like a rabbit caught in car headlights for at least three numbers – 'Let Me Entertain You', 'Let Love Be Your Energy' and 'We Will Rock You', until the slick professionalism of the practised entertainer kicked in. His voice may not have been at its absolute peak that evening but a gig of this size is all about overall effect. The man himself was reduced to tears by the warmth of the response to him.

The next day many of the papers concentrated on the problems fans had reaching the site forcing some to miss the event completely; or the five and a half hours it took others to get out of the car park. That was a pity as it detracted from Robbie's big night. The next night, which was filmed, was a much slicker affair from the smoother traffic control to Rob's own immaculate performance. It was as if the first night had been the dress rehearsal to iron out the gremlins. Even Jan had glammed up for the cameras and looked ready for a cocktail party when she was again called out to take a bow.

It will be very difficult for Robbie Williams, the professional entertainer, to top Knebworth 2003. The rest of the year was an anticlimax. The grind of the world tour had another four months to run, a couple more singles were released from the *Escapology* album and scraped into the top ten but they seemed to have been around for ever. By the end of the year there was a suspicion that Robbie Williams the pop product was being milked for every last drop. Everybody knows he was made 'rich beyond his wildest dreams' by EMI's reported £80 million deal. But this is big business and they will want to bank a handsome return on their investment.

Every last drop of Knebworth, for example, is being exploited. A *Live at Knebworth* CD has been a huge seller and the DVD *What We Did Last Summer* was premiered in Leicester Square in time for the Christmas sales rush. The CD did not include all the tracks from the concert giving rise to the cynical thought that a few were left off so that a *Greatest Hits* album could come out in time for Christmas 2004. There is even talk of a follow up to *Swing When You're Winning*.

At thirty, Robbie Williams has been in the entertainment business for nearly half his life. He has achieved what very few pop stars can boast of – being a top name for a decade. Many can manage half a decade, which in pop terms is a generation. The age groups represented in the Knebworth crowd, from small children to grandparents, demonstrated the extent of his appeal. Gareth Gates and Will Young seem to have been around for ages but it's only a couple of years.

His success in the UK as opposed to the US may have something to do with the way the two countries perceive celebrity. Robbie is the lad from Tunstall. He is one of us who we could easily imagine chatting to in the pub. David Beckham, the other great British male superstar of today is, despite his fabulous wealth and lifestyle, still an ordinary bloke who plays football. The US, it could be argued, prefer their stars to be Hollywood, fixed on a pedestal to be admired – all teeth and tan.

It seems weird that Rob, the real person, lives in Los Angeles. But he seems to be thriving on a life that revolves around feeling safe and secure, enjoying a degree of anonymity and walking his dogs. He still has to answer the relationship/fatherhood question time and time again. His latest response is that his first child will be called Sunny, regardless of sex – an ironic gesture from someone who, by their own admission, has been plagued by depression. He just may be able to find someone special in LA without the whole world instantly knowing and inspecting in minute detail.

My own over-riding impression after writing this book is that here is an immensely likeable man who has the priceless capacity to make you laugh or smile. He shares his problems with us and that makes him more appealing and more approachable. His fans seem forever able to forgive his excesses and fallings from grace. He is both a

little boy lost and a lad with a lager. He also has
unsurpassed star quality. My mother-in-law, Julia, adores
him. 'I love Robbie' she declared on our way back from
Knebworth. She wanted the DVD for Christmas.

Sean Smith
February 2004

Discography

Take That Singles featuring Robbie

Release Date	Title	Highest UK Chart Position
July 1991	*Do What You Like*	82
November 1991	*Promises*	38
June 1991	*It Only Takes a Minute Girl*	7
August 1992	*I Found Heaven*	15
October 1992	*A Million Love Songs*	7
December 1992	*Could It Be Magic*	3
February 1993	*Why Can't I Wake Up With You*	2
July 1993	*Pray*	1
October 1993	*Relight My Fire* (featuring Lulu)	1
December 1993	*Babe*	1
April 1994	*Everything Changes*	1
July 1994	*Love Ain't Here Anymore*	3
October 1994	*Sure*	1
April 1995	*Back for Good*	1

(*Never Forget* and *How Deep Is Your Love* were released after Robbie left Take That)

Take That Albums

Release Date	Title (track listings in parentheses)	Highest UK Chart Position
September 1992	*Take That & Party* (I Found Heaven, Once You've Tasted Love, It Only Takes a Minute, A Million Love Songs, Satisfied, I Can Make It, Do What You Like,	2

Release Date	Title (track listings in parentheses)	Highest UK Chart Position
	Promises, Why Can't I Wake Up With You, Never Want to Let You Go, Give Good Feeling, Could It Be Magic, Take That and Party)	
October 1993	*Everything Changes* (Everything Changes, Pray, Wasting My Time, Relight My Fire, Love Ain't Here Anymore, If This Is Love, Whatever You Do to Me, Meaning of Love, Why Can't I Wake Up With You, You Are the One, Another Crack in My Heart, Broken Your Heart, Babe)	1
May 1995	*Nobody Else* (Sure, Back for Good, Every Guy, Sunday to Saturday, Nobody Else, Never Forget, Hanging On to Your Love, Holding Back the Tears, Hate It, Lady Tonight, Day After Tomorrow)	1
March 1996	*Take That Greatest Hits* (How Deep Is Your Love, Never Forget, Back for Good, Sure, Love Ain't Here Anymore, Everything Changes, Babe, Relight My Fire, Pray, Why Can't I Wake Up With You, Could It Be Magic, A Million Love Songs, I Found Heaven, It Only Takes a Minute, Once You've Tasted Love, Promises, Do What U Like, Love Ain't Here Anymore [US Version])	1

Robbie Williams Singles

Release Date	Title (track listings in parentheses)	Highest UK Chart Position
July 1996	*Freedom 96* (**CD1**: Freedom [Radio Edit], Freedom [Arthur Baker Mix], Freedom [Instrumental], Interview 1	2

Release Date	*Title* *(track listings in parentheses)*	*Highest UK* *Chart Position*
	CD2: Freedom [Radio Edit], Freedom [The Next Big Gen Mix], Freedom [Arthur Baker's Shake and Bake Mix], Interview 2)	
April 1997	*Old Before I Die* (**CD1**: Old Before I Die, Better Days, Average B-Side **CD2**: Old Before I Die, Making Plans for Nigel, Kooks)	2
April 1997	*Lazy Days* (**CD1**: Lazy Days, She Makes Me High - Every Time We Say Goodbye **CD2**: Lazy Days, Teenage Millionaire, Falling in Bed [Again])	8
September 1997	*South of the Border* (**CD1**: South of the Border, Cheap Love Song, South of the Border [187 Lockdown's Borderline Mix], South of the Border [Phil 'The Kick Drum' Dane + Matt Smith's Nose Dub] **CD2**: South of the Border, South of the Border [Mothers' Milkin It Mix], Cheap Love Song)	14
December 1997	*Angels* (**CD1**: Angels, Back for Good [Live Version], Walk This Sleigh **CD2**: Angels, Karaoke Overkill, Get the Joke, Angels [Acoustic Version])	7
March 1998	*Let Me Entertain You* (**CD1**: Let Me Entertain You, Medley from *The Full Monty* by Robbie & Tom Jones, I Wouldn't Normally Do This Kind of Thing, I Am the Resurrection **CD2**: Let Me Entertain You [Six Different Remixes])	3

Release Date	Title (track listings in parentheses)	Highest UK Chart Position
September 1998	*Millennium* (**CD1**: Millennium, Love Cheat [Demo Version], Rome Munich Rome [Demo Version] **CD2**: Millennium, Lazy Days [Original Version], Angels [Live Version])	1
November 1998	*No Regrets/Antmusic* (**CD1**: No Regrets, Antmusic, Sexed Up [Demo Version], There She Goes [Live Version] **CD2**: No Regrets, Antmusic, Deceiving is Believing)	4
March 1999	*Strong* (Strong, Let Me Entertain You [recorded live at the Brit Awards '99], Happy Song)	4
November 1999	*She's the One/It's Only Us* (**CD1**: She's the One, It's Only Us, Coke & Tears, She's the One [Video] **CD2**: She's the One, It's Only Us, Millennium [Live version recorded at Slane Castle], It's Only Us [Video])	1
July 2000	*Rock DJ* (Rock DJ, Talk to Me, Rock DJ [Player 1 Remix])	1
September 2000	*Kids* [Robbie Williams/Kylie Minogue] (**CD1**: Kids, Karaoke Star, Kill Me or Cure Me **CD2**: Kids, John's Gay – Often, Kids [Video])	2
November 2000	*Supreme* (**CD1**: Supreme, United, Supreme [Live Version], Supreme [Video, filmed in Manchester] **CD2**: Supreme, Don't Do Love, Come Take Me Over, Supreme [Video, filmed in Manchester])	4

Release Date	Title (track listings in parentheses)	Highest UK Chart Position
April 2001	*Let Love Be Your Energy* (Let Love Be Your Energy, My Way [Live Version], Rolling Stone, My Way [Video filmed live])	11
July 2001	*Eternity/The Road to Mandalay* (Eternity, The Road to Mandalay, Toxic)	1
October 2001	*Somethin' Stupid* [Robbie Williams/ Nicole Kidman] (Somethin' Stupid, Eternity [Orchestral Version], My Way [recorded live at the Royal Albert Hall], Somethin' Stupid [Video])	1
April 2002	*My Culture* [1 Giant Leap featuring Robbie Williams on guest vocals] (My Culture [Radio Edit], My Culture [Goldtrix Main Mix], Racing Away [Album Version], My Culture [Enhanced Video])	9
December 2002	*Feel* (Feel, Nobody Someday, You're History – Robbie Photo Gallery and Robbie Video Clips)	2
April 2003	*Come Undone* (Come Undone, Get a Little Help)	4
July 2003	*Something Beautiful* (Something Beautiful, Berliner Star, Coffee, Tea & Sympathy)	3
November 2003	*Sexed Up* (Sexed Up [US Album Version], Get a Little Help, Appliance of Science)	10

Robbie Williams Albums

Release Date	Title (track listings in parentheses)	Highest UK Chart Position
September 1997	*Life Thru a Lens* (Lazy Days, Life Thru a Lens, Ego A Go Go, Angels, South of the Border, Old Before I Die, One of God's Better People, Let Me Entertain You, Killing Me, Clean, Baby Girl Window, [plus hidden track – Hello Sir])	1
October 1998	*I've Been Expecting You* (Strong, No Regrets, Millennium, Phoenix From the Flames, Win Some Lose Some, Grace, Jesus In a Camper Van, Heaven From Here, Karma Killer, She's the One, Man Machine, These Dreams, [plus hidden tracks – Stand Your Ground and Stalker's Day Off])	1
April 1999	*The Ego Has Landed [US Release Only]* (Lazy Days, Millennium, No Regrets, Strong, Angels, Win Some Lose Some, Let Me Entertain You, Jesus In a Camper Van, Grace, Killing Me, Man Machine, She's the One, Karma Killer, One of God's Better People)	N/A
August 2000	*Sing When You're Winning* (Let Love Be Your Energy, Better Man, Rock DJ, Supreme, Kids, If It's Hurting You, Singing for the Lonely, Love Calling Earth, Knutsford City Limits, Forever Texas, By All Means Necessary, The Road to Mandalay)	1
November 2001	*Swing When You're Winning* (I Will Talk and Hollywood Will Listen, Mack the Knife, Somethin' Stupid, Do Nothing Till You Hear From Me, It Was a Very Good Year, Straighten Up and Fly Right, Well,	1

Release Date	Title (track listings in parentheses)	Highest UK Chart Position
	Did You Evah, Mr. Bojangles, One for My Baby, Things, Ain't That a Kick in the Head, They Can't Take That Away From Me, Have You Met Miss Jones?, Me and My Shadow, Beyond the Sea)	
November 2002	*Escapology* (How Peculiar, Feel, Something Beautiful, Monsoon, Sexed Up, Love Somebody, Revolution, Handsome Man, Come Undone, Me and My Monkey, Song 3, Hot Fudge, Cursed, Nan's Song)	1
September 2003	*Live at Knebworth* (Let Me Entertain You, Let Love Be Your Energy, (We Will) Rock You, Monsoon, Come Undone, Me and My Monkey, Hot Fudge, Mr Bojangles, She's the One, Kids, Better Man, Nan's Song, Feel, Angels)	2

Robbie Williams Videos/DVDs

Release Date	Title
November 1998	*Robbie Williams Live in Your Living Room*
April 2000	*Rock DJ*
December 2001	*Robbie Williams Live at the Albert*
July 2002	*Nobody Someday*
March 2003	*The Robbie Williams Show*
November 2003	*What We Did Last Summer – Robbie Williams Live at Knebworth*

Chronology

13 Feb 1974 Robert Peter Williams born in the North Staffs Maternity Hospital, Stoke-on-Trent. He spends his first year in the family home in Victoria Park Road, Tunstall. His father, Pete Conway, a comedian, reaches the final of TV talent show New Faces.

1975 His parents take over the Red Lion, Burslem, close to Port Vale football club's ground.

1977 Makes his 'international' debut when he impersonates John Travolta singing 'Summer Nights' from *Grease* for a talent evening at the Pontin Continental, Torremolinos. His father Pete leaves home.

1981 Mother Jan takes him to his first concert, Showaddywaddy, at the Queen's Theatre in Burslem.

Sept 1985 Appears as Jeremy in *Chitty Chitty Bang Bang* at the Theatre Royal, Hanley. Afterwards he is introduced to the Lord Mayor backstage. Begins senior school at the St Margaret Ward Roman Catholic High School, a short walk from his home in Greenbank Road, Tunstall.

Oct 1988 Takes the key role of the Artful Dodger in *Oliver!* at the Queen's Theatre, Burslem. His father turns up unexpectedly and watches proudly from the stalls.

July 1990 Leaves school and secures a job as a double glazing salesman with best mate Lee Hancock.

August 1990 Sings a Jason Donovan song at an audition for a boy band in Manchester. Is chosen to join Gary, Mark, Jason and Howard to form Take That.

July 1991 Take That releases their first single, the undistinguished 'Do What U Like', which reaches No. 82 in the charts.

Feb 1993 Take That wins first Brit Award for 'Could It Be Magic', Best British Single.

Apr 1994 Sings the lead vocal on 'Everything Changes', Take That's fourth number one record.

June 1994 Secretly attends the Glastonbury Festival but spends the whole time hiding in a tent.

Dec 1994 Jan puts the home in Greenbank Road, Tunstall, up for sale. She cites a lack of privacy from Take That fans as the reason for moving to a smart address in Newcastle-under-Lyme.

June 1995 Attends Glastonbury Festival with bleached blond hairdo, a blacked-out tooth and a crate of champagne. Is pictured dancing madly on stage with Oasis.

July 1995 Robbie leaves Take That after a final meeting at the Cheshire Territorial Army Barracks in Stockport. Begins period of partying which leads to him being voted NME Ligger of the Year.

Aug 1995 Proves a big hit presenting *The Big Breakfast* on Channel 4.

Sept 1995 Dons black wig, high heels and white Y-fronts for a soft drink advert, which reportedly makes him £100,000. Appears as an extra in EastEnders, talking on the telephone in the Queen Vic.

Dec 1995 Begins dating his first serious girlfriend, make-up artist Jacqui Hamilton-Smith, the daughter of Lord Colwyn. They see each other for nine months.

Feb 1996 Reaches out-of-court settlement with BMG to enable him to pursue a solo career. The four remaining members of Take That split.

June 1996 Signs a four-album record deal with Chrysalis/EMI rumoured to be worth £1 million. Shortly afterwards parts company with manager Tim Abbot and hires IE Music to represent him.

July 1996 His first solo release, 'Freedom 96', a cover of a George Michael song, just misses the top chart slot. It sells a respectable 270,000 copies.

Oct 1996 Reveals he is being treated by celebrity therapist Beechy Colclough for drink and drugs problems.

May 1997 Robbie is pictured embracing actress Anna Friel on a hotel balcony in Rome but the romance is short-lived.

June 1997 Checks into the Clouds clinic near Salisbury in Wiltshire for his first serious stab at rehab. He stays six weeks.

July 1997 Attends High Court in London to face legal action from former Take That manager Nigel Martin-Smith, who is claiming £200,000 in unpaid commission.

Sept 1997 His first solo album, *Life Thru a Lens*, is finally released, more than two years after he left Take That.

Nov 1997 Meets Nicole Appleton of girl band All Saints on a TV show, soon after the release of the group's biggest hit, 'Never Ever'. The romance begins in earnest over the New Year.

Dec 1997 'Angels' reaches No. 4 in the UK chart. It spends thirteen weeks in the top ten and becomes his biggest selling single to date, selling more than 820,000 copies. *Life Thru a Lens* re-enters the album charts and goes to No. 1. Shares a stage with Gary Barlow at Princess Diana's Concert of Hope for a chorus of 'Let It Be'.

Feb 1998 Fails to win a Brit award but performs a show-stopping duet with hero Tom Jones. He describes it as the best five minutes of his life.

May 1998 Achieves ambition of scoring a goal in Port Vale colours when he plays in testimonial game for Dean Glover. He nets a penalty a few minutes into the second half. Minutes later he is sent off for arguing with the referee.

Sept 1998 Secures first UK No. 1 single with 'Millennium', which samples the theme from the James Bond film *You Only Live Twice*.

Dec 1998 Finally splits from Nicole Appleton after a rollercoaster year during which they had been engaged twice.

Feb 1999 Wins three solo Brits, having been nominated for a record six awards. Also wins two Ivor Novello Awards this year for 'Angels' (Most performed song) and Songwriter of the Year (with Guy Chambers).

April 1999 Buys his mother a £1 million luxury home in the village of Batley, near Newcastle-under-Lyme. The house has twenty-four acres of land around which Robbie, who does not have a licence, can drive his Ferrari.

May 1999 Flies back from the US to play in a testimonial football match for Port Vale hero Neil Aspin. He scores a goal in his side's 5-3 win over Leicester City. Efforts to kick-start a romance with Andrea Corr fail despite sending her two bouquets of 101 roses with the message 'What Can I Do to Make You Love Me?'.

August 2000 *Sing When You're Winning* is released and becomes his third number

one album. He dedicates it to collaborator Guy Chambers.

Nov 2000 Flies off for a holiday in Barbados after a bad night at the MTV Europe Music Awards in Stockholm, where he had a scuffle with a record producer and ended the evening passed out.

Feb 2001 A disturbed fan throws him off the stage during a concert in Stuttgart. To great acclaim, he refuses to abandon the concert. Dedicates Brit award for Best Video to his nephew Freddie.

May 2001 Puts on football boots again for Vale stalwart Martin Foyle's testimonial at Vale Park.

Oct 2001 Showcases his *Swing When You're Winning* album at a triumphant concert at the Royal Albert Hall, London. Lifelong friend Jonathan Wilkes joins him on stage to sing 'Me and My Shadow'.

Dec 2001 Achieves his first Christmas No. 1 when his duet, 'Somethin' Stupid', with Nicole Kidman tops the charts. Moves to Los

Angeles, initially as a temporary measure, but is still there and 'has never felt so well'.

June 2002 Steamy pictures of Robbie and a topless Rachel Hunter appear in the Sunday newspapers.

Oct 2002 Tells a press conference in London that he is 'rich beyond his wildest dreams', after announcing new contract with EMI, reputedly worth £80 million, the biggest deal in British music history. Splits from his songwriting partner Guy Chambers.

Nov 2002 His fifth album, *Escapology*, is released and goes straight in at No. 1. It becomes the biggest selling album of the year despite not being released until 18 November. 650,000 tickets for his 2003 European tour sell out in seven hours.

Feb 2003 Rachel Hunter confirms she has split from Robbie but that she will always 'absolutely adore him'. He wins a record fourteenth Brit award (Best British Male) and recites a joke Lonely Hearts advertisement as his

acceptance speech: '29-year-old Aquarian, slightly chubby, seeks boy or girl for nights of poker and AA meetings … See you next year'.

June 2003 Begins sell-out European tour at Murrayfield Stadium in Edinburgh.

Aug 2003 Performs for three nights at Knebworth before 375,000 people confirming his position as the UK's number one pop star. His mother Jan takes a bow and the crowd sings 'Happy Birthday' to his best friend Jonathan Wilkes.

Nov 2003 Tours Moscow in his role as a special representative for UNICEF as part of the organisation's End Child Exploitation campaign. Played a concert at the city's Olimpiisky stadium.

Dec 2003 The gruelling *Escapology* world tour ends in Sydney. He has performed for more than 1.2 million people in six months.

Feb 2004 Robbie Williams is thirty.

Photo Credits